British and Irish Women
Writers and the
Women's Movement

British and Irish Women Writers and the Women's Movement

Six Literary Voices of Their Times

JILL FRANKS

McFarland & Company, Inc., Publishers
Jefferson, North Carolina, and London

ALSO OF INTEREST: *Islands and the Modernists: The Allure of Isolation in Art, Literature and Science,* Jill Franks (McFarland, 2006). *The Poetry of Thom Gunn: A Critical Study*, Stefania Michelucci, translated by Jill Franks (McFarland, 2009). *Space and Place in the Works of D.H. Lawrence*, Stefania Michelucci, translated by Jill Franks (McFarland, 2002).

LIBRARY OF CONGRESS CATALOGUING-IN-PUBLICATION DATA

Franks, Jill, 1957–
    British and Irish Women Writers and the Women's Movement : Six Literary Voices of Their Times / Jill Franks.
      p.   cm.
    Includes bibliographical references and index.

    ISBN 978-0-7864-7408-0
    softcover : acid free paper

    1. Women novelists, Irish — History and criticism.
2. Women and literature — Ireland — History — 20th century.
3. Women and literature — Great Britain — History — 20th century.   4. Feminism and literature — Ireland — History — 20th century.   5. Women novelists, English — History and criticism.   6. National characteristics, Irish, in literature.
I. Title.
PR8733.F73 2013
820.9'92870941 — dc23   2013000244

BRITISH LIBRARY CATALOGUING DATA ARE AVAILABLE

On the cover: *top row* Doris Lessing, 1990s; Fay Weldon (both Photofest); Virginia Woolf (Wikimedia commons); *bottom row* Nuala O'Faolain, 1996 (photograph by Paddy Whelan, © *The Irish Times*); Elizabeth Bowen; Edna O'Brien (both Photofest); *background* Map of British Isles and compass (both iStockphoto/Thinkstock)

Manufactured in the United States of America

McFarland & Company, Inc., Publishers
  Box 611, Jefferson, North Carolina 28640
    www.mcfarlandpub.com

To my mother,
Mary Harris Franks

Table of Contents

Acknowledgments

Several people and institutions have supported me in this project. Austin Peay State University provided me with a paid professional development leave in spring 2011, and an award for scholarly achievement. Vanderbilt University made me a visiting scholar and gave me access to the Alexander Heard Library collections. Students in my spring 2012 literature course, Second-Wave Women Writers Around the Western World, fed my enthusiasm for the project by their close, personal readings of women's writing. They are the living proof of the fact that women's novels raise consciousness around feminist concerns. I am grateful to the graduate students in my fall 2011 seminar, Psychoanalytic Approaches to Literature, for their assistance and companionship in navigating the dark waters of the unconscious as we read Freud, Lacan, Chodorow, Klein, Kristeva, and Mitchell, learning about the psychopathology of everyday life, as well as the etiology of schizophrenia.

Colleagues Carrie Rohman, Eleanor Green, Kellie Bean, and Susan Wallace read and listened to drafts of the manuscript. My friend Susan Wallace comforts me by defending second-wave principles against third-wave circumlocutions, bringing real-life meaningfulness to my academic pursuits. Thanks go to Lee Arndt, whose good humor, friendship and originality demonstrate the positive aspects of the third wave. Jim Rogers at *New Hibernia Review* was always ready with a philosophical quip, editorial suggestions, and moral support.

I want to thank my friends in the southern branch of American Conference for Irish Studies, such as Marguerite Quintelli-Neary and Howard Keeley, for their work on Irish literature and their feedback on my writing. University College Cork scholars Maureen O'Connor and Pat Coughlan provided support and encouragement at a crucial time. Pat Coughlan's psychoanalytic approach to Irish women writers makes her projects meaningful and inspirational to me. Nancy and Jack Frazier provided hospitality and long discussions about writing, art, and the history of lobsters. I am grateful to Chuck

Knight for his perceptive comments, great sense of humor, sensitive psycho-analytic readings, and his loving support. My mother remains my role model and constant source of love, support, and inspiration. If it weren't for her, this voice that wrote this work would never be heard. It is to her that I dedicate this book.

Preface

My interest in comparative Irish and British literary studies arose from teaching the British surveys that all English majors are required to take. For years, I represented Modernism with two Irish texts, *Portrait of the Artist as a Young Man* and *Playboy of the Western World*, before moving on to the British classics. Feeling their underrepresentation, I longed to teach solely women's twentieth-century novels, and courses exclusively Irish. In a small department, it can take a few years to get any "specialty course" on the books. Thus, when I could teach "Twentieth-Century Irish Literature and the Construction of Gender and Nation," followed by "Twentieth-Century British Women Writers," and "Second-Wave Women Writers Around the Western World," I was happy. While teaching these courses, I felt challenged to articulate the differences in Irish and British women's voices, and to find reasons for them in social history, going beyond the obvious facts that Ireland was Catholic and colonized, while Britain was Protestant and colonizer.

This book is the result of that query. It contributes to the dialog about what makes Irish women's writing Irish, but is different from other studies in defining it against the English tradition. What makes Irish women's writing different from British? Catholicism and colonialism are the obvious answers; the challenge is to articulate how these ideologies influence feminist consciousness. My comparative approach addresses this question in a way that appreciates both national traditions, but is aware of the reductionism of any exclusive focus on gender to the neglect of class, ethnicity or race. Ethnicity and class identities inflect all of my subjects' styles of feminism, sometimes limiting the extent to which they are able to identify as feminist at all. In this statement, I use the term *ethnicity* to indicate not only Irish and British but also the Rhodesian roots of Lessing, the New Zealand origins of Weldon, the Bloomsbury coterie of Woolf, and the differences between Bowen's Ascendancy class and O'Brien and O'Faolain's Catholic backgrounds. The category "Irish" in this study necessarily contains two very different ethnicities, Anglo-

1

Irish and Gaelic-Irish, creating subdivisions within the broader categories that I address.

Feminism adds a complex third term to the other two terms presented in the title, Irish and British women writers. Knowing that I must study the entire twentieth century in order to show changes in consciousness through the three waves, I expected to find vastly different attitudes to feminism among my writers. What I did not expect, however, was the virulence against feminism that I found in some writers who generated worldwide affinity for their portrayals of women's problems. When I discovered that five out of six of my chosen novelists disliked feminism at some point in their lives, and that three of them made anti-feminist statements to the press, I wanted to understand how one's creative output can express a politics or awareness that one explicitly denies or denigrates. Contemporary psychoanalytic criticism and Marxist criticism such as Fredric Jameson's *The Political Unconscious* help such understanding by acknowledging that texts express a writer's unconscious life and the unconscious life of her culture. Cultural trends limit and influence many women's willingness to adopt the label "feminist" at a given time and place. It is a peculiarly loaded term.

Also helpful in understanding why the term *feminism* is so loaded is an appreciation of the many kinds of feminism that exist, some of which are antithetical to each other. Biological feminism posits that men and women are essentially, inherently, and genetically different, whereas constructionist feminism posits that social conditioning creates and maintains our differences. Liberal feminism trusts the legal system's capacity to bring equality to women in the public world, whereas socialist feminism distrusts the current economic structure and tries to change the state to a socialist model. Radical feminism separates women from men, believing that women flourish in isolation from masculinist values. Cultural feminism celebrates the unique contributions that women make to culture, and nurtures so-called female values.

My six authors fit some of these definitions, and they fit different categories in different times of their lives, but they do not all share the same ideological category. What they do share is what I am calling literary feminism. I am calling all six of my novelists "literary feminists" because their texts do the work of unsettling status quo patriarchy. These authors clearly posit differences between the genders, and do the cultural work of undermining patriarchy by exposing its ills. They revalidate undervalued female attributes such as self-understanding and the quest to understand one's relationships with others, while at the same time they want to understand and appreciate men. O'Faolain and O'Brien's heroines try against great Irish odds to rediscover their personal female worth. Woolf's and Bowen's protagonists see their worlds in male/female dichotomies that pain them, yet they lack role models to help them escape. Lessing lets Communism trump feminism, and Weldon turns the battle of the sexes into an occasion for satire, since she avows that each side is fatally flawed.

Cultural feminists exhibit awareness and appreciation of gender difference. However, cultural feminist politics are more radical than the authors I study. Although some of them overtly share the biological-difference feminism of cultural feminists, my selected authors are not separatists. On the contrary, they immerse their protagonists in heterosexual relationships, in which they experience men and women's differences, and suffer. Linda Alcoff defines cultural feminism:

> Cultural feminism is the ideology of a female nature or female essence reappropriated by feminists themselves in an effort to revalidate under-valued female attributes. For cultural feminists, the enemy of women is not merely a social system or economic institution or set of backward beliefs but masculinity itself and in some cases male biology.... Cultural feminist politics revolve around creating and maintaining a healthy environment —free of masculinist values and all their offshoots such as pornography —for the female principle [408].

Although difference is not the same as inequality, cultural feminism is uncomfortable for poststructuralists, because any description of gender can be essentializing. Even if the category of femininity carries all positive attributes, such as nurturance, peacefulness, and creativity, such categorization risks the catastrophic fall of individual women, from the pedestal of an ideal womanhood.

The authors I study, with the exception of Fay Weldon (who does it in jest), do not essentialize women, nor use their novels as propaganda platforms. Although all of the novelists demonstrate strong awareness of gender difference, they do not advocate the view that women are better than men. In fact, as skilled novelists, most of these writers create believable characters of both genders. Registering what Judith Butler calls the "melancholy of gender performance," they interrogate the restrictions that gender places on individuals. Nor do they advocate the separation that Linda Alcoff's definition describes. Unlike some cultural feminist theorists, my selected novelists do not bash men, nor do they argue extreme views, such as "Female energy needs to be freed from its male parasites" (Mary Daly).[1] In fact, Fay Weldon makes fun of such sentiments.

Yet in each of the novelists, I see a celebration of womanhood, even in those characters who most abhor their gender. For instance, Lessing's Anna Wulf is ashamed to write about women's issues, and O'Brien's Kate Brady hates being a woman, because she believes that women are self-involved.

Because of their struggles with female identity in strongly patriarchal environments, these protagonists illuminate both the struggle and the system of oppression. In their commitment to these characters' battles, I see the authors' celebration of womanhood. Their struggle is what I am calling literary feminism. The protagonist does not have to "succeed" at love, work or self-definition. The author uses her as a tool to question the assumptions of patriarchy. The readers' identification with the protagonists' struggles creates the possibility for feminist change. Christine St. Peter described this process simply as "one woman's creativity can inspire or enable another's" (9). Virginia Woolf's motto is also right on point: "thinking is my fighting." Besides being therapeutic for the writer, novel writing and reading effect change through the process of identification and motivation. I am defining literary feminism to signify this kind of political effect that the cultural product (in this case, novels) can have on a wide audience of readers. As a professor of literature, I see this kind of consciousness-raising in action, in both male and female students, who provide ample feedback on their reading's effects on their daily lives.

Recognizing that my selection is small — six novels, three from each nation — I do not intend for my conclusions to be monolithic. For instance, I have included only Irish writers from the Republic of Ireland, not Northern Ireland, because I have wanted to stress colonizer (England) versus colonized (Republic), and English Protestant versus Irish Catholic identities. Also, there are more Republic women's novels from the three waves to choose from. Christine St. Peter explained her own greater concentration on the Republic of Ireland than on Northern Ireland writers in a way that colorfully figures sectarian struggle and its wilting effects on feminism: "it is difficult for Northern women to insert their 'voices' into the extravagantly militarized 'masculine' discourses that still predominate [in the North]" (2).

Believing that literary popularity reveals widespread cultural conditions, I have intentionally selected the most famous authors of the two canons, which leaves out hundreds of good novelists. I have also limited the field by selecting literature over pulp fiction and similar genres such as romance novels. Further focusing my field, I have selected only the three decades in which the feminist waves peaked, thereby omitting important work that occurred in the other seven decades of the century. Despite these disclaimers, the selection of Virginia Woolf, Doris Lessing and Fay Weldon to illuminate aspects of twentieth-century feminist consciousness in England, and Elizabeth Bowen, Edna O'Brien and Nuala O'Faolain to do the same in Ireland, aims to make fruitful comparisons because of the high visibility and iconic status of these writers, and because their relationships with feminism reflect the spirit of their times and places.

Part of my intention in choosing Irish feminism (instead of American, French, etc.) to contrast with British is to reclaim the label *feminist* for Irish writers. Because the struggle for Irish women's rights has long been dominated by national and sectarian battles, and because Ireland's Catholic-nationalist hegemony predominated until at least the 1960s, many readers assume that Irish women writers simply are not feminist. My three Irish selections refute that assumption. All three Irish novels expose patriarchal ideologies and practices that female characters both internalize and resist. All three challenge the status quo. O'Brien's trilogy was burnt on the pyre of state censorship, Bowen's novels express homosocial longings, and O'Faolain's expose the ravages to a female psyche of what Seamus Deane calls the "typical Irish childhood" marked by alcohol, abuse, and guilt.

Introduction: Why Voices, Gynocritics and Biography Matter

Meanings of Voice

The concept of *voices* is central to feminist studies. *Voice* has many symbolic and metaphorical meanings, as well as its important literal one, of the sound a person makes when she talks. Voice is the vehicle by which women claim the right to be heard in public. It is also the inner self that is repressed in order to perform gender in ways that seem safe.

In Emmeline Pankhurst's time, *the voice* meant the interruption of public meetings for political purposes, similar to what we now call *intervention*.[1] The *Oxford English Dictionary* defines this meaning of voice as "the right of speaking in a legislative assembly, or more generally, the right of exercising control or influence." For Mrs. Pankhurst and the Women's Social and Political Union, heckling speakers at public meetings was the only way to be heard when the Prime Minister refused them audience. The story of British women attaining suffrage includes thousands of women's voices fearlessly raised in hundreds of venues to which they had been denied access.

Voice also refers to a literary style or tone, the characteristic sound and feeling of an author's work. The six novelists represented in this book offer six distinctive voices of their own, but my question is whether Irish women's literary voices share something that distinctly differentiates them from British voices. Before describing women's voices, or the voices belonging to women sharing a particular ethnic or national identity, it is important to establish one's reasons for isolating them from other voices. My purpose is to study feminist literary consciousness and history in two geographically-close but culturally-distant nations in order to better understand how historical conditions affect feminism. Although I could study feminist consciousness in men's novels of the three waves, I would not find a lot of subject matter.

Several studies validate the project of describing Irish women writers' voices as distinct from men's, such as Mary S. Pierse's *Irish Feminisms, 1810–1930* (2010), Heather Ingman's *Twentieth Century Fiction by Irish Women* (2007), Rebecca Pelan's *Two Irelands: Literary Feminisms North and South* (2005), *The Field Day Anthology of Irish Writing: Irish Women's Writing and Traditions* (2002), Christine St. Peter's *Changing Ireland: Strategies in Contemporary Women's Fiction* (2000), and Ann Weekes' *Irish Women Writers* (1990). Ann Weekes defends the project to study only women because she is "seeking the purposes the women share, the map of Irish female experience their words may reveal" (9). Pelan's project may invite more critical finger-pointing, since she seeks to define differences between Northern and Southern Irish women writers, potentially a more politically-charged mission than differentiating men's and women's literature. Pelan's intention is to "rectify biases against Northern Irish writing, which can seem impoverished and regressive if social conditions go unconsidered." Volumes Four and Five of *The Field Day Anthology* focus exclusively on women because there was a need to bring them back into the canon of Irish literature after the first three volumes excluded most women from its pages. Gayatri Spivak speaks of "strategic essentialism" as an appropriate reason to address the concerns of a group (for instance, women) and exclude other terms (such as men).[2]

Voice also has a psychological meaning. For feminist psychologist Carol Gilligan, *voice* means the core of the self. It is a powerful psychological instrument that connects self and other, a "litmus test of relationships and a measure of psychological health."[3] In her landmark study, Gilligan interviewed girls and women over the passage of several years, regarding important moral choices in their lives. Her conclusion: early in their lives, girls learn to suppress their real voices, replacing them with false feminine voices in order to protect their relationships. Gilligan refutes Freud's dictum that females are less moral than males, casting light on different exigencies that shape female development. Females undergo different developmental stages than males do. In their teens and twenties, girls and women prioritize maintenance of relationships over any other human value. This concern gives rise to an ethics of responsibility in girls and women, as opposed to the ethics of rights espoused by boys and men.

Carol Gilligan's term, *false feminine voice*, suggests that there is another, truer voice, which women repress in most of their speaking. The idea of women having two *voices* is also crucial to Elaine Showalter's work, which describes women's writing as a *double-voiced discourse*, containing both a dominant and muted story. Because women participate in two literary traditions, male and female, both voices are contained in the texts that they produce. Showalter borrows the concept of muted (female) versus dominant (male) groups from anthropologists Shirley and Edwin Ardener, who analyze societal power relations in terms of which group controls the channels of communication. Women are in a relatively inarticulate position, whose reality does not get represented. This non-representation does not mean that women are silenced, but that their reality cannot be expressed in the language of the dominant structure.[4] Showalter names a "wild zone" of women's culture, a place forbidden to men, which contains aspects of female lifestyle that are unlike those of men. The irony and parody found in many women novelists' work reflects this double-voiced discourse, in which the dominant discourse is both adopted and critiqued.

Feminism could be defined as the collective *voice-finding* of women, except that collectivity has been a sore point among and inside women's organizations throughout the three waves; this is in fact the subject of Fay Weldon's novel, *Big Women*, which I analyze in Chapter Five. Since feminism includes so much material, how do feminists agree on which material to prioritize in a collective struggle? First-wave feminists, agitating for the vote, found their groups split on issues of militancy versus pacifism, and nationalism versus suffragism. Second-wave feminists diverged on several issues, including radical versus liberal methods, sexual orientation and sexual lifestyles, socialism versus capitalism, and whether Ireland's Troubles or women's oppression should be the priority of their organization. Third-wave feminism aims to correct white, middle-class, heterosexual biases of feminism by celebrating the plurality of *voices* of individual women, emphasizing those of minority races, working class, and lesbian, bisexual and transgendered persons.

Consciousness-raising (CR), the main tactic of the early seventies' Women's Liberation Movement, invited women to hear their own *voices* for the first time. In CR, women gathered to discuss taboo subjects such as sexuality, abortion, contraception, marital discord, depression, and low self-esteem. Recalling their experience of CR today, many women refer to it as a life-changing event, their first opportunity to feel that their voices were heard, supported, accepted, and therefore normalized for having ambivalent or even hostile feelings to their prescribed roles. Hearing their true voices in women-only groups gradually helped liberate them from their sense of oppression.

In Defense of Gynocritism

Gynocriticism is, like it sounds, the study of women's literature. It needs to be defended because any project that separates women from men raises the red flag of essentialism. In "Towards a Feminist Poetics" (1979), Elaine Showalter coined the term *gynocriticism*.[5] A feminist criticism concerned with "the history, themes, genres and structures of literature by women," it addresses "the psychodynamics of female creativity; linguistics and the problem of a female language; the trajectory of the individual or collective female literary career; literary history; and of course studies of particular writers and works."[6]

Like cultural feminism, poststructuralists criticize gynocriticism for essentializing women's writing. Because it characterizes a body of writing, there might be a tendency of gynocritical approaches to homogenize diverse experiences. The fear of essentialism applies not only to making diverse groups of women seem similar to one another, but also to making women's voices seem ineluctably different from men's. Poststructuralists try to avoid essentialism because of its links with biological determinism, which gave strong support to programs of racism, imperialism and sexism in the nineteenth century. In the 1910s and 20s, cultural anthropology led the shift from biological towards cultural determinism. Margaret Mead studied diverse New Guinean tribes, whose different cultural ascriptions of gender roles proved her thesis that culture rather than biology determined gender difference.

The fear of stereotyping is very real, and pertains to all academic disciplines. However, the various projects that might call themselves gynocritical, such as writing women's literary history, or describing and comparing women's writing, whether to men's or other groups of women's writing, are usually undertaken for legitimate purposes rather than to entrench polarities. For instance, Christine St. Peter's purpose, in *Changing Ireland*, is to establish a women's tradition of writing to foster creativity, because "one woman's creativity can inspire or enable another's" (9). Heather Ingman's purpose, in *Twentieth Century Fiction by Irish Women*, is to place the dialog between Irish feminism and nationalism in a wider theoretical context (3). Ann Weekes' stated intention, in *Irish Women Writers*, is to describe a neglected female Irish literary tradition. Rebecca Pelan's intention, in *Two Irelands*, is to assess the relationship between a body of written work and the society that produced it. Angela Bourke's intention, in *Irish Women's Writing and Traditions*, like Weekes', is to educate: "Irish women are entitled to know about their history, culture and traditions."[7] The benefits of gynocritics, a focus on women's writing, appear to far outweigh its dangers. In the hands of a careful critic, a gynocritical approach has the benefits of reclaiming neglected work, understanding relationships between production and culture, and exploring gender identity, as well as making gender a less oppressive category.

In Elaine Showalter's gynocritical book, *A Literature of Their Own* (1977), she studied British women writers' voices in the context of literary history. Responding to G. H. Lewes' suggestion that women should express their real experiences instead of imitating the styles and subjects of men, Showalter maintains that there always has been a female tradition, one that passed through three distinct stages, from imitating males' writing (18th century), through feminist struggle (19th century), to woman-centered writing (20th century). These three centuries of British women writers constitute a literary tradition separate from men's. Women enjoy a subculture unified by values, conventions, experiences, and behaviors.[8] The task for Showalter's new "feminist poetics" was to describe that tradition of women writers, giving voice to the muted female half of literary history, and affording it its own legitimacy and style: "Gynocritics begins at the point when we free ourselves from the linear absolutes of male literary history, stop trying to fit women between the lines of the male tradition, and focus instead on the newly visible world of female culture" (383).[9]

Besides its attention to neglected literature and history, another asset of gynocritics is its interdisciplinarity. Feminist literary criticism utilizes research in other fields, such as feminist history, anthropology, psychology and sociology, all of which describe a female subculture that may both internalize and resist patriarchy's constructions of femininity while also creating its own network of inter-female relations and ideas. For Showalter, women's literature contains feminine values that "penetrate and undermine" the masculine systems that contain them. This is precisely the type of feminist work that I locate in the six novels in this study. Despite their affiliations (class, religion, party) that compete with their feminist identity, my six authors create texts that undermine patriarchy by exposing its ills.

Besides the risk of essentialism, gynocriticism has been disapproved for its dependence on Freudian concepts of woman, such as penis envy and envy of men's social power. However, gynocriticism does not stop at Freud; it embraces the many feminist revisions to Freudian developmental psychology produced in the past thirty years, particularly those by Nancy Chodorow and Carol Gilligan. Chodorow reverses Freudian lack by positing that the female child identifies positively with the mother in the pre-Oedipal phase, while the male child suffers in this primary relationship by his difference from the mother. Gilligan corrects Freudian phallocentrism, as discussed earlier, by establishing that there exists a different pattern of moral development in females. In my studies of O'Brien and O'Faolain's novels, I interpret the protagonists' psychic processes using terms and concepts of psychoanalysts Julia Kristeva and Melanie Klein, both of whom challenge Freudian misogyny.

Another awareness one should cultivate when studying women's novels is the intersectionality of oppressions. Besides gender, other categories of identity and oppression exist, such as race, class, orientation, age, and physical ability. Third-wave feminism was founded because of dissatisfactions with the second-wave movement's domination by white, middle-class, heterosexual women, whose work did not represent the needs of these other categories. Kimberlé Crenshaw coined the term *intersectionality* to express the perception that people are oppressed simultaneously by several different systems of power. Since identity is formed by this intersection of factors, we must look at all of them in order to understand oppression. My current study does not address certain oppressed groups, especially Irish Travelers, and Northern Ireland women living in sectarian-apartheid communities, and women of color. Far from isolating gender from other categories of oppression, however, the central point of this book is that the gender awareness of the selected women writers intertwines with their ethnic, class and national identities to such a degree that it creates quite different feminisms in Ireland and Britain.

The Uses of Biographical Criticism

Like gynocriticism, biographical criticism is also unpopular with those who fear reductionism or a too-close attribution of the author's work to the author's life. In the 1930s, New Criticism defined the biographical fallacy as the assumption that the text was equivalent to the author's life. But using biography as a background to interpretation is different from assuming without examination that the text is the story of the author's life. New Criticism cautioned against a reading of the text alongside or intertwined with the author's biography. Fortunately, psychoanalytic criticism, particularly popular in the 1960s and 70s academy, reversed this bias, making the text *all about* the author's Freudian neuroses. Neither extreme approach is particularly useful. In the 1980s, post-structuralism opened up the ways in which critics perceived the interpreting profession, and the material conditions of producing texts became the focus of interpretation. Marxist, feminist, postcolonial, and race theory gained ground as legitimate, and even politically essential ways to analyze literary texts. Psychoanalytic literary criticism evolved and expanded from pure Freudianism to include feminist psychoanalysis, Object Relations theory, and Lacanian theories of language in its relation to the unconscious. Jacques Derrida's contribution to post-structuralism involves the instability of textual meaning, and the tendency of the text to deconstruct its own apparent meanings. Michel Foucault understands texts as discourses about power, and Frederic Jameson personifies the text, saying it contains its own political unconscious. All of these poststructuralist interventions make psychoanalysis a newly viable literary approach, insofar as psychoanalysis can occur at the level of the text's language and discourse, and be removed from the unsuspecting author who is not there to defend herself. Additionally, due to the popularization of psychoanalytic terms and concepts from the 1960s onwards, we now see writers who with varying degrees of earnestness or flippancy, analyze themselves in their novels. Fay Weldon (flippant) and Nuala O'Faolain (earnest), the authors whom I have chosen to represent the turn-of-the-21st-century period, are strong examples of this tendency to self-analyze as an aspect of their fictions.

In this study I use biography in conjunction with psychoanalytic concepts to understand the relation of my subjects to their times and places, and to feminism. Although Freud provided the foundations for all twentieth-century developments in psychoanalysis, I focus on two female psychoanalytic theorists, Julia Kristeva and Melanie Klein, whose work built on Freudian foundations to give nuanced interpretations of abjection (Kristeva) and object relations (Klein). I provide extensive biographies of the authors, not in order to diagnose their neuroses, but rather to establish their individual relations with cultural phenomena that affect their writing. For instance, Doris Lessing's love affair with communism handicapped her affiliation with feminism. The story of her involvement with the Rhodesian Communist Party is germane to my argument about her novel's deeply conflicted protagonist, as well as my comparison of Lessing's communist experiences to O'Brien's Catholic indoctrination.

Biography is the history of one life, as it interacts with others. But history, the narration of events in time, is as important to my project as the biography of individuals. Hence, the first two chapters of this book are historical accounts of the women's movement in its three waves in Ireland and Britain. Feminism does not stand on its own; it has close ties with other progressive movements such as national independence for Ireland and socialism in England. The three waves manifest very differently in Ireland and Britain; their histories are a necessary grounding for literary criticism of the selected novels.

Review of Chapters

Beginning with the Ladies Land League in 1880, and ending with Mary McAleese's presidency in 2011, Chapter One covers key movements, organizations, events and figures in the Irish women's movement during the long twentieth century. Before the creation of the Free State in 1922, the women's movement has difficulty attaining any significant separate status from nationalist causes. The leaders of the movement, such as Maud Gonne, Constance Markievicz and Hanna Sheehy Skeffington, differ in the degree to which they perceive suffrage as a separate issue from republicanism. Many women were deluded by their republican ideals and comrades into thinking that achieving an independent Ireland would automatically bring about equal relations between men and women. The conservative post-Independence government proved them wrong. Ireland's new leaders relied on Ireland's chief difference from England — its Catholic faith — to help create a distinct identity of Ireland as spiritual leader of the world. In 1937, staunch Catholic Prime Minister Eamon de Valera codified women's role as mothers, wives and housekeepers by amending the Constitution to state that women's place was in the home. In the 1970s, the Irish Women's Liberation Movement brought international attention to Irish women's plight with events such as the Contraception Train, but the movement was short-lived, and gave way to the antifeminist backlash in the 1980s, as experienced in other countries as well. Third-wave Irish feminism is not "sex-positive"[10] in its orientation as is America or Britain's; at least until the Peace Accord (1998), the women's movement continued to focus on sectarian violence in Northern Ireland (rather than sex) as a main issue. The female presidencies of the past three terms give a somewhat distorted view of female presence in Irish politics, as President is a ceremonial role in Ireland. Women's showing in the *Dáil Éireann*, or Irish assembly, where significant decisions are made, is still minimal.

Chapter Two covers British women's movements, starting with the suffrage (first-wave) campaign of the Pankhurst family and their organization, the Women's Social and Political Union (WSPU). Because the Pankhursts' story accentuates the troubled relations between classes, political parties, and feminism in the United Kingdom, I include the biographies of the three Pankhurst sisters, one of them socialist, one socialist-turned-imperialist, and the third an impassioned rhetorician who switched causes from suffrage to patriotism to Seventh Day Adventism. In second-wave British feminism, I highlight the activities of a charismatic leader, Germaine Greer, whose contributions reflect conflicts within the movement over sexuality, class difference, and leadership itself. To counterbalance Greer's heavily sexual emphasis, I describe the women's peace movement, which combined spiritual ecology with feminism in an historic attempt to stop nuclear war. Deciding to remain at Greenham Common Peace Camp until the Prime Minister agreed to meet them, thousands of women took turns living outside the nuclear base for a period of nineteen years. In the 1980s, Margaret Thatcher's two terms as Prime Minister ushered in a socially conservative era that was not kind to feminism. Third-wave British feminism includes negative aspects, such as the normalization of sex industries, and positive aspects, such as organized attempts to improve women's lives. Britain suffers from the rumor that feminism is dead, but a recent study by Catherine Redfern and Kristin Aune suggests that feminism is still strong at a grassroots level.

In Chapter Three, I shift to literary analysis, starting late in the era of first-wave feminism, the 1920s. *Mrs. Dalloway* (1925) by Virginia Woolf and

The Last September (1929) by Elizabeth Bowen dramatize their protagonists' conception of gender in relation to their respective nations and classes. Upper-class Mrs. Dalloway's sympathy for the working class is limited, but in turn, her imagination of other, radically different lives is extraordinary. The premise of the novel depends on the protagonist's ability to imaginatively suffer with a World War I trauma victim as he struggles to communicate his worldview to his doctor. When he is unsuccessful at this communication, this veteran chooses death (suggesting how important *voice* is, in rehabilitation of trau-matized veterans). Surprisingly, his death liberates Clarissa Dalloway from her own depressive outlook, at least for an evening. Woolf's privileged posi-tion within Bloomsbury may have insulated her from material cares, but her perception of patriarchy's oppressions found expression in her novels and her nervous breakdowns. In contrast to Woolf's, Elizabeth Bowen's class pres-tige is more historical than actual. When the novel takes place, her protagonist Lois Farquhar is living in the last months of Anglo-Irish Ascendancy. Amidst IRA-British army skirmishes, Lois tries to conduct a love affair with a British soldier, but finds she cannot ascribe to his British absoluteness about gender and national merits. Her dissociation from her own feelings reflects her dying social class. Her emotional anesthesia resembles the dandy pose popularized by Oscar Wilde in the 1890s. The apparent frivolity of a dandy comes to seem more absurd in the face of the Irish War of Independence; even the pose must die in wartime. Bowen's satiric mode expresses her intentional detachment from politics and exposes the fall of her class in Ireland. The political uncon-scious of the text spells out Anglo-Irish colonial guilt, even as its gentrified characters dance on the Big House driveway.

Chapter Four moves to second-wave feminism, comparing Doris Less-ing's *The Golden Notebook* (1962) to Edna O'Brien's *The Country Girls Trilogy* (1964) in terms of their protagonists' debilitating heterosexual relationships. Because of their indoctrination in Communism and Catholicism, these char-acters are unable to analyze (and thereby dissolve) their painful relationships through a feminist lens. Using Julia Kristeva's explication of the psychological term *abject* and Antonio Gramsci's development of the Marxist term *hege-mony*, I describe how the Irish-Catholic construction of femaleness as abject becomes a self-destructive force in O'Brien's heroine Kate. Her early child-hood experience of trauma dovetails with her cultural teachings to make masochistic sexuality her mode of coping. Similarly, Lessing's heroine Anna internalizes Communism's abjection of "female" qualities of self-interest to the extent that she suffers a writer's block. She thinks that her novels of self-exploration are a women's subject, and therefore base and bourgeois. Although she confronts her hypocritical allegiance to the Communist Party, she is unable to conquer her addiction to hyper-masculine men and her own masochistic sexuality. Despite their disavowals of feminism, both authors' texts dissect and critique patriarchy, especially as it manifests in abusive, addictive, heterosexual relationships.

Chapter Five moves to third-wave feminism, comparing Fay Weldon's *Big Women* (1997) and Nuala O'Faolain's *My Dream of You* (2002). The novels' opposite approaches to the crisis in feminism reflect the different nature of feminism in Britain and Ireland. Weldon satirizes second-wave idealism in her portrait of a feminist press that lacks solidarity. O'Faolain uses confessional realism, a genre common in American third-wave publications, yet her Irish ethnicity and upbringing make her concerns quite different from American or British Gen Xers or Millennial Generation feminists. Instead of rejecting second-wave calls for authenticity in her romantic engagements, she marries her interrogation of her feminized weakness with an exploration of the positive potential of her Irish identity.

Using Ann Weekes, David Bakan and Max Weber's definitions of Protestant versus Catholic cultural identity-formation, I examine how O'Faolain's middle-aged, self-exiled protagonist seeks meaning through communal identity with other Irish, while Weldon's six feminists fail to identify strongly enough to sustain community. Weekes states an important difference in Catholic and Protestant values, theorizing that Catholics value communal experience, while Protestants find their salvation in individualism. In regard to individualist versus communal values, the structures of *My Dream of You* and *Big Women* are opposite. O'Faolain's protagonist starts off intensely lonely, but achieves community by the end, while Weldon's six protagonists start out by forming a collective, but end up alone, albeit wealthy. *My Dream of You* features a lone protagonist whose journey *seems* to entail the loss of one important relationship after another, yet she both consciously and unconsciously establishes many fertile bonds, enabling her to recreate a more healthy psychic community than the Irish family she had intentionally fled. I use Kleinian Object Relations theory to describe O'Faolain's psychic reality.

The Conclusion makes explicit the implied comparisons found throughout the rest of the chapters. Although I grant equal space to Irish and British subject matter in this book, the forging of an Irish feminist identity is a motivating factor of my study, given the marginalization of Irish women's literature and Irish feminism. Internationally, academic feminism relies on Anglo-American and French theories, but because of Ireland's different history, not all aspects of these theories fit Irish culture. Similarly, postcolonial theory tends to concern itself with nonwhite populations, marginalizing Ireland even further. Nonetheless, contemporary theoretical debates form a strong part of Irish women's studies programs. Their challenge is to integrate Ireland's cultural and historical specificities with international theoretical concerns, taking aspects that are useful, while growing recognizable Irish identities. I am a literary scholar who believes strongly in the assets of comparative approaches; any studied term can be seen more sharply when another term is analyzed beside it. Hoping to contribute to our understanding of both Anglo and Irish women's literary history, I offer a comparison of selected British and Irish women's writing to trace trends of feminist consciousness in Britain and Ireland.

CHAPTER ONE

"Cherish all the children of the nation equally": The Irish Women's Movement

"Cherish all the children of the nation equally" was the high-minded intention of Ireland's liberators in the 1916 Uprising, as expressed in the Proclamation of Provisional Government of the Irish Republic. Suffragettes joined with nationalists to overturn British rule in Ireland, some never doubting their male comrades' esteem of women. But women's struggle for equality did not end with the vote in 1918, nor the Free State in 1922, nor the election of President Mary Robinson in 1990, nor the right to divorce in 1995.

Because this chapter is a condensed history of more than one hundred years, I treat dramatic events and colorful figures, rather than detailing each new development and the many players who contributed to history. In studying these Irish figures and events, I notice certain patterns of behavior and outcomes. Particular tensions develop in and among groups fighting for social change, making the language of the 1916 Proclamation particularly bittersweet. "Cherish all the children of the nation equally" was an idealistic goal that was never attained, and one that is difficult to attain by any group of human beings. In the sphere of women's organizations, there is a constant friction between the struggle to gain national independence and the fight for women's rights in the early century. This conflict returns in second-wave feminism between those who want to address every category of oppressed person, on the one hand, and those who believe that feminist issues deserve a single focus, on the other hand. Some second-wave feminists in the Republic believed that endeavors to aid their sisters in the North should predominate, others believed that the partition issue should remain totally outside the scope of feminism, and yet another group believed that drawing attention to women's issues at all was a petty bourgeois distraction from the fight for a united and free Ireland.

In both early and late century, these tensions splintered groups, both within and outside the women's movement. For the national struggle, this could have disastrous consequences, such as the misunderstanding between the Irish Volunteers, the Irish Citizen Army and the Irish Republican Brotherhood, as to when the Easter Uprising should take place — and who was in control. Because of miscommunications of orders to mobilize, there were only a thousand men in Dublin to take the city and proclaim the Republic. With these low numbers, the Uprising lasted just one week. British forces retook the city and executed the revolutionary leaders, inadvertently creating martyrs that strengthened the Republican cause. Within nationalism, the dividing line was between those who advocated the use of physical force, versus those who advocated only the use of legal channels to attain independence.

The high points of the Irish women's movement in the twentieth century include the battle for a free Ireland in the first two decades, and the dramatic pronouncements and direct action tactics of second-wave feminism in the early seventies. The backlash of the eighties was followed by several achievements in the past two decades, including two female presidents; women's studies programs in Trinity College, University College Dublin, Limerick, Galway, and Cork; the founding of *Irish Feminist Review*; the launching of Cork University Press' series in Irish gender and women's studies; recent global interest in Irish culture; and economic benefits from the Celtic Tiger phenomenon of economic growth.

Irish Independence and First-Wave Feminism, 1880–1937

In addition to first-wave suffrage and second-wave activism, any account of the women's movement must describe the War of Independence and the Civil War in some detail, for two reasons. First, women were heavily involved in these endeavors (for instance, forty women occupied the General Post Office in the week of the Easter Uprising, and seventy women were arrested after the event). Second, the relationship of nationalism and feminism in Irish history is so intertwined and perplexed that it is central to any analysis of Irish feminism.

The key historical events and political organizations in this sub-chapter are the Ladies' Land League (1881–82); the Irishwomen's Franchise League (founded 1908); the first women's newspaper, *Bean na hEireann* (1909–11); the 1913 Strike and Lock-out; the Daughters of Erin (*Inghinidhe na hEireann*), 1900–1914; League of Women (*Cumann na mBan*), founded 1914; the Easter

1916 Uprising; the First and Second *Dáil* (Assembly); the Anglo-Irish Treaty (1922); the Civil War (1922–23); and the 1937 Constitution. Colorful female figures of this period include Anna Parnell, leader of the Ladies' Land League; Maud Gonne, "Ireland's Joan of Arc"; Hanna Sheehy Skeffington, the one pure feminist; and Constance de Markievicz, warrior and friend of the poor.

Ladies' Land League (LLL) and Anna Parnell, 1880–82

The twentieth-century Irish women's movement had its roots in the nineteenth-century organization that first proved to republicans that women were good at organizing to change Ireland's social structure, in this case, by helping the poor to resist abusive landlords. Perhaps more significantly, the Ladies' Land League proved that women organized and followed through more efficiently than men. Males' negative reaction to female success also foreshadowed a pattern in Irish politics: most male politicians, soldiers, and activists did not want women to assume equal roles in the fight for independence, and would underhandedly orchestrate the suppression of women's organizations.

For decades after it was technically over, the Famine had a direct impact on tenants' poverty and their superstition of landlord/tenant laws. The Great Famine of 1845–52 occurred when a water mold, *phytophthora infestans*, caused potato blight, obliterating the crop upon which one-third of Irish people depended as an exclusive source of food. Over one million died from disease and starvation; between one-and-a-half and two million emigrated. England's response to her colony was harsh. Throughout the Famine, landlords evicted tenants for non-payment of rent, and required that Ireland export her other food crops instead of eating them. Based on evidence that British government intended to create mass starvation, to "destroy in substantial part" the Irish people (so that the British could take over their lands), their behavior meets the definition of *genocide* under the 1948 Hague Genocide Convention. Framed in this way, it becomes easier to understand nineteenth-century republicans' animosities towards the British, and their long-lasting efforts to oust them from Ireland.

Since they had barely recovered from the Great Famine of the forties, the 1879 potato failure hit tenants hard. Michael Davitt led the Fenians (republicans with a physical force tradition), who joined with Charles Stewart Parnell and the parliamentarians (who used legal channels) in a campaign to give peasants ownership of the land they planted. On October 21, 1879, the Irish National Land League elected Parnell its president, aiming to reduce rack rents (extortionate rates) and change tenancy to ownership. Land Leaguers encouraged peasants to negotiate rent reduction; if the landlord didn't agree, tenants should pay only at the point of a bayonet. Tenants could make evictions and confiscations somewhat difficult by hiding livestock and blocking roads, but the negotiating techniques of the Land League were not very successful. Nonetheless, the British instituted a Coercion Act that required "arbitrary and preventative arrest" of anyone involved in the Land League. When Land League leaders understood that they would soon be imprisoned, they passed leadership to women, assuming that females would not be suspected of political agitation, and therefore be free to assemble and travel throughout the country.

Without consulting her, Michael Davitt assigned Anna Parnell, Charles' 28-year-old feminist sister, the task of running the Ladies' Land League (LLL). The daughter of an American feminist and an Irish Protestant landowner, Anna chafed at the conditions of her gender and class, such as her dependency on her brother for an allowance. With her mother and sister, Anna traveled to America to solicit monies for famine relief, until summoned back home to lead the LLL. Although Charles Parnell believed that women were inferior, Michael Davitt attested to their superiority in direct-action endeavors such as the League: "They have more courage, through having less scruples, when and where their better instincts are appealed to by a militant and just cause" (Ward 310). Davitt was one of very few Irish leaders to celebrate women's aptitude for revolution.

Since women characteristically relied on the men in their families, Anna's first task was to instill confidence in women workers. In LLL's early days, Anna Parnell's distrust of men was apparent in her speeches. This uneasiness would only grow as she observed men's reactions to the success of her organization. She found that women were more willing than men to resist their landlords and risk bodily harm. To prevent men from paying rent, Anna advised women to pay for groceries with their husband's wages. Meanwhile, the imprisoned male National Land Leaguers offered no assistance to the women leading the movement in their absence. The first order of business for LLL was to clean up inaccurate records. They compiled a new survey of landlords and tenants so that they could assist peasants to resist, reduce, or pay rents. The women Leaguers made it a point to be present at evictions. Their services ranged from advising tenants about passive resistance, paying their court costs, and constructing wooden huts that evicted tenants could move into. Women were keener on providing these alternative dwellings than the National Land League had been.

Since it often cost more to resist rent than to pay it, Anna Parnell soon tired of the inefficiency of these methods. Advocating a no-rent policy, she was surprised at the male leaders' reluctance to organize. She later understood the reason for this: to the men, the Ladies' Land League was only meant to offer a semblance of authority, because "that was all the Land League itself had achieved."[1] It was more important to the male Leaguers to uphold their reputation than to save tenants from eviction and starvation. Given the confused state of records, it was difficult for the LLL to determine which tenants deserved charity. The League's coffers were strained by the costs of bringing the prisoners meals, and feeding the prisoners' families.

When Charles Parnell issued a No-Rent Manifesto from jail without consulting Anna Parnell, she was enraged. The manifesto stated that no Land League money would go to tenants who paid any rent whatsoever. Anna believed this was just a "cover whereby the male leaders could withdraw from the impasse they had placed themselves in, while at the same time maintaining a fiction of a continued opposition" (Ward 21). Later, Anna Parnell wrote *The Land League: Tale of a Great Sham,* telling the story of the conflict between the two leagues, but it remained unread until 1950. During the war, police confiscated her records; not until 1950 did the "Sham" resurface for public viewing. Meanwhile, newspapers denounced the "immodest behavior" of League women traipsing around the countryside and resisting authority. But by December 1881, the LLL had achieved some positive press. On the other hand, this same publicity caused the British government to suppress the women's activities. On December 16, 1881, England extended the Coercion Act to the Ladies' Land League, stating that, "where any females are assembled, such meeting is illegal." Margaret Ward distinguishes the women's reactions to this threat from the men's. While the men "melted away," the women defied the Act with weekly Sunday assemblies, holding mass meetings in several locations throughout the country to publicize their work.

When women were arrested, they were treated worse, in the press and in jail, than men. They were either placed in solitary confinement, or with low-class criminals such as prostitutes and vagrants. On the outside, this government hazing of women backfired, since it caused many angered women to volunteer for the LLL. In turn, police increased their surveillance, arresting LLL members just for erecting shelters. Michael Davitt believed that the women's activities fomented more peasant violence than the men's. The threat of agrarian "outrages," as they were called, motivated officials to negotiate a treaty with Charles Parnell. In return for Parnell using his influence to stop agrarian crime, the government would release prisoners and amend the Land Act to include leaseholders. Once released from prison, however, the National Land Leaguers blackmailed the Ladies' Land League. The women were told that LLL's debts would remain unpaid unless the organization folded. At this point, Anna referred to the National Land League as her enemy. She never recovered from the frustrations of working with (or more accurately, without) her brother and his colleagues. After the Treaty was signed, she moved to

England, taking an alias for the rest of her life. She and her brother never spoke again. Much later, the popular Fenian John O'Leary told Maud Gonne that the National Land League had suppressed the Ladies' Land League because "they were honester and more sincere than the men" (Ward 37). The women's good work made the men's mediocre achievements look bad.

Inghinidhe na hEireann (Daughters of Erin) and Maud Gonne, 1900–1914

The story of the women's movement before World War I can be told partly through the life of the most prominent female nationalist leader, Maud Gonne, so central was she to the twin goals of achieving an independent Ireland and asserting women's right to take part in its formation. Not a pure feminist like Hanna Sheehy Skeffington, Maud believed that the fight for suffrage should not be separate from the fight for Ireland's independence. She thought that women had a right and a duty to participate equally in the "larger" human rights movement, the fight for a free Ireland.

Born in England in 1866, to Captain Thomas Gonne and Edith Cook Gonne, from County Cork, Maud lost her mother to tuberculosis when she was five. Due to Maud's own weak lungs, her father sent her and her sister Kathleen to live in Cannes with a French governess who inculcated the values of republicanism, egalitarianism and philanthropy. In her teens, Gonne visited her aunts in Paris and London. Being a great beauty, she was "launched" into a cosmopolitan crowd. Her first romance was with right-wing Parisian lawmaker Lucien Millevoye,

Maud Gonne, 1901 (Library of Congress).

whose cause was to regain French control of Alsace-Lorraine. Because he was married and had a political career, Lucien could not marry Gonne. Yet he supported her fight for Irish independence, in return for her support of his own political cause.

During a liaison lasting eleven years, Gonne had two children by Lucien. The first died of meningitis, while the second, Iseult, had to be presented to the world as Maud's niece, in order to avoid the stigma of illegitimacy. Lucien finally tired of distance, secrecy, and competition with Gonne's love for Ireland; he moved on to another affair. Two years later, Gonne married Captain John MacBride, who had returned triumphantly from the Boer War where he had supported the Boers against the British. They quickly had a son, Sean. Within a few years, the marriage was ruined by MacBride's alcoholic rages and abuse, possibly including incest upon Iseult. With two conflicted relationships behind her, Gonne was through with romance. After her separation from MacBride, she was afraid to move back to Ireland, lest he kidnap Sean. Nor could she leave delicate Sean alone with servants for any length of time, although she had left Iseult for years.

Being away from Ireland, Gonne missed much of the preparation for the Uprising, but she did her best to contribute, from abroad, by writing articles and utilizing her many connections. One biographer, Samuel Levenson, believes that Gonne lost her key role in Irish politics after her 1905 separation from MacBride, because of Catholic attitudes to divorce, and because of her necessary absence from Ireland during such important events as the establishment of Sinn Fein, the recruitment of Irish Volunteers in the North and South, the beginning of the modern labor movement with the 1913 Lockout, and the 1916 Easter Rising.

Comparing the lives of Iseult Gonne and her younger brother Sean MacBride through a feminist lens, we note the differences in their education and the relative encouragements they had to carry the Irish banner flown by their mother. Early in his childhood, Gonne made her son part of her political life. He eventually became a famous defender of political prisoners, then a senator and a Nobel Peace laureate. As a girl, Iseult did not share the same intimacy with her mother, nor did she enjoy the same career support. After turning down a proposal of marriage from 52-year-old William Butler Yeats (whom her mother had already refused five times), 24-year-old Iseult married a teenaged poet, who later left her and their two children for a German Jew. The acquaintance with Yeats was a positive influence on Iseult's self-expression. Yet Iseult did not follow through on her initial creative promise, publishing only a few poems, a short play, and some translations from Bengali. Iseult suffered from being second to Sean in her mother's affections. As Amanda French notes, descriptions of Iseult Gonne "portray her less as a personality than as an embodiment of some abstraction, some constant companion to other, more vivid human lives [especially those of Willie Yeats, her mother Maud, and her husband, Francis Stuart]" (13). Gonne's letters to Yeats indicate that she was far more concerned to keep Iseult productively occupied (first with translations, then with nursing, both of which Iseult quit) than to look after her emotional life.[2]

Although Levenson and others argue that Gonne is known far more for her relationship with W.B. Yeats than for any contribution to Ireland's independence, this assessment is debatable, and reflects a sexist view of both history and biography. Because of his bias, Levenson's biography provides important material for a feminist scholar precisely because it illustrates the process of devaluing women that Irish historians have long engaged in. Levenson praises Gonne for her initiative, character, and commitment to an independent Ireland, but he questions why she would not submit to Yeats' repeated attempts to make her his wife: "Was it because she lacked emotional depth, sensitivity to another's woes? Was it because he did not seem to her masculine enough? In many women there seems to be a mechanism that converts pity into love. Why was there none in Maud?" (253). But Gonne's experience of love does not suggest emotional superficiality. On the contrary, the biography meticulously details her agonies of separation, submission, toleration of infidelity and assault in her long-term relations with Lucien Millevoye and John MacBride. She certainly showed a "woman's dedication," body and soul, to them. She also showed enormous sensitivity to others' woes when she campaigned tirelessly for prisoners' rights in the years following the Civil War. Instead of calling her unwomanly in refusing Yeats, Levenson might have noticed that they were poorly matched in their beliefs and values. Yeats was not committed to the freedom fight, nor did he share her strong identification with the Catholic poor, cemented by her conversion to Catholicism in 1902.

Gonne's contributions to the Republican movement are numerous and persistent. As founding President of *Inghinidhe na hEireann* (Daughters of Erin), she helped create the first women's group to fight for Irish independence, in 1900. This contribution alone makes her an active agent of revolution, rather than an interesting object of Yeats' frustrated romantic desire. The Daughters' constitution ambitiously aims "to re-establish the complete independence of Ireland; to encourage the study of Gaelic, of Irish literature, History, Music and Art, especially among the young, by organizing the teaching of classes; to support and popularize Irish manufacture; to discourage the reading and circulation of low English literature, the singing of English songs, the attending of vulgar English entertainments at the theatres and music hall, and to combat in every way English influence, which is doing so much injury to the artistic taste and refinement of the Irish people; and to form a fund called the National Purposes Fund, for the furtherance of the above objects" (Ward 51).

The requirements of membership in Daughters of Erin were strict, in interesting contrast to the Irish Women's Liberation Movement (1970), to be discussed later. First, one must be of Irish birth or descent, and willing to adopt a Gaelic alias to avoid detection. Candidates had to make a definite commitment, and be supported by two members. The Daughters' first job was to stage the Patriotic Children's Treat, a grand feast for 30,000 Dublin children, which was meant to subvert the gala offered for Queen Victoria's visit of April 4, 1900. The political implication was that children who paid tribute to England's sovereign were not truly Irish. Gonne understood that the best time to grow new patriots was at a very young age; she started parading Sean in Irish gear when he was three. At the Treat in Clonturk Park, Gonne spoke to the young audience of her hope that Ireland would be free by the time they grew up, leaving no uncertainty about who was responsible for carrying on that mission. In her autobiography, Gonne proudly recalls that forty years later, people still thanked her for inspiring them at that occasion. It had changed their lives.

Although providing food and festivities for children is typical women's work, Gonne also challenged grownups, especially police. One of her memorable patriotic demonstrations was named the Battle of Coulson Avenue, another protest of British royalty's visit to Dublin, and a critique of the hypocrisy of the Dublin Corporation (city government) who chose to honor them. The incident typifies Gonne's insouciance towards the police. On July 20, 1903, the day before King Edward was to arrive in Dublin, Gonne took umbrage at the British colors displayed across Coulson Avenue in honor of the King. To counteract such false patriotism, she hung a black petticoat on a broomstick from her living room window. When this was confiscated, she hung another, and told police they were trespassing. Using a perfume atomizer that looked like a gun, she defended her property and right to free speech. Appealing to the policemen's religious conscience, Gonne said that today, every other Catholic nation was displaying flags at half-mast for the Pope's death, while in Ireland, the English King "who has taken an oath against our religion" is honored with the Union Jack. When news of Gonne's predicament reached a Daughters' meeting, its members joined the *Cumann na Gaedheal* (League of Ireland), Celtic Literary Society, and National Council, in a march to her home. Fearing their patriotic zeal, the twelve policemen disbanded, while the Daughters (affectionately called the Ninnies) made tea to celebrate Gonne's petticoat victory.

Gonne's work extended far beyond the distaff world of ninnies, petticoats, treats, and tea. Her radical ideas showed colleagues the quickest way to proceed towards Irish independence. In 1898, she was the first republican who advocated abstentionism (withdrawal of Irish MPs from English Parliament as a way to contest England's sovereignty). She was a strong proponent of direct action. Encouraging starving Mayo peasants to steal sheep from their landlords, she cited Scripture to defend the right of a starving person to steal. Levenson believes that one of the most important ways in which Gonne influenced Irish history was by subsidizing Arthur Griffith when he launched the *United Irishman* newspaper. Again, his bias should be noted. While there is no question that supporting this pro–Republican publication was important, calling it the *most* important act is to minimize Gonne's active and courageous moves to ensure independence. She acted on her own behalf, not just for men. Philanthropy was part of her role as a revolutionary, but it would have been far less useful had she not done active things like cooking in school kitchens in a campaign to gain state subsidies. Gonne was not an armchair philosopher; she was present and active wherever she perceived the need for protesting, proselytizing, nursing, fighting, organizing and inspiring others.

In addition to direct-action protests and strikes, Maud gave hundreds of public speeches, believing her role was to teach Irish people to "look on English law and justice with contempt and defiance" (Levenson 155). She organized protests in front of agrarian courts. She instructed farmers to disobey laws forbidding public assembly. A brilliant public speaker, she was equally gifted with her pen. Her most famous article appeared in the April 6, 1900, *United Irishman*, on occasion of protesting the Queen's visit. The following lines prove her rhetorical skill:

> In truth, for Victoria, in the decrepitude of her 81 years, to have decided, after an absence of half a century, to revisit the country she hates, whose inhabitants are the victims of the criminal policy of her reign and the survivors of 60 years of organized famine, the political necessity must have been terribly strong. For, after all, she is a woman, and however vile, selfish and pitiless her soul, she must sometimes tremble as death approaches, when she thinks of the countless Irish mothers who ... watching their starving little ones, have cursed her before they died [quoted in Levenson 168].

Here Gonne combines several rhetorical devices, including strong language; clever use of numbers (81, 50, and 60 years); and the appeal to pity, not just for the children themselves, but for the Queen who is killing them, presumably against her maternal instincts. This makes it appear that she condemns the behavior, not the person.

As well as a mellifluous, passionate voice, Gonne had a beauty that ignited the patriotic fires of both women and men. Yeats wrote of her power to compel action: "when men and women did her bidding they did it not only because she was beautiful, but because that beauty suggested joy and freedom ... an element in her beauty that moved minds full of old Gaelic stories and poems, for she looked as though she lived in an ancient civilization where all superiorities whether of the mind or the body were a part of public ceremonial, were in some way the crowd's creation" (quoted in Levenson 124). Many admirers mention the nobility of her character as well as her physique.

Although her nationalist activities surpassed her interest in suffrage, Gonne did sound a feminist note in her interview with the *New York Evening World* after her separation from MacBride:

> If a woman really has something worth while doing in the world, I say unhesitatingly that marriage is a deplorable step, or is likely to prove so until after she has accomplished her work. If she is an ordinary, commonplace woman, then she might as well marry as not.... Man is so inherently selfish, that no matter how loving he is when he first marries, he is sure to become jealous or sarcastic about his wife's career. In the end, he is likely to make his wife's life a hell.... In these days the woman is likely to be better educated than her husband. It is a fatal error for such a woman to take on such a man. If you question 100 husbands on the street, 75 would be quite happy, whereas at least 95 of the wives would be unhappy or feel their lives were incomplete owing to their husband's congenital conviction that the main thing in the world is his content and comfort [Levenson 231].

Clearly, her two sexual partnerships with men had left Gonne convinced that men rule women in marriage.

Bean na hEireann (Woman of Ireland) (1909–11), the Irish Women's Franchise League, and Hanna Sheehy-Skeffington

Like Gonne, most female nationalists put suffrage second in priority to national independence. Socialist Helena Moloney edited *Bean na hEireann*, the first Irish women's paper (1908), to which Countess Constance Markievicz contributed a column called "The Woman with the Garden." Constance parodied the uses of nationalist propaganda: "A good nationalist should look upon slugs in the garden much in the same way as she looks on the English in Ireland" (Ward 69). Although most of the articles were dedicated to the nationalist struggle, one proclaimed that the objective of *Cumann na mBan* (League of Women) should be "Freedom for Our Nation and to remove all disabilities to our sex" (Ward 69). This statement reveals the common belief of most women involved with politics in the day, that the two struggles were intertwined.

The problem with suffrage, however, was that the only body capable of giving votes to women was the English Parliament, and many republicans did not believe in petitioning to the British government, even for a right as fervently desired as the vote. This attitude mirrored the republican rejection of Home Rule, based on grounds that (a) Britain may write the bill, but never enforce it; (b) the limited Irish sovereignty the bill provided was not enough for the republicans, who wanted an entirely Irish nation; and (c) accepting legislation from Westminster was tantamount to accepting England's sovereignty over Ireland. Finally, and I think most antifeminist in its sentiment, was the republican fear that women would dilute the energy of the independence movement by fighting for women's independence. In the same mistaken reasoning as that of Marx and Engels, republicans pretended to believe in all human rights. They assumed that the new utopia of an independent Ireland would automatically make women equal, so that there was no need to claim women's rights before the victory was won.

The woman most prominent in publicizing the opposite view — that women needed the vote in order to participate as equal citizens in the nationalist movement — was Hanna Sheehy Skeffington. A frequent writer for *Bean na hEireann*, and co-founder in 1908 of the Irishwomen's Franchise League, she tried to open women's eyes to the fact that they were second-class citizens. The nationalists wanted women to think that they were equal because they were fighting for a common objective with men, but the jobs given to women were always "women's work," and secondary to men's. The Gaelic League appealed to mothers to make sure that their homes were as Irish as possible, by teaching their children Gaelic and buying Irish products. Women were recruited for women's work, such as teaching, feeding and clothing the poor, taking care of prisoners' dependents, and nursing wounded soldiers. Women were allowed to be members of *Sinn Féin* (Ourselves Alone), a new party committed to attaining independence, but not to progress to the higher ranks. No woman sat in local government or Parliament until Constance de Markievicz was elected Labor Minister in 1919.

When speaking of patriarchy, Hanna's language was strong and direct, like other female leaders of her time. It was imperative for women to organize separately and "refuse any longer to be the camp-followers and parasites of public life, dependent on caprice and expediency for recognition" (quoted in Ward 72). She understood the implications of Ireland's Catholicism for women's role in society. In a rural Catholic society, women were economically and socially disadvantaged, and most politicians wanted to keep them that way. For Hanna Skeffington, franchise was the very keystone of citizenship. Until women had the vote, they would not truly participate in decisions about the independence of Ireland. Although women (over thirty) did get the vote in 1918, Skeffington's predictions were prescient, as women still had huge battles to fight, including extending suffrage to age twenty-one, getting women elected, and attaining employment, contraception, and divorce. After the Treaty, nationalist women painfully learned that their nationalist brothers were not the egalitarian humanitarians that they had supposed. Even the leader of the revolutionary party, Eamon de Valera, shamelessly publicized his misogyny.

Cumann na mBan (League of Women, 1914 to the present), The Uprising, and Countess Constance Markievicz

Dublin's Strike and Lockout of 1913 provided strong impetus for the 1916 Uprising. Residents were disgusted by the police brutality used to suppress strikes. Dublin Castle wrote harsh laws to deal with protesters. In early summer 1913, the transport workers' union commenced a strike when the owner of The Tramway Company refused to heed their demands. William Murphy, the richest man in Ireland, immediately locked out sixty employees. Other employers followed suit, until most of Dublin's labor force was fired. Through the bitter months of winter, unemployed men and their families ate in soup kitchens run by Countess Markievicz and Hanna Sheehy Skeffington. Finally, in August, Labor Leader Jim Larkin publicly burned the Magistrate's proclamation forbidding union meetings, appearing at his next Sunday gathering in contravention of the law. Dublin Castle was so threatened by the number of agitators that it authorized a baton charge. That day, casualties numbered two dead and 478 injured. Named Bloody Sunday, this day's brutality motivated labor leaders to establish an Irish Citizen Army (ICA) to defend workers from future police aggressions. In three years' time, ICA was one of three armed bodies that staged the Easter Monday Uprising.

The Easter Uprising was an attempt to declare Ireland a Republic with its own Constitution and no ties to England. But, due to hasty planning and miscommunication between ICA leaders in Dublin and Volunteers leaders in Cork and Kerry, the attempt was costly and unsuccessful. Germany's efforts to provide ammunition backfired when their shipment of revolvers was destroyed in Galway Bay. Orders to mobilize the ICA were delivered, then cancelled, then reinstated and re-cancelled. Because of these communication failures, an insurrection that was intended to be nationwide ended up occurring in Dublin alone.

Republican leaders encircled the downtown area by occupying several key buildings. Future long-term Prime Minister Eamon de Valera famously refused to allow women volunteers into his post at Boland's Mill. The heart of the battle was the General Post Office in O'Connell Street; from its steps, schoolteacher Patrick Pearse proudly read the Proclamation of Provisional

Government of the Irish Republic. Only a small number of men were willing to risk treason by signing it — Tom Clarke, Sean MacDiarmada, Thomas Mac-Donagh, Patrick Pearse, Eamonn Ceannt, James Connolly, and Joseph Plunkett. Yet sixteen leaders were found to be traitors by the British government. Of these, fifteen were executed on the rooftop of Kilmainham Gaol a week later. Constance de Markievicz was pardoned because of her sex, while Eamon de Valera was not technically a traitor to the British government because of his American citizenship.

The Proclamation was an important document to feminists, for its words promised an equality that never materialized: "The Republic guarantees religious and civil liberty, equal rights and equal opportunities to all its citizens ... cherishing all the children of the nation equally" (Owens 113). Despite its egalitarian language, the Proclamation's concern stemmed more from awareness of laborers' than women's rights. Clearly institutionalizing Ireland's gender discrimination, the 1937 Constitution would legalize a distinction between men's and women's rights that would plague women for decades to come. The dream of a free Ireland in which women were valued as equals to men was not to come true.

In the void left by Maud Gonne's absence, another woman leader stirred the hearts and minds of nationalists. Constance Markievicz neé Gore-Booth was born to money, yet made an alliance with the poor. Her father was a benevolent Anglo-Irish landlord who provided food for his starving tenants, and refused to seize their homes when they went to the poorhouse. Constance, nicknamed Con, grew up in horsey upper-class society; her greatest delights were riding and shooting. Her mother tried to rein her in, and Markievicz's diary expresses frustration about parental controls on her life, as she fervently wishes to earn her own living. Finally allowed to attend St. George's Art School in Paris, Constance meets Count Casimir Markievicz, a wealthy Polish *bon vivant*. His friendly personality and aristocratic background make him acceptable to her parents, so the young couple marries without opposition. Although her family will later oppose her republican activities as "unbefitting her womanhood," Constance's sister, Eva Gore-Booth, remains a spiritual supporter of Constance's mission throughout her life. Eva herself is a suffragette living with another woman, and involved with the labor movement in Manchester.

Markievicz's nationalist activities include joining the Daughters of Erin in 1908, helping Helena Molony edit *Bean na hEireann*, joining the Irish Citizens' Army in 1909 (open to women because of James Connolly's progressive stance), and organizing the *Fianna na hEireann*, a paramilitary boy scout group, in 1909. Like Gonne, Markievicz knew that nationalism should be planted in young minds, because boys respond well to patriotic appeals. Most historians agree that organizing this boy-scout group was Markievicz's greatest contribution to Irish history, because it was a training ground for soldiers in the War of Independence and Civil War. When the scouts came of age, their *Fianna* membership automatically transferred to the Irish Republican Army.

Also like Gonne, Markievicz encountered working-class distrust of her aristocratic status. Unafraid of publicity, she was a persuasive public speaker, and drew men into the cause by her beauty and poise. As a tomboy, her image did not receive the same mythological projections of goddess and saint as Gonne's. In fact, Markievicz was known for un-statesmanlike behavior; she was so frank and "boyish" in her direct style of communication that she usually got what she wanted. If she were unsatisfied, she would start a fight. Her motto was "organize, and make a row;" thus, it is not surprising that she spent much of her time in jail.

Constance was first arrested at a protest of King George's 1911 visit to Dublin. On July 4, Markievicz stole a Union Jack from Leinster House, then cut it and wrapped it around her waist. Police tried to wrest this symbol of British power from this iconic figure of Irish rebellion. When she burned the flag, police arrested a male bystander rather than this scion of Ascendancy privilege. Helena Molony did manage to get arrested for throwing stones at pictures of the King and Queen, and for calling King George "one of the worst scoundrels of Europe." At this point, Markievicz was arrested too, for being Helena's co-conspirator.

Labor leader James Connolly helped draw Markievicz further into the ranks. In 1913, she joined the Irish Citizen Army, in part because of Connolly's charisma. He believed in the equality of poor and rich, and of women and men, even in their military capability. Connolly's messages and personality appealed deeply to Markievicz, reminding her of her benevolent father who respected his tenants. During the 1913 Lockout, she helped Maud Gonne operate soup kitchens at Liberty Hall.

At this time, the threat of impending Home Rule aroused northern Irelanders to form the Ulster Volunteer Force to defend the union. The Irish Republican Brotherhood was glad of this occasion, believing it would persuade the milder of Irish nationalists that force, not faith in England's liberals, would be required to effectuate the Republic. At a November 25 meeting of 6000 people, the Irish Volunteers constituted themselves as a counterforce to the Ulster variant, their objective "to secure and maintain the rights and liberties common to the whole people of Ireland." Since the Volunteers banned women, a group of fighting women formed their own *Cumann na mBan* (League of Women) on April 5, 1914, as an auxiliary group. The primary aim of the *Cumann* was "to advance the cause of Irish liberty" and "assist in arming and equipping a body of Irish men for the defense of Ireland" (Ward 164). Markievicz was a prominent member of both *Cumann na mBan* and the Irish Citizen Army, the latter giving her the physical outlet she needed, since the women's organization did not give permission to fire arms. The *Cumann* women were only involved with arms to the extent that they procured and delivered them to men.

Because of her proven abilities, and her visibility within the nationalist community, Markievicz was made a Lieutenant in the ICA, being appointed second-in-command to Michael Mallin. During the Uprising, their unit commanded St. Stephen's Green, where they dug trenches and built barricades to little avail. British sniping from the surrounding buildings overpowered them, so their small troop moved headquarters to the adjacent Royal College of Surgeons, where they held out for six days. During this period, Markievicz had an epiphany about the Catholics with whom she had been working for the past eight years. Admiring the strength they drew from faith, she experienced a personal conversion in the midst of battle, and was baptized by a priest upon her departure from Aylesbury Prison. This conversion was yet another step away from her Anglo-Protestant upbringing, one that would further distress her mother — with whom Markievicz's daughter Maeve was living.[3]

Upon receiving Patrick Pearse's surrender order, Markievicz and Mallin were escorted through the Dublin streets to Kilmainham Gaol. There was very little popular support for the Uprising, and Dubliners hissed and booed these "heroes" as they passed. But the events of the next month shifted public opinion. The murder of Francis Sheehy Skeffington, Hanna's pacifist husband, was an arbitrary police action. He had been in the streets during the Uprising only to help prevent looting. For no official reason, he was brutally murdered by British Captain Bowen-Colthurst. Also incendiary was the execution of the fifteen Uprising leaders on the roof of Kilmainham Gaol. Unlike Captain Colthurst's brutality, this killing at least had a legal rationale, but Dubliners considered it excessive punishment for the heroes who had proclaimed the freedom of Ireland. Markievicz was not proud of being treated differently than her male counterparts. Upon hearing of her pardon, she told the British officials, "I wish you lot had the decency to kill me." Adding to the people's resentment was the imprisonment of 3,197 men and 77 women by July 1. Of these, 1,862 were interned without trial. These outrages gave new vitality to *Sinn Féin*.

Thirteen months after their internment, the government released Markievicz and the other Uprising detainees. Upon release, Markievicz became President of the women's group, *Cumann na mBan*, which was planning further insurrection. The work of the *Cumann* women was to keep the faith in a free Ireland, by popularizing the memory of the 1916 leaders, organizing prisoner relief agencies, and opposing conscription. Members of *Sinn Féin* (where Markevicz was Head of Labor), the Labor Party, and Irish Parliamentary Party banded together to resist England's Conscription Act of April 16, 1918. On April 23, all Ireland stopped work to protest conscription of Irish men for an English war. Prime Minister Lloyd George was so alarmed by these numbers and the potential for violence that he ordered police to arrest anyone who seemed suspicious. He concocted The German Plot to establish grounds for arresting Irish republicans, but this was a mere pretense, for in actuality the anti-conscriptionists were not in communication with the German enemy. These arrests landed seventy-three *Sinn Féin* leaders in jail on May 17–18, including Markievicz, Gonne, and Kathleen Clarke (widow of a 1916 martyr). After considerable protest, the three women managed to arrange adjacent cells and the right to association. It was during this time that Gonne discovered she was not as resilient as Markievicz, who wisely distracted herself by gardening, painting and reading. In prison, Gonne's health deteriorated. Meanwhile, Hanna Sheehy Skeffington was arrested under the Defense of the Realm Act for having entered Ireland from the U.S. without a passport, and spent one day in jail with her fellow revolutionaries.

In February 1918, British Parliament gave suffrage to women over thirty, and in November of that year, the right of women to be members of Parliament was also granted. Immediately, *Sinn Féin* nominated Markievicz to run for office, and the *Cumann na mBan*, Volunteers, and Irish Women's Franchise League all canvassed for her while she was in jail. *Sinn Féin* was the majority party at this election, and made a courageous gesture for Irish independence. Both Woodrow Wilson and Prime Minister Lloyd George declared that World War I was being fought to achieve the rights of small nations. Ireland was a small nation. Eamon de Valera and Count Plunkett declared that the newly elected *Sinn Féin* officials would treat it as such. An independent Irish parliament, the *Dáil Éireann* would convene regardless of Britain's sovereignty. At the *Dáil's* first assembly, 36 members were still imprisoned by the enemy. The *Dáil* sent three members to the Paris Peace Conference, in part to solicit America's support in declaring Ireland an independent nation. But President Wilson needed British support for the League of Nations, so he ignored Ireland's cause. Once again, Ireland learned that she would have to fight her battle with arms. At the *Dáil's* second assembly in March, Eamon de Valera was elected President and Constance de Markievicz, Minister of Labor. As part of Ireland's proclaimed independence, *Sinn Féin* determined to take over the judiciary, and went about establishing Ireland's own land courts and magistrates.

Now the War of Independence started in earnest. On March 25, 1920, British authorities unleashed a mercenary police force called The Black and

Tans (for the colors of their boots and uniforms) to terrorize republicans into submission. Known for their brutality, this force indiscriminately destroyed homes, shops and animals, and murdered men, women and children. In turn, IRA volunteers ambushed British forces, while women performed the open-air tasks of carrying dispatches, scouting, and collecting intelligence. Women could travel more openly than men because they were not suspected of political activity.

On June 24, 1921, after more than a year of brutalities on both sides, Lloyd George capitulated to international pressure to call a truce. *Sinn Féin* selected Arthur Griffith and Michael Collins to represent them during treaty negotiations. Sadly, after their London meeting, these deputies returned with terms unacceptable to many republicans: (1) a Free State, but with dominion status; (2) a partition of the six counties of Ulster from the twenty-six of southern Ireland; and (3) the requirement that all *Dáil* deputies swear an oath of allegiance to the English crown. For some, these conditions were sufficient for the time being; full independence could be achieved at a later date. For others, anything less than full Republic status was unacceptable. The oath of allegiance was the turning point in their decision to fight the treaty. In fact, more debate was heard about the oath than the partition, although the partition has caused more trouble ever since. The female *Cumann na Ban* deputies to the *Dáil* voted against ratification of this treaty, manifesting their strong republican ethos. However, many male voters undermined the *Cumann* position by saying that these soldiers' widows were crazed by grief. Once again, women's contributions to the cause were ridiculed rather than respected.

The women's side lost. On January 6, 1922, the *Dáil* ratified the Anglo-Irish Treaty by a vote of 64 to 57. Eamon de Valera was anti–Treaty, so he resigned as President of the *Dáil*. Griffith became President of the Free State, and Michael Collins, Minister of Finance. When the first pro-treaty parliament met, *Cumann na Ban* women demonstrated outside of Mansion House. The status of Ireland was not their only issue; they also asked that the new Parliament extend the women's vote to age twenty-one *before* the people's vote on the Treaty, so that women's voices could be heard on this vital issue of national definition. President Griffith angrily declared that they were trying to "torpedo the Treaty" by fronting the suffrage issue. He proceeded to call the referendum before voters had a chance to read the new Constitution, introducing undemocratic methods in the new government from its very inception. With these events, women became the scapegoat of the pro–Treaty faction. Calling them the Furies, *Sinn Féiner* P.S. O'Hegarty said, "The women were the implacable and irrational upholders of death and destruction.... We know that with women in political power there would be no more peace" (Ward 177).

The Civil War that ensued over the treaty issue was heartbreaking to Irish people who had so recently bonded together to fight a common enemy, only to turn arms against each other. Aided by British weapons and troops, the pro–Treaty faction (Free Staters) had the clear advantage. Shooting took place in both Dublin and the countryside for ten months. Even more than during the War of Independence, women became involved as messengers and spies. Because the male opponents were well known to each other, the IRA had to fragment itself into very small groups, which created an ineffective defense. Old safe houses were no longer viable, and IRA men had to be constantly on the run. When the army's chief-of-staff Liam Lynch was killed, De Valera finally surrendered to the Free Staters. Yet the new government continued to make arrests, their causes as spurious as those of the Black and Tans before them. Women continued to protest, get arrested, and go on hunger strike. They were beaten and raped in jails. Yet men, not women, received accolades for the fight. Speaking of a women's commemoration of the 1916 freedom fighters on Easter 1923, Margaret Ward remarks: "As the cult of martyrology has always been a powerful motivating force in Irish history and it has always been men who have paid the supreme penalty, this sacrifice of male lives for the national cause has obscured the continual yet less dramatic sacrifices made by women working for the same cause" (Ward 193). Women continued to be recognized for their organizing efforts, but only as auxiliaries, not in their own right.

The 1937 Constitution and Eamon de Valera

The ten years following the Civil War saw a continuation of police brutality. Authorities harassed political activists with impunity. The Coercion Act, Article 2D, permitted arrest for any suspicious activity, and the new President, William Cosgrave, still found the anti–Treaty people suspicious, even after the end of the Civil War. He would attempt to rule both their minds and bodies: in 1929, the Censorship Act allowed the government to censor media (literature, art, journalism, film) on moral grounds, promising an Irish barrier against *evil* continental influences upon the minds and souls of the *pure* Irish people. For the first forty years of the Free State, official Ireland was principally concerned to express its differences from Britain — a pattern noted by scholars to be inevitable in newly independent states. Finally, in 1932, De Valera's party, *Fianna Fáil*, won the election and he became President of the *Dáil*, putting an end to the repressive Cosgrave government. At first, he made reforms that mollified republicans, such as abolishing the oath of allegiance, suspending Article 2A, firing unpopular Police Commissioner O'Duffy, and instituting pensions for veteran republicans.

However, De Valera's social vision was regressive from the point of view of feminists and other liberals whose hopes resonated with the democratic words of the 1916 Proclamation. De Valera and his party aimed to maintain Ireland's cultural isolation from the world, by censoring their media, making them speak Gaelic, and being faithful to the directives of their conservative Catholic Church, "which liked the idea of Ireland as a spiritual oasis in the modern world" (Killeen 66). A staunch Catholic and avowed misogynist, De Valera's plan was to write "a Catholic constitution for a Catholic people." Through legal loopholes, he revised the people's constitution of 1922, expressing his own ethos and that of the majority of his constituency.

The most frightening regression that came out of this autocratic assertion of power was a distinction between male and female rights in Article 41. It was De Valera's heartfelt belief that women's place is in the home. He had barred women from Boland's Mill during the Easter Uprising; he had disregarded women's contributions to the Civil War; and he believed the Church's teachings on women's inferiority. These beliefs are encapsulated and made law by the provision of Article 41, which states, "By her life within the home, woman gives to the State a support without which the common good cannot be achieved.... The state, shall, therefore, endeavour to ensure that mothers shall not be obliged by economic necessity to engage in labour to the neglect of their duties in the home" (Ward 238). The practical effect of this law was that women could be forbidden employment, which was especially advantageous to men at this time of economic depression.

The *Cumann na mBan* and other women's organizations did not make a strong showing against the constitutional revision. Historians ask why. Margaret Ward believes that women were distracted by their protest of George V's coronation as King of England, Wales, Scotland and Ireland. Technically, Ireland had dominion status within the Commonwealth, so the King's inclusion of Ireland in its domain was legal. Yet this reminder of what was *not* achieved by the 1922 Treaty provided an opportunity to keep the republican fires burning. There was, however, a small anti-constitution protest by some liberal members of the women's movement. In 1938, the Women's Social and Progressive League distributed an *Open Letter to Women Voters of Ireland*, asking them to interrogate any candidate about his stance on Article 41 before voting for him. This letter contains the statement, "Under the Constitution our position has deteriorated and is further menaced by the implications of Clauses 40, 41, and 45," indicating that the legal implications of De Valera's wording were fully understood (Connolly 73). Yet the Irish Women Workers' Union withdrew from the Article 41 protest because its female leader had an ambivalent attitude to women in the workforce.

De Valera's reworking of the People's 1922 Constitution into the Catholic

1937 Constitution gave his government *carte blanche* to write discriminatory statutes. Soon thereafter, Ireland enforced a marriage ban on teachers and civil service workers — married women could not hold these good jobs. This ban continued in force until the second wave of feminists removed it in the 1970s. The failure of women's organizations to fight Article 41 to its death is extraordinary when we consider how persistent, vocal, fearless and united they were in the fight against the British presence. However, demographics explain this apparent paradox. Many Irish — especially of the working class — were so relieved to see the end of war and the ousting of the Cosgrave government that they accepted the "smaller" setbacks of De Valera's initiative to send women back home after their magnificent contributions to achieving independence. The wording of Article 41 was not upsetting to most good Catholics. For those unaware of the subtleties of the law, the Article seemed like a benevolent attempt to support families, not an invitation to discriminatory legislation. The next period of Irish history sees the women's movement in abeyance, although several women's organizations concern themselves with the economies of the home during yet another economic downturn.

The Women's Movement in Abeyance, 1922–1968

In the years between the birth of the Free State and the meetings of second-wave feminists in 1968, the women's movement changed focus. This era is known as the abeyance period. So closely allied was the first wave with nationalism and suffrage that once those goals were achieved, feminists lost unity and purpose. As Ireland struggled through the Great Depression and its aftermath, she tried to rebuild an economy that had been devastated by six years of war and the partial withdrawal of its British investors. People focused on survival. Revisionist historians are keen to prove that the women's movement did not die and go away, but that in the 1940s, a marginalized feminist base, consisting of first-wave activists and new recruits, produced the leaders of second-wave feminism. Linda Connolly, a University of Cork sociologist, maintains that there is continuity in the movement from first to second wave.

Because of the repressions of De Valera's government (such as Act of Censorship, Article 41, marriage ban, and Catholic hegemony), the narration of the abeyance period lacks the verve of the century's first two decades. Liberalism goes underground, as does the radicalism of the IRA and republican movement. However, the underground activities are well worth our attention, since they explain how such a powerful feminist consciousness could erupt in the early seventies. Historians and sociologists strive to correct narratives that say that the abeyance era is completely repressive, or that women are totally submissive to the Church. Although this revisionism can go too far in the direction of justifying De Valera's regime, the documents discussed are open to interpretation.

Mary Daly, for example, suggests that the impact of first-wave feminism has been greatly exaggerated because of the visibility of its highly educated leaders. The realities of working class women have been ignored. More controversial is her assumption that "in turn, the repressive nature of the new Irish state may also have been overstated" (in Connolly 84). This makes sense only insofar as suggesting that Cosgrave and De Valera used repression *differently* than the British had done before the Free State. However, both Presidents still used demonstrably repressive measures to keep women in their place.

The female leaders of both the suffrage and the freedom movements in the early century were primarily educated, middle-class women, and this demographic would also predominate in the abeyance period. The Irish Housewives' Association (IHA), for example, was established in 1942 "to unite housewives, so that they may realize, and gain recognition for, their right to play an active part in all spheres of planning for the Community" (Connolly 74). There is a remarkable difference in ambition between the word "community" and the word "nation," the sphere in which first-wave feminists and republicans conceptualized their role, but the advent of the Depression helps explain this downsizing of political ideals. At IHA's inception, Ireland was experiencing the second of two blows to its economy in the abeyance period: first, the Depression, and second, economic stagnation due to its neutrality during World War II. While this neutrality saved Irishmen's lives, it also reduced the availability of money, food and fuel. The IHA's first action was to form coalitions that put pressure on government to address consumer issues such as social welfare, public health, education and the law, particularly family law. The IHA included more feminist members than other women's organizations, and its work provided a basis from which second-wave organizations were built. Their most important contribution was the creation of a Consumer's Association in the 1960s, which protested rising prices and nominated candidates to the *Dáil*.

However, the IHA's feminist consciousness was sometimes squelched by censorship. As Linda Connolly relates, "the publication of feminist analyses of women's situation was largely impeded and political sentiments were frequently misinterpreted" (75). Because they worked to provide food for the poor, the IHA's intentions were misconstrued as communist during Ireland's version of America's Red Scare. Founding member Hilda Tweedy notes, "These continuous allegations of communism, or of communist leanings, were extremely upsetting and disruptive for our members, especially in the climate of the time. Not only did it frighten many of our members, but also their husbands who feared that their livelihoods might be affected" (Connolly 75).

Two other women's organizations, the Irish Countrywomen's Association (ICA), and the IWWU (Irish Women's Worker's Union), were both more conservative than the IHA. Founded in 1910, the ICA is the largest women's organization in Ireland; its objectives are to provide social and educational opportunities for women, and to improve the standard of rural and urban life in Ireland. A recent study of the ICA by Diarmaid Ferriter challenges the assumption that the 1950s were socially and culturally stagnant, while recognizing that women's sphere of activity was social and cultural, rather than political. Linda Connolly's overriding concern as expressed in *The Irish Women's Movement: From Evolution to Devolution* is that "selected aspects of this history could be taken up in a tokenistic or incomplete manner." To correct this tendency, we need to realize that women's organizations of the abeyance period were moderate in their politics because of rigid constraints on women's participation in the public sphere. They needed to be cautious in order to remain in existence (Connolly 86).

Second-Wave Feminism (1968–1980) and the Irish Women's Liberation Movement

The peak activism of second-wave feminism was intense and brief, lasting a mere two years, 1970–71. As in America and Britain, there were two main strands of second-wave feminism: women's rights (liberal feminism) and women's liberation (radical feminism). The women's rights strand was more centrally organized, using legal channels to push for social change. In contrast, the women's liberation strand consisted of many small, radical, autonomous, loosely structured groups that used direct-action techniques such as protest and picketing to publicize their demands, as well as consciousness-raising to change the social fabric, one mind at a time. Women's liberation had an ideological orientation, and was influenced by simultaneous American anti-war, free love, back-to-nature, and women's movements. Although it was spiritually powerful, the lack of structure in the women's liberation strand affected its ability to lobby effectively.

Council for the Status of Women (CSW), 1972

Historical periodization always invites challenges, because history does not move in blocks. It grows organically, through strands of thought and chains of events. However, the years 1968 to 1971 were history-makers. As in other European countries, 1968 is a clear banner year in Ireland, marking increased government receptivity to women's demands. At their 1968 annual London conference, the International Alliance of Women, of which IHA was an affiliate, asked its members to examine the status of women in their respective countries, and to lobby their governments to set up national commissions on the status of women. After intense lobbying by IHA and other women's organizations, Irish *Taoseich* (Prime Minister) Jack Lynch established the First Commission on the Status of Women in 1970. The language of its mission challenges Article 41 of the Irish Constitution by exhorting members "to make recommendations on the steps necessary to ensure the participation of women on equal terms and conditions with men in the political, social, cultural and economic life of the country." The Commission's August 1971 report recommended removal of the marriage bar and implementation of equal pay. To institute these measures a Council for the Status of Women (CSW) was formed to "provide liaison between government departments and women's organizations, provide educational and developmental programs for women, examine cases of discrimination against women, and consider legislative proposals of concern to women" (Connolly 99).

These idealistic goals were only gradually achieved. One problem was a lack of funding; CSW didn't obtain government funding until 1977. Another obstacle was state recognition. In Linda Connolly's words, "the State was by no means permeable to the CSW's moderate demands" (102). CSW moved forward only when the media paid attention, and that impetus came only through international bodies, such as the United Nations. However, the CSW did begin to enact social change through institutions, a *modus operandi* in direct contrast to that of the women's liberation movement. The CSW used politics of persuasion and non-confrontational tactics like talking to the government, while the Irish Women's Liberation Movement members, many of whom had been involved in left wing, Republican parties, used direct-action, confrontational tactics.

The Irish Women's Liberation Movement (IWLM), 1970–71

In her small, unpretentious Dublin restaurant on Baggot Street, Margaret Gaj provided the right atmosphere for the Irish Women's Liberation Movement, which met there on Monday nights. The IWLM was visible, courageous, and effective — at least in raising consciousness. The group grew organically out of the kinds of conversations typical of the restaurant patrons. Whores, robbers, doctors, aristocrats and social workers were the unusual mix that frequented Gaj's to hold political discussions with a leftist orientation. At Gaj's, waiters were hired on probation to see whether they were temperamentally suited to work shifts that began with story-telling, but might end in overturned tables. Mrs. Gaj functioned more as a social worker than a cook or businesswoman. She was a socialist who "never saw why you needed to make more money than you needed to live decently." Mrs. Gaj advocated for friends on trial, and co-founded the Prisoners' Rights Organization in 1973 with Joe Costello.

On this fertile ground, the IWLM began with a phone call from Máirín de Burca to her friend, journalist Mary Maher, in August 1970. De Burca was an activist working with several groups, including *Sinn Féin*, the Dublin Housing Action Committee, the Irish Voice on Vietnam, and the Irish Anti-Apartheid Movement. Although a pacifist, de Burca was well-versed in direct-action tactics like shouting at politicians and defacing property. She first served time for smashing bottles of cow's blood on the steps of the American Embassy, and burning the American flag in protest of the Vietnam War. Her most important contribution to women's rights was the successful Supreme Court challenge of the law forbidding women jurors; she worked on a legal team headed by Mary Robinson, the future President of Ireland.

News of American consciousness-raising, or CR, inspired De Burca to begin the IWLM. Betty Friedan's *The Feminine Mystique* and Germaine Greer's *The Female Eunuch* were her feminist bibles. She and Mary Maher organized a feminist discussion group, to convene on Monday nights at Gaj's. Mary Maher was the first editor of the *Irish Times* women's page; she dropped the recipes and fashion advice, switching to discussion of women's rights and problems, including single motherhood, deserted wives, equal pay and contraception, a taboo subject in Ireland.

The third feminist in the phone chain was Máirín Johnston, a working mother who cared passionately about working-class issues, and was distrustful of middle-class women. She did not believe that people of privilege sympathized with her own class. Once Johnston started attending consciousness-raising sessions, she was able to break down her barriers and sense of inferiority. In addition to her working-class point of view, she offered organizational skills, particularly attractive for those who feared that sitting around and talking about experiences was not productive for the movement.

The fourth founding member was Dr. Moira Woods, a wealthy physician, mother of six, and passionate civil rights activist. Her commitment to causes despite her own life of economic ease convinced Máirín Johnson and others that not all wealthy people were selfish. Johnson was also surprised to hear that, despite her privilege, Woods encountered sex discrimination in her daily life. When the issue of contraception arose, Woods' medical knowledge made her invaluable. Her extensive education made her an eloquent and fearless speaker. In the mock trial of Richard Nixon for his crimes against the Vietnamese, held on the steps of the American Embassy, Moira played the role of judge. Another admiring member, Mary Kenny, suggested that Woods' combination of beauty, privilege, and character were reminiscent of Maud Gonne and Constance Markievicz: "She is well in the Anglo-Irish tradition of beautiful, passionate, radical women who are willing to storm the gates of any establishment for The People" (Stopper 61). In this chapter, I have described these radical women in detail because Irish patriotism has always taken inspiration from the heroes of past centuries, and I believe that Irish feminism might benefit from a similar project.

Although IWLM eventually disbanded for its want of organization, it did produce a pamphlet that made waves. *Chains or Change*, a compilation of the inequalities suffered by Irish women, was meant to enrage readers and incite them to action. The pamphlet made six demands: equal rights in law; equal pay and removal of the marriage bar; justice for widows, single mothers, and deserted wives; equal education; contraceptive rights; and one-family-to-a-house for subsidized living (Stopper 71). Of these, the issues that didn't touch directly on the Church's teachings were considered reasonable by many Irish people, whereas the right to contraception and rights for single mothers were controversial, as they appeared to condone immorality.

Even in a group of radical feminists, abortion was too volatile to address. Much like The Troubles, the subject of abortion was deeply divisive. After interviewing several founders, journalist Anne Stopper expressed it this way: "Not one of the IWLM founders remembers the topic of abortion ever even surfacing and being rejected as too damaging to the group — it simply wasn't even on their radar" (75). The strength of this abortion taboo is underlined by the fact that members would talk about other deeply personal issues as a matter of course.

IWLM meetings followed the standard format of consciousness-raising, which required an honest response by each member to any question on the table. By now, this method has been so popularized that most consumers of entertainment media have seen something like it on TV or in the movies. Group members sit in a circle and take turns telling a personal story in response to a question. To avoid patriarchal hierarchy, there is no leader. Everyone must speak, and no one must be interrupted. The method is quite simple, yet the effect can be extraordinary. Several women expressed a feeling of euphoria when they discovered that their problems were not unique to them, but shared by other members of the group. This was the real-life proof of the feminist credo that "the personal is political."[4] Women's suffering of injustice at home or at work is often a result of patriarchy, rather than a personal failure. Even years later, some founding members recall the power of bonding in these sessions; one compared it to falling in love, saying that "a change takes place in the psyche that is often that complete and profound" (54).

From the cauldron of these sessions arose three direct-action projects that helped publicize the members' awareness to a very large public sector: their appearance on Gay Byrne's *Late, Late Show* on March 6, 1971; the Mansion House meeting on April 14, 1971; and the Contraceptive Train on May 22, 1971. These dates are important, because they indicate the momentum that the movement gained in a very short time. After the Train, the group dispersed, partly in response to the sheer magnitude of interest demonstrated at Mansion House, which was beyond their ability to organize. Gay Byrne's show, originating in 1963, was a forum for the most intense issues in Ireland: the border, Irish language, and eventually, divorce and contraception. De Burca and Maher felt it was an appropriate forum in which to air the aims of the IWLM, though they had qualms that their two "live wires," Mary Kenny and Nell McCafferty, might damage their reputation. Each of these speakers lived up to her reputation.

On air, Mary Kenny made the contentious statement that *Dáil* members didn't care about women's problems: "I think that they resist changes in any of these areas up to the hilt, because I don't think that they give a damn" (Stopper 11). This prompted *Teachta Dála* (Senator) Garret FitzGerald to rush from his house to the studio in order to refute Kenny's assertions. He said that the fault wasn't the senators', but the women's, as they didn't put enough pressure on legislators to change. Given that the IWLM included some members who had spent years putting pressure on various governing bodies, the exchange turned into a good fight, with Byrne fanning the flames and audience members shouting and laughing. At this, De Burca's fears were realized, that the TV-watching public would see women speaking emotionally about their concerns! Many of Stopper's interviewees consider the IWLM appearance on the *Late, Late Show* to be a turning point in their lives, as it was the first time they had heard such opinions aired, or seen women stand up for themselves.

The adrenaline from the *Late, Late Show* spurred IWLM to their next project: a large meeting to explain their aims and sign up new members. The Mansion House meeting was larger than expected, exceeding 1000 people and lasting three hours. Like the format of *The Late, Late Show*, the Mansion House meeting invited input from the audience. Master-of-ceremonies Nell McCafferty presented the microphone to women who were eager to speak of their experience. The simple statement "I am a single mother and I am proud" aroused such thunderous applause and tears that McCafferty believed "the silence of centuries was broken" (Stopper 141). Because of audience participation, this mass meeting had some of the characteristics of a very large consciousness-raising session. Its success catapulted IWLM's ambitions to the next level: taking on contraception, the most risqué issue of the day.

The Contraceptive Train was simple in its logistics: cram a train in Dublin with as many feminists as possible (in the event, only forty-seven dared), go to Belfast to buy contraceptives, return to Dublin, wave this contraband in the face of the authorities, and distribute condoms to a crowd. However, the subject of contraception was divisive for IWLM. Some thought that single women shouldn't participate, because buying contraception implied they were having sex before marriage. IWLM wanted to reveal the hypocrisy of the state's refusal to repeal the ban despite its failure to enforce it; as expected, no arrests were made that day. The birth control pill was the only legal contraceptive in Ireland, but the prescribing doctor had to write "for cycle regulation" so it would not appear to be a contraceptive. Yet the medical community knew that the Pill could be harmful, and was too expensive to be used by the lower classes. Even though the condom was far safer than the Pill, both Nell McCafferty (a lesbian) and Mary Kenny (the most outrageous of the group) found something vulgar about waving condoms in police's faces. Their mixed feelings about the Train protest had much to do with the disbanding of IWLM. There was no declaration of an ending, but after a summer meeting of the founders, no more meetings were held. Founders continued to visit branch meetings, but the heyday of the IWLM was over.

Even though IWLM activism lasted for less than a year, the supreme confidence and courage of its leaders is what people remember about it. Their actions were an inspiration to Irish women. As a sociological study, IWLM shows the difficulty of sustaining a group without a structure. Their motto was "No leaders, no constitution, no spokespersons," because these were all trappings of patriarchy. This looseness gave them the freedom to speak, and perhaps to trust each other, but it prevented effective action over the long term. The group, and others like it, was characterized by freely expressed differences of opinion.

Irishwomen United (IWU) 1975–77

The next group to work for women's equality was the IWU. Formed in Liberty Hall on June 8, 1975, it was more radical than the IWLM. These women had the same agenda, but were more politicized, less interested in consciousness-raising. Contraception was their pivotal issue, and they achieved major advances. They set up an abortion referral agency and rape crisis centers.

They demanded free contraception, self-determined sexuality, equal pay, and the establishment of women's centers. Yet, the ideological schisms in IWU were more pronounced than in IWLM. The list of factions included nationalists, liberals, socialists, and lesbians, and they all disagreed on what constituted appropriate feminist aims. Liberals said that women's rights were most important, while nationalists claimed that helping women interned in Northern prisons should be their main goal. Socialists wanted connections with trade unions, but not with Northern Ireland, because they felt that the women's rights struggle had been damaged by republicanism. Lesbians felt that sexuality was the most important issue in feminism.

These beliefs were fervently expressed, and there was open anger and friction. One IWU member said, "There can be a lot of abusive behavior in feminist organizations.... Power struggles, politics and also the fact that women are very jealous of their position.... In order to maintain their position they become quite abusive of other people" (Stopper 138). If there was pettiness, there was also a positive sense of passionate commitment. Another member said, "Feminism is like climbing over a very high wall ... once going over it there really is no going back ... it becomes part of your soul and pervades everything you do" (Stopper 134).

Ultimately, the nationalist and lesbian questions split IWU apart. Lesbians found more support from international alliances than Irish groups. Indeed, it was so uncomfortable to live in Ireland that many of the most outspoken lesbians emigrated to England or America. The International Lesbian Caucus mobilized Irish lesbian feminists, giving them an understanding of gender as a social construct, thus removing the pathological label from lesbianism, much as the IWLM's consciousness-raising had done for feminism. Nationalism as a topic tended to be avoided. Members found it so divisive that they agreed not to talk about it, much as IWLM had implicitly agreed not to discuss abortion.

Although there were shortcomings in the 1970s women's movement, feminists achieved much recognition. Skillful activists in all three organizations (CSW, IWLM and IWU) understood that until they publicized issues of women's inequalities in Ireland, they wouldn't have an adequate support base to get laws changed. The task was to raise the consciousness of women and men regarding the inequities rampant in the system. In the seventies, the differences between the women's liberation strand of the movement and the women's rights strand were clear. But by the 1980s, the movement had gone mainstream, thanks to the efforts of second-wave feminists to publicize it. Now the two strands merged. Both liberal and radical feminists were willing to use both legal channels and direct action to effect change. They petitioned, lobbied, sued, and held mass meetings. Yet, just as goals began to seem attainable, another substantial segment of the Irish population lashed out at feminists' "insult" to cherished Irish traditions. This backlash was not an isolated Irish phenomenon, occurring in the United States, England and Europe as well.

Backlash, Third Wave Feminism (1980–present), the Kerry Babies, and Divorce and Abortion Referendums

The 1980s saw the mainstreaming and professionalization of the women's movement. The eighties also produced a conservative counter-movement, which challenged the work of 1970s feminist organizations, and helped to pass the 1983 Referendum that made all abortions illegal except in cases where the fetus' birth would kill the mother. The wording of the Referendum, which became Article 40.3.3 of the Constitution, has been interpreted by some to value the life of the fetus over that of its mother: "The State acknowledges the right to life of the unborn and, with due regard to the equal right to life of the mother, guarantees in its laws to respect, and as far as practicable, by its laws to defend and vindicate that right" (Connolly 243).

Strangely, the urgency of feminism declined as the strength of the Right grew. There was a decline in grass roots activity and direct action. The sphere of feminist action narrowed to the abortion issue. When pro-choicers lost on the 1983 referendum, many disillusioned feminists chose to leave their country. However, the great publicity of the Kerry Babies case in 1984 brought awareness to Ireland and the world of the ongoing misogynist practices of the Church, the medical establishment and the law (both police and judges) that conspired to debase and defame women. A companion case, the Ann Lovett death, made many Irish people examine their consciences about just how far their religious culture could go to create unchristian, inhumane outcomes.

Ann Lovett was a fifteen-year-old convent student in the small town of Granard, County Longford, who miscarried and died of exposure in January 1984, in the Grotto of the Virgin. Whether the child was engendered by Lovett's father or by her boyfriend is unknown, but the reason why none of her nuns, teachers, friends, doctor, or family helped her is better understood. Teen pregnancy was so frowned upon that Lovett chose to go through pregnancy and death alone rather than be humiliated. In initial inquiries, nuns, family members, and even her doctor testified that they did not know she was six months' pregnant, though upon an investigation ordered by the Minister for Women's Affairs, certain townspeople admitted to knowing of her obvious pregnancy. Historian Moira Maguire speculates that the reason Lovett was so isolated was because her family was not accepted by townspeople, since they were from another county, and didn't attend church or social functions. Mr. Lovett was known to be an abusive alcoholic. The community did not want to pry, not because they respected the Lovetts' privacy, but because they feared social deviance.

National media ran coverage of Lovett's death, sparking a surprisingly large and emotional response. Letters poured into the newspapers from all over the country, debating the moral issues surrounding the case, returning always to the question, why didn't someone help Lovett? The people of Granard felt attacked by this attention, believing that their response was no different than any other self-respecting Irish town's. Nuala Fennell, the *Dáil*'s Minister for Women's Affairs and former IWLM member, called Lovett's death a national tragedy and demanded an inquiry. However, there was nobody to indict for this tragedy, only a generalized attitude of Irish people that says avoiding shame is better than letting a fellow human being suffer. Publicity was its own form of consciousness-raising, although it was unlike the kind practiced by the IWLM. Whereas women's libbers sought to raise their consciousness, the awareness of provincial neglect was forced upon the Irish public by tragedy, rather than intentionally sought. The event improved public awareness just at the time of an even more gruesome case, the Kerry Babies.

On April 14, 1984, two unrelated events occurred which the *Gardai* (police) of Tralee and Abbeydorney (County Kerry) linked together in their attempts to solve a murder case. A newborn infant was found stabbed to death on the Cahirciveen shore, and Joanne Hayes visited her local hospital (fifty miles distant) to be treated for excessive uterine bleeding following a miscarriage. The baby on the beach was not hers; she had buried her dead fetus on her family's farm. After receiving blood tests of all parties—the babies, Joanne, and Joanne's baby's father (who was married to another woman)—the prosecutor dismissed the case for lack of evidence.

However, for over a year, the *Gardai* and a special tribunal persecuted Joanne and her family. The case generated much media attention, as well as local protests, and national support in the form of letters, flowers, and attendance at court. The upshot of this national coverage was to imprint upon the minds of Irish people the degree to which the triumvirate of Irish medicine, law, and church conspired to defame women for their sexuality, or, as journalist Nell McCafferty put it, to defame women for being women.

In a travesty of judicial procedure, the tribunal was meant to investigate charges of police misconduct, but soon turned into a persecution of Joanne Hayes. Police coerced confessions from Hayes and her family that she had killed her own baby. Prosecution used a super-fecundation theory to argue that the dead baby in Cahirciveen was also hers. To do this, they had to prove that she had sex with two different men in a 48-hour period, producing twins by different fathers (the theory appealed to the salacious imagination of the prosecution). Fortunately, their expert witness refused to validate the theory. Nonetheless, the hearing that was meant to vindicate Hayes turned into a sex scandal that titillated several of the legal players.

At the end of six months' tortuous testimony, only four of the judge's forty-three findings related to police misconduct; the rest related to the conduct of Hayes and her family. The judge found Joanne guilty of murder without evidence. In fact, the blood type of the Cahirciveen baby was incompatible with Joanne's, and her own fetus, the one she buried, was found to have collapsed lungs, a sign that the baby had been stillborn, not murdered. So Joanna was "free" to live a normal life if she and Ireland could ignore this tribunal's judgment on her character as a promiscuous baby-killer. In her book, *A Woman to Blame: The Kerry Babies Case*, Nell McCafferty describes the prosecutor's heckling. On the stand, Joanne answered personal questions that had nothing to do with the *Gardai*'s misconduct. Her privacy was invaded, and when she broke down, she was criticized for emotional instability. She was framed as a woman of loose morals and a child murderer, but as McCafferty argues, "[Joanne] had been charged with no crime, but womanhood itself was on trial in Tralee.... The perfect excuse had been found to pin a woman under the microscope and have a good look at her" (127).

Historian Moira Maguire notes that the Ann Lovett and Kerry Babies publicity effectuated a remarkable shift in Irish attitudes towards the interventions of church and state in the private lives of individuals. Following Lovett's death, a number of agencies were founded to deal with crisis pregnancies as well as to raise awareness about their prevalence and to fight prejudice against unmarried mothers. Maguire describes this shift: "For the first time since the emergence of the independent Irish state in the 1920s, there was a wide-scale challenge to the long-held conviction that the Catholic Church alone should determine the social and moral values that informed Irish social policy, particularly in areas of sexuality, reproduction, and family life" (358).

In 1992, "Miss X" tested the new secularism of the Irish courts. Miss X was a fourteen-year-old victim of sexual abuse who petitioned to travel to England for an abortion, with her parents' consent. The High Court enjoined her travel, but was overturned by the Supreme Court. Article 40.3.3 permitted abortion in the case of risk to mother's life, and Miss X ran the risk of suicide should she be required to continue the pregnancy. There was massive public demonstration about this decision; a crowd of 100,000 marched down O'Connell Street to Parliament. Following a tide of public approval for abortion in severe cases, the government enacted the Abortion Information Act in 1995 with little debate. The AIA allows doctors, family planning clinics and other health professionals to counsel on abortion in crisis pregnancies and to provide information on English abortion services. The Irish courts' commitment to allowing abortion in extreme circumstances was re-tested in the 1997 "C" case, when a thirteen-year-old Traveler was raped, and later sheltered by a state agency. The High Court ruled that she be allowed to travel to England for an abortion, and be accompanied by her state-paid social worker — proof that the ruling on Miss X was being respected five years later.

Despite Moira Maguire's optimism about Ireland's increasing liberalization, there remains a fifty-fifty split on abortion issues. The 2002 Abortion Referendum was defeated by only 1 percent of voters. It called for the reversal of the Miss X ruling. In 2005, three women who had already procured abortions in England contested the constitutionality of Article 40.3.3 in the European Court of Human Rights. The International Court heard this case, named *A., B., and C. v. Ireland*, on December 9, 2009, and ruled that only Plaintiff C's rights had been violated, as her medical history of cancer posed a risk to her health if her pregnancy was brought to term. In its decision, the Court confirmed that there is no international right to abortion, disappointing the hopes of Ireland's pro-choice constituency.

The Wave of the Future: Two Female Presidents in Ceremonial Roles

Following Maguire, I see a deep division between Ireland's conservative majority and liberal minority. Irish government often pays lip service to demands for equal rights and women's rights. Since her entry into the European Economic Community (now the European Union) in 1973, Ireland's token liberalism has progressed at a reasonable pace, considering the Catholic background of the country. The right to divorce was finally achieved in 1995. Two female presidents have been elected since 1990, Mary Robinson from 1990 to 1997 and Mary McAleese from 1997 to 2010. Their election does not mean that women have real power. The presidency of Ireland is largely a ceremonial role. The President's powers to act are almost entirely limited by the necessity of the *Dáil*'s approval. The Prime Minister has much more power than the President; no woman has filled that role yet. The *Dáil* is only 14 percent female, while the Northern Ireland Assembly has 16 percent women legislators.

In February 2010, Margaret Ward spoke to the *Guardian* about the status of women in Ireland. She regrets that women have worked so hard for so long without achieving adequate representation or rights. Ward commented on the scarcity of women's representation in either the *Dáil* or Northern Ireland Assembly, and the "hidden diaspora" of women travelling for abortions (90,000 from the Republic since 1980; 80,000 from Northern Ireland since 1968). Another hidden statistic is domestic abuse, which Myrtle Hill estimated in 2003 occurs at the rate of one-fifth to one-third of all Irish women, although figures could be higher, given that many women are afraid to speak up about their abuse (Ryan 97).

What is the prognosis for the future of women in Ireland? Are Irish women beginning to feel enough support to be able to speak up, not only about domestic violence, but also about other areas of life in which they have traditionally been oppressed? There are many signs that this is the case. For instance, when the three-volume *Field Day Anthology of Irish Literature*, edited by Seamus Deane, was published in 1991, a group of academic feminists pressured him to rectify the omission of Irish women writers, resulting in the publication of a fourth and fifth volume of women writers. The sheer indifference to women's contributions that characterized the initial project shows how easy it was for Ireland's top intellectuals to omit women. Seamus Deane thought the anthology represented unprecedented inclusiveness, but his concern was for the balance of North and South, not men and women. Nine years after this historic event of sexism, I attended a university seminar at University College Dublin on "Modern Ireland, 1880–1930," led by Seamus Deane and Kevin Whelan. Ireland and England's academic elites shared the lectern, at the ratio of about nine men to one woman. When one brave participant intervened and asked why women's contributions were being omitted from a period so rich with women's history, no answer was given. An effort to rectify the omission was rebuffed. It appears that the lesson of the *Field Day Anthology* needs to be taught again and again.

On the other hand, the amount of literature by Irish women has seen a significant increase in the past two decades. I end this chapter with Christine St. Peter's encouraging words about the robust health of Irish women's literature:

> In the last decade, we have seen a prodigious growth in the number and diversity of women's public voices. Nowhere has this phenomenon been more apparent than in the works of fiction that women have, for the first time in history, published in huge numbers. This success is no accident. It happened because large numbers of women have ... managed to acquire the necessary material conditions for creative expression: education, some time and privacy at their own disposal, newly available access to publishing houses, or equally significant, the creation of such Irish firms as Arlen House in the 1970s and Attic Press in the 1980s and 1990s dedicated to producing women's writing ... and women readers with the desire and money to buy books by women [7].

CHAPTER TWO

"Deeds, Not Words": The British Women's Movement

"Deeds not words," proclaimed Emmeline Pankhurst, founder of British militant feminism and the Women's Social and Political Union (WSPU) in 1903. The dramatic nature of the suffragettes' campaign, including hunger strikes and bombing, helped publicize women's persisting determination to achieve the vote. Later in the century, second-wave feminism produced another campaign, this time peaceful, but nonetheless compelling. The Greenham Common Peace Women's nineteen-year campout around the fence of the RAF Base in Derbyshire rivals the Pankhursts' efforts in its feisty, creative, and attention-getting character. These two campaigns highlight my chapter on feminist movements in Britain. Key figures to be discussed include the Pankhurst family, Germaine Greer, and Natasha Walter. Greer's life and work, especially *The Female Eunuch* (1970), illustrate a portion of radical second-wave ideology, but by no means all. The chapter ends with reflections on British third-wave feminism. As Natasha Walter's 2010 title, *Living Dolls: The Return of Sexism*, suggests, a widespread attitude of sexism remains today, despite several legal gains during the century.

Striking similarities exist between first- and second-wave feminisms in Ireland and Britain, such as the physical courage of Irish freedom fighters and British militant suffragettes. Women in both countries put aside their feminist campaigns to aid their brothers in war, the Irish for their War of Independence, and the British for the troops in World War I. In both nations, women's organizations faced exclusion and discrimination from men's groups whose causes they believed in, such as the Land League in Ireland, and the Labour Party and New Left organizations in Britain. Both British and Irish feminist groups suffered from internal conflict and breakdown, resulting in split-off groups with different ideologies. In Britain, this was most pronounced in the constitutional NUWSS (National Union of Women's Suffrage

Societies) versus the militant WSPU, whereas in Ireland, conflict surfaced between feminist nationalists and feminists who prioritized suffrage. An additional battle between sisters in the two nations occurred between 1910 and 1914, when the British WSPU tried to persuade the IWFL (Irish Women's Franchise League) that their objectives were one and the same. In effect, the WSPU used Irish suffragists to bolster their own cause, without adequate sympathy for the underlying colonial positions that differentiated them.[1]

Yet the differences between the two countries' movements are more interesting than their similarities, as they point to the nature of colonialism and its influence on feminism. First, the British movement was blessed with more financial support. Patrons Frederick and Emmeline Pethick-Lawrence worked for WSPU, contributing magnanimously to their funds. As the WSPU gained national attention, subscriptions from sympathetic middle and upper-middle-class supporters were paid to that organization. Funding bought publicity, which allowed larger and showier demonstrations. Second, the British movement was divided along class lines, with the working class often campaigning through socialist organizations like women's trade unions, while middle-class women tried for several years to affiliate with the Liberal Party. Instead, the Irish movement was divided by ideologies of nationalism versus unionism, especially in the north of Ireland. Third, Irish women were more tentative about sexual liberation, whereas the power to speak publicly about sex came much earlier to their Protestant sisters in Britain. As early as 1918, Marie Stopes' book *Married Love* encouraged Englishwomen to find pleasure in their sexual relations and to space out their pregnancies, whereas even in 1971, many staunch Irish feminists blanched at the Contraceptive Train demonstration. Irish lesbians felt so threatened in Ireland that many of them moved out of the country, whereas British lesbians had more voice, even so far as dominating discussions in the 1977 and '78 national conferences. Fourth, there was a three-decade difference in the attainment of sexual rights. Britain legalized no-fault divorce in 1967, Ireland not until 1995. British women got legal contraceptives in 1952 (the pill in 1961), Irish women not until 1980. Britain legalized abortion in 1967, whereas Ireland forbade information about getting English abortions until 1995.

These material differences reflect philosophical differences in feminist consciousness. We would expect that the richer country could afford to place greater emphasis on the personal lives of women (sexual rights and freedoms, quality of domestic life, and so on), while the poorer country would have to focus on public reforms that would allow more women to work outside the home for better pay. In actuality, greater wealth or a higher GNP does not mean that Britain has achieved greater rights for women in public life, for reasons that this chapter will elucidate.

Suffrage Campaign and First-Wave Feminism, 1903–1918

First-wave feminism did not arise suddenly at the turn of the century; a long line of foremothers paved the way. Mary Wollstonecraft is often chosen as the first British feminist, though this ignores earlier writers, such as Julian of Norwich (b. 1342) who believed that God is our mother; and Aphra Behn (1600s) and Eliza Haywood (1700s), who earned their living by their pens, creating strong female fictional characters. But Wollstonecraft is the first British woman to claim women's natural right to education. In a book-length essay (*A Vindication of the Rights of Women*, 1790), she argues that women can only be equal to men if they are educated to the same degree. Wollstonecraft enjoyed a better reception for her work because of the *Zeitgeist* of 1790s Britain. Influenced by the French Revolution, the English intelligentsia made human rights the theme of the day.

Nineteenth-Century Requests for Women's Suffrage

John Stuart Mill's essay, *The Subjection of Women* (1869), takes up Mary Wollstonecraft's point nearly a century later, the difference being that he is in a position to do something about it. As Liberal Party MP, Mill introduces an amendment to the Representation of the People Act in 1867, the first time that a petition for women's suffrage has been entered at Parliament. His grounds for female suffrage are that the days of "separate spheres" — women in the home, men in the world — are over. Women and men have become companions who advise and trust one another. The vote would make women good citizens, and "unless women are raised to the level of men, men will be pulled down to theirs" (Van Wingerden 13). When Mill presented the amendment, the age-old objections to female emancipation echoed through the House: first, that women didn't want the vote (this required the speaker to ignore the women's deputations or demonstrations outside the door); second, that women were not suited to the brutality of public life; third, that even if women *did* adapt to public life, it would degrade their sexual characteristics (especially the qualities of tenderness and submission, from which men greatly benefit).

An industrial city in northern England, Manchester was more of a hotbed for revolutionary politics than London. Workers' strikes and demonstrations were frequent, and many of the women who began the suffrage movement had their first experience of direct action in Manchester. Emmeline Pankhurst herself said that seeing the gallows where three Irish Fenians were hanged made a deep childhood impression. In 1867, it was Manchester women who formed the National Society for Women's Suffrage. One of their first actions was to interpret the word *man* in the 1867 Reform Act as including *woman*, and on this basis, to convince registrars to register 5,100 women voters in municipal elections. When their names were tossed out, these women brought a court case, *Chorlton vs. Lings* (1868), in which Dr. Richard Pankhurst (later Emmeline's husband) eloquently argued via precedent. Women had voted in the middle ages, and common law made that precedent binding in the courts of the present. The judge disagreed, holding that unless Parliament expressly articulated that women had the right to vote, no such right existed. Despite the ruling, the Municipal Vote was granted to women in 1869.

One of the earliest Manchester suffragists, Lydia Becker, founded the *Women's Suffrage Journal* in 1870. Together with Dr. Pankhurst, she authored numerous petitions to Parliament requesting the vote. Arranging mass meetings in Manchester and London, Becker gave women experience in public speaking, an activity much frowned upon by Victorian standard-holders. Speaking in public was believed to unsex women, and "no one believed that a woman's voice could be heard," both literally (she was trained to speak softly) and figuratively (men and women were trained to consider a woman's opinion of little value) (Van Wingerden 25). Becker later headed the NUWSS. In 1880, she staged a series of women's demonstrations at the Manchester Free Trade Hall, the same venue where Christabel Pankhurst would spit at a police officer at the beginnings of militant suffragism.

When the Boer War broke out at the end of the nineteenth century, suffragists suspended their campaign. Fifteen years later, suffragists would again suspend their campaign in order to help their country in World War I. In Ireland, the same phenomenon occurs, in the Uprising, the War of Independence, and the Troubles. Patriotic Irishwomen suspend their feminist campaigns in the mistaken belief that their interests are taken seriously by the movement for a free and united Ireland.

Emmeline, Christabel, Sylvia, Adela, and Harry Pankhurst

Mrs. Pankhurst, as she liked to be called during her suffrage campaign, is the leading lady of the suffrage movement, not because she agitated longer or harder than someone like Lydia Becker, but because she garnered the most publicity. Arguably, she shared that privilege with her eldest daughter, Christabel, but their styles were quite different, and in some ways, Emmeline appears the more committed fighter, even though it was Christabel who initially and persistently advocated militancy. Martin Pugh maintains that after Christabel joined the campaign, her mother always deferred to her judgment, so Christabel may have begun to dominate the movement. In any case, as undisputed leaders of the WSPU, Christabel and Emmeline set the policy for the militant campaign, determining when to increase violence, and serving prison sentences for obstruction. Mrs. Pankhurst also served the beginning of a three-year sentence for counseling the destruction of property, whether or not she knew of the specific intent of persons to bomb Lloyd George's unoccupied home in Walton Heath.

Christabel and Emmeline Pankhurst (Photos.com).

Biographers are drawn to Mrs. Pankhurst because she embodies an interesting set of contradictions. The most striking is her shifting political identity. While a young woman, she is Liberal; in mid-career, she gravitates to Labour; during and after World War I, she becomes a Conservative. She enjoys a happy marriage to Richard, a prominent lawyer and suffragist, yet she knows that marriage is a compromise or trap for most women of her time. She believes that women have admirable virtues such as benevolence and nurturance, yet she snubs her father and her daughter Sylvia when they disagree with her, and exiles her daughter Adela. She wants women to have the vote so that they can improve the democratic flavor of British governance, yet she runs her own organization as a dictatorship. She believes in the power of organization and collective action, yet she splits her group over policy questions. She is elegant and beautiful, yet never alludes to her own romantic life in her friendships or speeches. She is soft-spoken, and iron-willed. She adopts abandoned babies during World War I, yet she disowns Sylvia for having an illegitimate child. She manages the richest women's political organization in history, yet manages her own finances poorly, making business failures of her restaurant and furniture store.

Born to a Manx mother and an Irish father, Emmeline was steeped in radical politics from childhood. The Isle of Man Parliament afforded women the vote in 1881. Her mother read the *Women's Suffrage Journal* and took Emmeline to her first suffrage meeting at the age of twelve. Her father owned a calico factory, and was a town councilman in Salford, a suburb of Manchester. Active in several human rights causes, he campaigned against slavery during the American Civil War. Going to school in Paris increased Emmeline's propensities to romanticize political activism. She roomed with Noémie, the daughter of one of the most prominent leaders of the Paris Commune, Henri Rochefort, who had escaped from exile in New Caledonia. Identifying with the women who stormed the Bastille, Emmeline changed her birth date to coincide with Bastille Day.

Returning to Manchester, Emmeline married Richard Pankhurst, a barrister known for his enthusiastic dedication to social reform. Although she initially proposed a free union instead of marriage, Richard convinced her that this would stigmatize them and hurt their political careers. Emmeline campaigned hard for her husband in three MP elections, but his radicalism prevented him from gaining the vote. Believing in free education, the disestablishment of the Church, the abolition of the monarchy, full suffrage and Home Rule, Richard couldn't get elected by Independents, Radical-Liberals, *or* Labour. He slacked in his law practice, preferring to spend time on his various political causes. When Emmeline's father's business suffered as a result of his son-in-law's politics, Richard lost a key source of support. The young family moved out of Emmeline's parents' house, and Emmeline snubbed her father for the rest of his life. As biographer Paula Bartley comments, "throughout her life, she was to place politics above people; she was never afraid to break with those dear to her if they disagreed with her own fundamental values or beliefs" (34). A stereotype that feminists often confront is that they are uncompromising ideologues that do not forgive human frailties. It is interesting to note that many political leaders, not just feminists, match this description.

Emmeline was not a frigid suffragist stereotype. Over the course of nine years, the couple had five children. The sons both died, Frank at age two and Harry at age twenty, while Christabel, Sylvia and Adela worked alongside their mother in the suffrage campaign. The previous chapter describes the favoritism that Maud Gonne showed to her son, and suggests a pattern of strong women politicians neglecting their female children. Emmeline's case exemplifies the pattern. The problem of work-life balance, especially for mothers, is a key issue in feminism today.

Emmeline nurtured her pretty eldest daughter Christabel, making her the poster child for the cause, much as Maud Gonne did with little Sean. But Emmeline's relationships with her second and third daughters, Sylvia and Adela, are painful to read about. She disowns Sylvia for approaching suffrage through a socialist framework and having an illegitimate child, and she banishes Adela to Australia, with nothing more than twenty pounds and a letter of introduction to suffragist Vida Goldstein. Yet Sylvia's is a more painful case, since she works in closer proximity to her mother, and longs for her affection from an early age. Clearly, Emmeline is placing politics before persons when she ousts Sylvia from WSPU, saying: "those who wish to give an independent lead, or to carry out either a program or a policy which differs from those laid down by the WSPU must necessarily have an independent organization of their own" (Bartley 158). Christabel's animosity towards her youngest sister is no less hostile than her mother's, when she tells Sylvia: "I would not care if you were multiplied by a hundred, but one of Adela is too many" (Mitchell 190).

The two oldest daughters, Christabel and Sylvia, were able to bond during childhood. But Adela, born three years after Sylvia, felt completely left out of her parents' and older sisters' life, becoming both despondent and rebellious at an early age. Her father was less available to Adela and Harry, being older and sicker during their childhood, and both younger children were afraid of him. Despite her fear, Adela dared to defy her father's atheism, by attending church and teaching Sunday school. Her younger brother Harry did not fare better. Although Harry offered to work for suffrage, Emmeline rejected his participation because she felt he was weak. Ignoring his preferences, she found work for him as builder and farm laborer, trades that didn't suit his delicate constitution. After two years of work, Harry succumbed to polio and died. Although Emmeline remained in the United States during Harry's illness, she was devastated by his death. At the funeral, "she is broken as I had never seen her; huddled together without a care for her appearance, she seemed an old, plain and cheerless woman," writes Sylvia (Pugh 206). Emmeline's *dishabille* is the more striking because she prides herself on her elegance, using it as a marketing device for suffrage.

Biographer Pugh defends Mrs. Pankhurst's coldness to her children by claiming it is normal for her time. Victorian parents thought children should have the moral and emotional maturity of adults. It was common practice to send children to relatives or acquaintances that could establish them in some career, or in any event get them off their parents' hands. Adela sadly remembers being sent, at six, to live with her mother's servant in a boarding house. This was a foretaste of her mother's later banishment of Adela from the movement and the country at age twenty-eight. But Emmeline herself was not brought up in this cold way. She was the apple of her father's eye, so it does not make sense that she would consider her neglect of Adela an emotionally sound course. Instead, it seems that she was so taken up with her cause that she put personal concerns aside, an ideology reminiscent of revolutionary Marxism, which considers sentimental relations to be bourgeois and counterproductive to the achievement of revolution. The serious emotional repercussions of Mrs. Pankhurst's neglect are well documented by Sylvia's autobiography, and by Adela and Harry's nervous conditions.

Deeds Not Words: The Switch to Militancy

After Dr. Pankhurst's death from a perforated ulcer in 1898, Mrs. Pankhurst moves the family to smaller lodgings, finding successive jobs as Poor Law Guardian and Registrar of Births and Deaths. These jobs raise her awareness of working women's living and employment conditions and she becomes an active member of the Manchester Independent Labor Party (ILP). Meanwhile, Christabel meets socialists Eva Gore-Booth and Esther Roper, who convince her, as her mother never had, that she is fit to lead the fight for suffrage. Needing a lawyer for their cause, they persuade Emmeline to allow Christabel to study law at Manchester University.

An event in October 1903 brings three of the Pankhurst women together in common cause. Artistic Sylvia has been commissioned to decorate the Dr. Pankhurst Memorial Hall in North Salford, but Christabel and Emmeline resent the fact that the ILP has banned women from that space. Refusing to work for the sexist ILP, Mrs. Pankhurst announces to a handful of women:

"We must do the work ourselves. We must have an independent women's movement. Come to my house tomorrow and we will arrange it" (Mitchell 47). Thus, the Women's Social and Political Union (WSPU) is born. The choice of the word *political* in their name was meant to suggest that action, not rhetoric, was intended. There were a few simple, but very strict rules. There would be no men, and no party affiliations. "Deeds not words" was to be the permanent motto. Secretary and treasurer were appointed, but leadership was in the hands of Emmeline and Christabel. There would be no constitution, no democratic procedure, nor any formal accounting of donations and subscriptions. Besides the Pankhursts, six working-class women attended the first meeting.

The primary audience for the WSPU was local trade unions. The goal was to muster their support for woman's suffrage by revealing that the labor movement was anti-women. In 1905, the first mildly militant action of the WSPU was Mrs. Pankhurst's protest meeting outside Parliament, where MP Henri Labouchere talked out a bill on women's suffrage by focusing on a bill about traffic lights. There was some disagreement about who performed the first militant action. Christabel claimed that *she* performed the first militant act when she spit at a policeman. Christabel and Annie Kenney (her devoted disciple) asked Liberal Party members at a political meeting whether they would take steps to give votes for women? (Van Wingerden 72). The question was simply ignored. When Annie repeated it at the end of the meeting, men howled and ejected them from the hall. Christabel decided that the most ladylike way to get arrested for assault was to spit in a policeman's face. Rather than accept her mother's offer to pay bail, Christabel insisted on serving her sentence.

Getting arrested was an intentional ploy to call attention to the movement in a more dramatic way than peaceful protest. Thus began a series of direct-action techniques that would, over the next twelve years, result in the vote. Some detractors argue that, far from obtaining the vote, militancy delayed it. Others believe that the Pankhursts' support of the government's military campaign in World War I was what really gained suffragettes the vote. Another voice says that the British custom of "gradualism"—Parliament relenting to pressures over time—led inexorably to the 1918 Bill's enactment.

As the plan for agitation grew, the Pankhursts knew they must establish headquarters in London. In 1906, they sent Annie Kenney to scout possibilities for a new home base. Kenney stayed with Sylvia Pankhurst, who was studying art at the Royal College of Art; together, they rented Caxton Hall, with a capacity of 700, for their first meeting. Soon, Emmeline and Christabel moved to London, found wealthy sponsors in Frederic and Emmeline Pethick-Lawrence, and established the new WSPU headquarters. For the next two years, WSPU staged many protests. In 1906, 11 were arrested and sent to Holloway Prison, on fortnight-long sentences for obstruction. In 1907, the number of arrests increased to 130. WSPU held its first annual Women's Parliament, in which women would summarize Parliament's annual agenda, and plan protests and deputations to MPs. As WSPU continued to grow, receive large donations, and lead the way for the militant approach, other special interest suffrage groups proliferated, such as the Artists' Suffrage League, the Men's League for Women's Suffrage, Women's Freedom League, Gymnastic Teachers' Suffrage Society, and Women Writers' Suffrage League. Among these, the WSPU held the place of pride. The Pankhursts intended to foster the heroines of the movement, those who would eventually give their lives for the cause.

Protests and deputations did make some headway in Parliament, as various women's suffrage bills passed in the House of Commons. However, these bills would stall or be defeated in discussions of the Whole House (House of Lords and House of Commons), or by the Prime Minister's fiat. The PM at this time was openly anti-suffrage and anti-women. Herbert Henry Asquith was Liberal Party Prime Minister from 1908 to 1916. Pugh believes that Asquith's deep-seated misogyny arose from his life at "a comforting series of all-male clubs," including Balliol College, the London Bar, and the House of Commons. Asquith's distaste for women was compounded by his indiscreet wife's meddling in politics (174–5). The Pankhursts soon learned to distrust Asquith, who promised repeatedly that he would introduce a suffrage bill "with the possibility of amendment for women's suffrage," yet each time manipulated the schedule so that there was no time for debate, or cleverly worded the bill so that the House would vote against it. Most Liberal and Labour members wanted a bill that would extend the male vote as well, so by careful packaging, Asquith could scuttle the bill. He repeatedly refused to see women's deputations, yet audience with the Prime Minister was the only legal recourse suffragists had, since they had no representation in the legislature.

The year 1908 marks a turning point in militant suffragism. The Pankhursts instituted a policy of greater violence, which increased the number of imprisoned suffragettes. One woman devised an easy way to remember the difference between suffragists and suffragettes. The latter are militant; included in their name is the word *get*, meaning while suffragists may want the vote, suffragettes are determined to get it. The need for the two branches to have different names reflects the ideological division between them, and the embarrassment that liberals felt towards their radical sisters. To them, it was embarrassing when Edith New and Mary Leigh broke two of Asquith's windows at No. 10 Downing Street. Muriel Matters interfered with a session of the House of Commons by chaining herself to the grille in the Ladies'

Gallery. Perhaps most significant for the future flavor of the movement was Marion Wallace Dunlop's hunger strike. Dunlop was sentenced to one month's imprisonment for printing the text of the Bill of Rights on St. Stephen's Hall. She demanded to be treated as a political prisoner. The conditions for Division One political prisoners were better; they had more privileges than the criminals in Divisions Two and Three. In Division One, prisoners could wear their own clothes, talk with fellow prisoners, have writing utensils, and receive visitors. Upon denial of Dunlop's request for political status, she began a hunger strike that lasted for ninety-one hours, at which time she was released for ill health. In the following six years, hundreds of women would follow suit, striking for the right to be regarded as political prisoners rather than hardened criminals. The hunger strike became emblematic of suffragettes' courage and their captors' cruelty.

Fasting was one source of pain, but forcible feeding was much worse. In 1909, *Leigh vs. Gladstone* legalized forcible feeding of the suffragettes, ostensibly to save their lives, but clearly to force them to serve out their full terms rather than being released for ill health caused by fasting. In actuality, forcible feeding was quite dangerous to health, causing bleeding gums, jaundice, ulcers, and degradation. One woman died when the tube was directed to her lungs rather than her stomach. Many prisoners died later, from complications of forcible feeding. Even though several doctors attested to its risks, forcible feeding remained in effect for four years, until the Cat-and-Mouse Act put an end to it. Sylvia Pankhurst was force-fed many times, while her mother was deemed too old and weak-hearted to sustain it. Christabel avoided it by avoiding prison. Sylvia writes of one incident when six wardresses held down her shoulders, wrists, hips and ankles while several doctors introduced a clamp between her teeth so they could force a tube down her throat.

> A steel instrument pressed my gums, cutting into the flesh. I braced myself to resist that terrible pain. "No, that won't do"—that voice again. "Give me the pointed one!" A stab of sharp, intolerable agony. I wrenched my head free. Again they grasped me. Again the struggle. Again the steel cutting its way in, though I strained my forces against it. Then something gradually forced my jaws apart as the screw was turned; the pain was like having the teeth drawn. They were trying to get the tube down my throat, I was struggling madly to stiffen my muscles and close my throat [Castle 116].

The resemblance of this act to rape is hard to miss. Male authorities such as wardens, doctors, politicians, and newspaper editors may have considered forcible feeding a symbolic comeuppance to women attempting to break the law and achieve the vote.

Given their very different personalities, Sylvia accepted this sacrifice for the cause, while Christabel removed herself to Paris when WSPU headquarters were raided. She justified her escape as politically necessary, since someone had to remain out of jail to run the campaign. At the same time, she was absenting herself from the horrors of prison that her sisters, real and figurative, were undergoing. In her lifetime, Christabel's mother underwent no fewer than ten hunger strikes.

The next year, 1910, saw an interesting challenge to prison authorities that reflected on British class attitudes as well as executive interference with the judiciary system. Lady Constance Lytton decided to protest differential treatment of prisoners based on class. Arrested in Newcastle for throwing a stone at what she thought was Lloyd George's car, she was soon released because of her social status. Lady Lytton wanted to serve time in Division Three so that she could report on the treatment of lower-class prisoners. Disguised as a poor seamstress, Lady Lytton threw a stone in Liverpool and was sentenced to fourteen days in the Third Division, where she was forcibly fed eight times before being discharged in a state of collapse. She was now able to publicize her treatment in the press. Lytton did not mind letting WSPU use her to gain publicity for the cause.

Another 1910 event constituted a turning point for suffragettes. Black Friday was the name given to a rally that turned exceptionally violent. Three hundred women were protesting Lloyd George's dismissal of the Conciliation Bill, when the event turned into a free-for-all, with police and bystanders assaulting women. Using the rough East End police in place of the ceremonious Westminster patrol, authorities staged a campaign of their own. According to biographer David Mitchell:

> As the campaign lengthened and tempers shortened, near (and sometimes actual) rape became a hazard of the tussles in Parliament Square ...
> clothes were ripped, hands thrust into upper and middle-class bosoms and up expensive skirts. Hooligans, and occasionally policemen, fell gleefully upon prostrate forms from sheltered backgrounds. Wasn't this, they argued, what these women really wanted? Perhaps in some cases, and in a deeply unconscious way, it was [160].

The attitude that all women unconsciously want to be violated is one of the hazards of men writing biographies of suffragettes. However, I choose Mitchell's biography, as I chose Levenson's of Maud Gonne, precisely to illustrate how women's history has been constructed by male desire, and the threat to male sexual fulfillment that can be read into women's fight for emancipation. In any case, there are first-hand accounts of sexual (what Mitchell calls *sensual*) violations, such as an elderly Mrs. Solomon's account of a policeman grabbing her by the breasts to throw her down. Another Mrs. S testified that a policeman grabbed her between the legs. A third woman, Cecilia Haig, was sexually assaulted and died from her injuries.

From her safe-point in Caxton Hall, Christabel watched and determined that "mild militancy" was over. The new *modus operandi* would take suffragettes out of the streets to protect them from assault. After Black Friday, WSPU protests became less confrontational, but more violent. Emily Wilding Davison set fire to three mailboxes, a prelude to a wider campaign involving arson on public buildings and destruction of the post. After a sustained mailbox campaign, the police retaliated by raiding WSPU headquarters and confiscating books, letters, mail lists, and pamphlets. To avoid arrest, Christabel fled to Paris; she would not be extradited because France gave political asylum. She continued to run the militant campaign from her comfortable lodgings. After Black Friday and several more failures of the Conciliation Bill, suffragettes gave up on deputations and took their case to the country.

By 1913, the militants did not trust Asquith to keep any promises regarding a suffrage bill. Their only recourse was to raise public awareness to such a degree that government officials would fear for their own re-election. Working under cover, suffragettes committed acts of property destruction of increasing magnitude. It was guerrilla warfare. They smashed shop windows in posh Regent Street. They slashed paintings in the National Gallery. They interrupted church services, asking that people search their conscience for a reason to deny women the vote. The suffragettes proved to be creative in the variety of ways they could increase their threat. The rank-and-file dreamed up these outrages, but the Pankhursts did not stop them. They smashed the glass case containing the Crown Jewels in the Tower of London. They vandalized golf courses, the refuge of Parliamentary politicians. They set fire to government buildings. In the ultimate act of destruction, Emily Wilding Davison ran in front of the King's Horse at the Derby, sustaining injuries that led to her death. Mrs. Pankhurst took full responsibility for a bomb detonated in Lloyd George's country house, declaring, "We have tried blowing him up to wake his conscience" (Bartley 146). She was sentenced to three years for inciting and counseling destruction of property. By now, she was skilled at using her trials for publicity, taking the opportunity to explain the suffragettes' war. Immediately upon imprisonment, Mrs. Pankhurst began a hunger and thirst strike. Depriving the body of water is even more dangerous than fasting. Sylvia went a step further, refusing to eat, drink or sleep. She walked circles in her cell until she collapsed.

In 1913, the government found a way to end the negative publicity about torturing women. It passed the Prisoners' Temporary Discharge for Ill-Health Act, which allowed wardens to release hunger strikers when their health was in danger, only to bring them back when they were healthy enough to finish their sentences. This new absurdity was quickly dubbed the Cat-and-Mouse Act for its resemblance to a cat playing with its prey. Using the subterfuge tactics they had learned in their destruction-of-property campaign, the suffragists on probation hid from the law. Disguise and running from the police became a way of life for some women.

From January to August 4, 1914, violence reached a peak. There were 107 acts of arson, 11 mutilations of art, and 14 other outrages. Pressured to his limit, Home Secretary Reginald McKenna considered three alternatives: letting suffragettes die in prison, deporting them, or committing them to insane asylums. He did not consider just giving them the vote. Police raided WSPU headquarters and confiscated subscriber lists; the WSPU had to move several times. The week before the war, the Government threatened to sue subscribers and publishers of *The Suffragette* on the grounds that it incited violence.

War and Compromise: Suffragette cum Jingoist

On August 4, 1914, Britain enters World War One. Biographer Mitchell's characteristically sour attitude to militant suffragism informs his description of this event: "one of the minor blessings [of the war] was to end a barren struggle [the suffrage campaign] which reflected little credit to either side" (246). On August 5, NUWSS' leader Millicent Fawcett called a truce: "Let us show ourselves worthy of citizenship whether our claim to it is recognized or not" (247). On August 10, Home Secretary McKenna freed all of the suffragettes from prison. On August 13, Mrs. Pankhurst proclaimed a temporary suspension of WSPU activities: "With that patriotism which has nerved women to endure endless torture in prison cells for the national good, we ardently desire that our country shall be victorious" (248). The leaders of the two suffrage organizations offered their vast financial and organizational resources to relieve wounded soldiers and their families. No one could have foreseen how far the Pankhursts would go in the opposite direction. Hating Germans with a vengeance, Mrs. Pankhurst and Christabel quickly turned into super-patriots.

Mrs. Pankhurst's battle against her daughters Adela and Sylvia also saw its most dramatic crisis in the months just before the war, when she excommunicated Sylvia from the WSPU and banished Adela to Australia. In both cases, Mrs. Pankhurst felt that the sisters' socialism interfered with the suffragette cause by diverting attention away from attaining the vote "on equal terms as men." Socialists did not want the vote for women on equal terms as men; they wanted to extend franchise to non property-holders, male and female. WSPU wasn't necessarily concerned with the rights of working women. Because of their concern for the welfare of working women, Sylvia and Adela took an anti-war stance. During the war, Sylvia's East London Federation of Suffragettes (ELFS) continued suffrage work. Its newspaper, *The Woman's Dreadnought,* put forth its pacifist view that "we must keep perfectly clear in our minds that this war is wicked. It is wicked because murder is wicked, and murder is wicked because hatred is of the devil" (Van Wingerden 157). Exiled in Australia, Adela took part in an anti-conscription campaign. The pacifist-suffragist argument against war stated that women were naturally peace loving; they had nothing to do with the war, so they shouldn't interrupt their suffrage campaign for it. The socialist-pacifist-suffragist argument stated that war was the tool of capitalists, and the primary mode of exploitation of the working classes. Working class women, who were doubly excluded from power in capitalism, could not benefit from war, didn't believe in war, and would not support it.

Some suffragettes supported the war because they believed that there could be no peaceful democracy at home if Germany took over Britain. They felt they must support the war and defer the suffrage campaign till war was over. Not all suffragists followed the party line, however. In 1915, Mrs. Pankhurst announced that WSPU funds would be used to provide adoptions for fifty orphaned war babies. A group of suffragette ex-prisoners protested, saying this was a usurpation of a State function. Another group demanded to see an accounting of WSPU funds, since they were clearly being diverted to the war effort. Mrs. Pankhurst refused on the ground that it was undesirable to issue a record of suffrage work done before the war, since the suffrage war had been suspended during the national war (Mitchell 251). It was not important for her to make perfect sense; she had always asserted her right to run the WSPU without member input. She reiterated: "WSPU is at war, and a fighting body must have an autocratic control if it is to wage war successfully. That is how the WSPU has been run and that is how it will continue to be run. Any member who does not approve of our plans must acquiesce or go" (Mitchell 251). Mrs. Pankhurst went so far as to have Annie Bell arrested for attending a WSPU meeting after she had been banned from the organization (for asking for an apology).

Even before the war, Mrs. Pankhurst and Christabel loved France and hated Germany. During the war, they rechanneled their hatred, from the Asquith government to Germany, with no loss of intensity. *The Suffragette* ceased publishing on the suffrage issue, renaming itself *The Britannia* and publishing patriotic, anti–German propaganda. The inner core of WSPU — Mrs. Pankhurst, Christabel, Annie Kenney, Grace Roe, and Mrs. Drummond — traveled throughout Britain, castigating men as shirkers, and handing out white feathers to those who hadn't enlisted. They campaigned to purge all Germans from the British government, including the Chief of the Imperial General Staff. The Pankhursts suspected all persons of German origin to be infiltrators and spies. Christabel combined feminism with her German phobia, saying that "German culture means the supremacy of the male ... carried to the point of absurdity." Women must resist the takeover of Britain by this masculinist menace, which would be worse than the Asquith government

(Van Wingerden 162). Hearing of their patriotic enthusiasms, King George asked the Government to use Mrs. Pankhurst (Mitchell 259). Once sworn enemies, now the Pankhurst duo became allies of Lloyd George, who was promoted from Minister of Munitions to War Secretary, and finally to Prime Minister in 1916. The PM asked Mrs. Pankhurst to compile a list of suffragettes for munitions work. She coordinated a Women's Right to Serve March, exhorting women to work for their country, and recruiting 110,000 workers by July 1915. Lloyd George also used Mrs. Pankhurst to persuade mine- and factory-strikers to be patriotic by returning to work. Although her speeches to industrial workers were not always successful, Lloyd George praised Mrs. Pankhurst in a letter to Bonar Law, saying, "They [the WSPU] have been extraordinarily useful to the Government — especially in the industrial districts where there has been trouble during the last two very trying years. They have fought the Bolshevist and Pacifist element with great skill, tenacity and courage" (Bartley 197). In a final act of loyalty, Emmeline Pankhurst supplied the names of ringleaders of a Newcastle strike to Lloyd George, who promptly sent them to the battlefront.

Mrs. Pankhurst and her followers' loyalty and patriotic activities finally won Asquith's acquiescence. In August 1916, Asquith proposed to give all servicemen the vote. The WSPU immediately piggy-backed the reform measure, and Asquith relented, admitting that "women fill our munitions factories, they are doing the work which the men who are fighting had to perform before, they have taken their places, they are the servants of the State, and they have aided in the most effective way in the prosecution of the war" (Van Wingerden 167). The House of Lords and Commons held a Conference on Electoral Reform, revised The Representation of the People Bill, and sent it to vote. It afforded only partial suffrage, as women voters had to be over 30 years old, pay rent or own a home, or be the wife of a man who did. The WSPU was content with this stopgap measure, while the socialist suffragists were dismayed by the exclusion of the average working woman. The age requirement disqualified some of the most energetic and courageous street fighters for suffrage. It took ten more years for women's suffrage to be granted on equal terms to men's, in 1928.

Return to Femininity: The Interwar Years, 1919–1939

What Happened to the Pankhursts?

Filled with drama and personalities, the story of the Pankhursts and the militant campaign is difficult to leave behind. It is fascinating to see how each one of the Pankhursts' personal destinies played out, particularly as each woman's life story expressed tendencies established in youth. Mrs. Pankhurst spent most of her last ten years in North America. Hired by the Canadian National Council for Combating Venereal Disease, she traveled for six years, speaking about the interrelationship of Bolshevism, immorality, and social disease. No longer did she believe that women's vote would cure the immorality of modern life. She became a eugenicist, believing that the state should control reproduction by monitoring the sex life of its citizens: "We shall not get a cure until the people have taken it up along with their other racial responsibilities and insure against the passion of those who communicate diseases to innocent victims" (Bartley 214).

Returning to England in 1925 exhausted from a grueling lecture schedule, Mrs. Pankhurst decided to try her hand as a restaurateur. With her longtime friend Mabel Tuke, she opened The English Teashop of Good Hope in Juan les Pins, France. Soon this business failed. Returning to England, Mrs. Pankhurst stood for Parliament as a Conservative candidate for Whitechapel. Explaining her transition from Labour to Conservative, she reflected, "My war experience and my experience on the other side of the Atlantic have changed my views considerably. I am now an imperialist" (Bartley 221). She believed that the moral greatness of England gave it a responsibility to improve the rest of the world. Biographer Bartley explains her political turnaround: "By now she was in an ideological vacuum: she had left Liberalism far behind, especially during her suffragette years, and any vestige of loyalty towards the Labour Party had disappeared during the First World War. In her view, socialists were now a discredited force, discredited by pacifism and pro–Germanism. There was only one viable party left, the Conservative, which had been in power since 1924" (222). Because of her public stature, no lesser lights than Nancy Astor, first female MP, and Conservative Prime Minister Stanley Baldwin supported her candidacy, but Mrs. Pankhurst lost her life before winning a seat. At age sixty-nine, she died of septicaemia in a private London nursing home. It was June 1928, just one month after suffrage had been extended to women on equal terms as men, giving the vote to women (with property qualifications) of twenty-one and above.

Christabel Pankhurst's deviation from human rights work is even stranger than her mother's. Languishing without a cause, she takes up Second Day Adventism with fervor equivalent to her former feminism. Like her mother, she repudiates the idea that women voters can change the world. Only the Second Coming of Christ could deter the coming fascist era. By publishing several books on biblical prophecy and lecturing in America, Christabel was able to retire comfortably in Los Angeles, surrounded by acquaintances. Martin Pugh believes that she achieved just the right amount of social involvement for one of her personality. Too reserved to form friendships, she nevertheless had a social life. Americans adored her English accent and dowdy style of giant hats and floral print dresses. They appreciated her praise of their country.

Sylvia was the only one of the four Pankhurst women to remain committed to her initial convictions. Attending the Second Congress of the Third International in Moscow in 1920, she criticized Lenin for compromising the revolutionary line when he urged European Communists to infiltrate their nations' parliaments. Sylvia had become so distrustful of governments that she considered parliaments bourgeois; revolution was the only way to serve the people. She turned ELPS into the Workers' Socialist Federation, from which she was eventually expelled for publicizing her disagreements with Lenin. Too ill to go on hunger strike, she served a six-month sentence in a prison infirmary for seditious articles published in the *Workers' Dreadnought*.

In 1924, Sylvia fell in love with Silvio Corio, an Italian socialist who had been exiled for political agitation. Refusing to marry for socialist reasons (Engels was a vociferous opponent of marriage), Sylvia and Silvio had their child, Richard Keir Pethick Pankhurst, out of wedlock. For this act of defiance, Mrs. Pankhurst finally disowned Sylvia. After expulsion from WSF, Sylvia turned her energies to ousting Mussolini from Ethiopia. She helped that nation restore its economy and health services, spending her last seven years as a respected resident of Addis Ababa. Her son became a professor of Ethiopian Studies, first at University of Addis Ababa, where he founded an Institute, later at the London School of Economics.

Adela's political trajectory is more similar to her mother's than Sylvia's, as she eventually repudiates Communism and joins the Australian Women's Guild of Empire before the Second World War. In 1914, when she first arrives in Australia, Adela briefly works for the Women's Peace Alliance, demonstrating excellent public speaking skills. Her experience with hecklers in Britain had prepared her to handle the soldiers who harassed her during Melbourne peace rallies. Quickly adopting the cause of Australian nationalism, Adela does not believe that Australia should be part of the British Empire; thus it should remain neutral in war. In 1917, she marries Tom Walsh, a staunch Communist and leader of the Seamen's Union. Marriage to a union organizer plunges her down the economic scale, as she is suddenly responsible for his three children by another marriage, to which they add four of their own. For the remainder of her life, Adela's family will often subsist near the poverty line, on a diet of tea, bread, and butter, especially when Tom is forced to leave the Union because of bitter rivalries with a more extremist leader. These discouraging experiences turn Tom and Adela against Communism. Briefly, Adela supports the family by speaking for the Industrial Peace Association, a 180-degree turn from her work for Tom's union, but Adela argues that she is still working for the poor.

Completing this reversal, Adela accepts a paid position for a right-wing organization, the Women's Guild of Empire, in the early 1930s. Their platform includes combating Communism, securing industrial peace, upholding Christian ideals, promoting awareness of the values of British citizenship, and developing Australia as part of the Empire. However, Tom and Adela's pro–Japanese sentiments made them emphatically unpatriotic at the outbreak of World War II. Since Japan was a major export destination for Australia's wool and wheat, they believed that an Australian alliance with Japan afforded the best protection of Australia's economic interests, as well as the best defense against Communism. The next organization that hired Adela was the unpopular Australia First Movement, which tried to keep Australia out of the war. When charged with treason, Tom was too ill with cancer to serve his sentence, while Adela (at 57 years old) underwent a hunger strike to be removed from an internment camp to a hospital. After Tom's death, Adela found it hard to escape her reputation as a fascist sympathizer, and could obtain only minimum-wage jobs. Adela may not have enjoyed an illustrious political career like her mother and sisters (Pugh even accuses her of not understanding political theory), but she was the only one who enjoyed domesticity, remaining with her beloved Tom till his death, and raising seven children. Pugh writes, "[She] was a warm, affectionate mother ... the children never felt neglected.... Adela possessed more awareness of other people's feelings than any other Pankhurst; indeed she once remarked that she had to be nicer towards her stepchildren than to her own" (388). The Pankhurst stories are valuable to this study because these women were instrumental to women's suffrage. In studying them, we also learn how many different ways there are to be feminist, and how challenging the assumption of a feminist identity has proven to various women at various periods of history.

The New Femininity: Between the Wars

Despite the attainment of the vote, the interwar period does not bring equality between the sexes. Similarly to post-independence Ireland, a new wave of conservatism sweeps Britain, one that will last for fifty years. Postwar Britain is traumatized by the experience of destruction. People suspect that the German threat is still alive, and they predict that fascism will spread. Men are increasingly fearful of the power women gained while men were at war. Officially, the Sex Discrimination (Removal) Act of 1919 made it possible for women to enter the professions, but in effect, women had to prosecute potential employers to activate that right. They had little success in doing so.

The prevailing sentiment in the employment sector was "Women, go home." The Restoration of Pre-war Practices Act in 1919 revokes the right of women to work in factories, while the enactment of the marriage bar in teaching, nursing, and civil service excludes married women from these fields. The notoriously misogynist Labour Party did not fight these laws, while the National Federation of Women Workers joined with the General and Municipal Workers Union. In addition to four million demobilized soldiers entering the workplace, thousands of workers were displaced from textile industries in the northern shires when the world market for British cotton and wool plummeted (Pugh 80). Under these conditions, for a married woman to insist on the right to work was considered unpatriotic. An unmarried woman's intervention in the male world of employment was both unpatriotic and unfeminine. Separate spheres ideology resurfaced, and the new femininity was born. As the excesses of feminists like the Pankhursts were overshadowed by the horrors of the Great War, women were expected to be content in their roles of mothers, wives and housekeepers.

Fortunately for women, birth control was increasingly available, so that their return to domesticity was not as overwhelming as it might otherwise have been. In the thirties, the birthrate dropped to one or two children per family. Although it wouldn't be named the "feminine mystique" until 1963, the phenomenon of depressed women living isolated lives in suburbs grew in tandem with the trend of home ownership. Rather than encouraging women to remain single and fight for better employment opportunities, the leading feminist of the day, Eleanor Rathbone, argued that women should be compensated for staying in the home. Author of the concept of "family wage" and "family endowment," Rathbone proposed that men's employers pay their salaries directly to the women of the family, to ensure that each child had enough to eat. However, she did not support women's equal pay in isolation from families. Equal-rights feminists argued against this separate-spheres feminism on the grounds that it codified women's primary role as that of mother and housekeeper.

Although they had gained the vote, it would take much more to make women happy. In the 1930s, many suburban women suffered depression and guilt from their feelings of incompleteness as wives and mothers, resulting in what social workers called "suburban neurosis" (Bruley 74). The phenomenon was noticed mostly in the upper-working class, and lower-middle classes, probably because more affluent women could afford to go outside the home to volunteer in churches, local councils and schools. If they received pay for their endeavors, women were expected to keep the fact a secret, so as not to insult the husband in his breadwinner role.

During these years, the equal-rights branch of feminism was smaller than separate-spheres, but it achieved an important milestone: the removal of the marriage bar for teachers. The nucleus of equal-rights feminism was in the three groups, Open Door Council, Six Point Group, and the Women's Freedom League. They supported national and local female representatives and pushed for abortion and contraception rights. The work of these women was essential for keeping women's issues in government's awareness until the second wave once again made the movement visible to the public.

Women in World War II

Like the previous war, the Second World War had a huge social impact on Britain. World War II is sometimes called "the people's war" (as opposed to an imperial war) because of popular consensus that Hitler was unspeakably evil, and must be stopped. The second war caused more disruption to the physical lives of British citizens because of the Blitz and evacuations. In the 1940–41 bombings, 60,000 civilians were killed and more injured. Two hundred fifty thousand homes were destroyed. In anticipation of air raids, 1,250,000 citizens were evacuated in the first three days of Britain's entry into war (Bruley 109). The government mandate to all citizens to host evacuees caused a disruption of British classes, just as food rationing leveled all citizens into one category. Yet few would say that Britain's social structure changed permanently because of the disruption.

As in the previous war, a great number of women entered the workplace, particularly in munitions factories. The Essential Work Order (1941) was a form of non-combatant conscription for women, requiring females aged 20–24 to choose between the women's services, civil defense, or the munitions industry. Millions of women volunteered to clear rubble and recuperate bomb victims. Women were permitted to serve in the armed services, but without arms. As in Ireland, they were permitted access, but only in auxiliary roles to men. With so many women working outside of the home, the government set up 1500 nurseries (though they withdrew funding at the close of the war). Other provisions for war wives included reduced hours, canteens, family allowances, and abolition of the marriage bar in the civil sector, yet discrimination continued in the form of lower wages for women. Even among bomb victims, there was a difference of seven shillings a week between male and female recipients.

It is partially true that women were empowered by men's absence from the job market and the home during World War II. More women entered and remained in the work force after World War II than World War I. After the war, the Labour Party was elected to government and made a dynamic change in Britain's economic policy by sponsoring a welfare system. The National Insurance Act of 1946 provided compulsory employer and employee contributions for sickness, unemployment, maternity, widows' and old age pensions, with the government funding the balance. Unlike post–World War I, the government expected a labor shortage after World War II, and did not reinstate the marriage bar after the war. Several industries in the Midlands and South East, such as engineering, aircraft and railways, continued to prosper after the war; they found it profitable to retain their already-trained women workers. The welfare state created many new clerical and administrative posts, in fields like real estate, banking, and law. An economic boom increased the demand for teachers and nurses.

However, the increased number of women in the workforce did not mean equality of pay or quality of occupation. Most of women's work was temporary and part-time, much of it in unskilled, low-paid labor. Women were still far behind men in attaining higher education; by 1951, only 27 percent of university enrollment was female. Perhaps the greatest difference for women in employment after World War II as opposed to World War I was that the stigma of the job-stealer was removed, since there was enough work for both genders.

Women's Liberation Movement (WLM), 1968–1970s, and Germaine Greer

WLM and the Seven Demands

According to Martin Pugh, the proximate cause of the women's liberation movement was not women's frustration with marriage and gender roles, but the impact of radical civil rights and disarmament movements in both Britain and America. The British Campaign for Nuclear Disarmament (CND) claimed many women members in the 1950s and 1960s. Although Britain did not join America in the Vietnam War, Prime Minister Harold Winter did not repudiate the United States' bombing campaign. The moral apathy of their government radicalized many young people in the sixties, who formed direct action campaigns against armament. Pugh sees these as training grounds for the Women's Liberation Movement. Women in the CND and other New Left organizations were dissatisfied because their brothers in the cause were anti-women. The New Left was a term for groups of activists who opposed the authoritarian politics of pre-war leftist parties (such as the Communist Party), and organized groups along more democratic lines to fight for social change. Black Panther Stokely Carmichael sums up the New Left's misogyny when he announces that the right position for women in the civil rights movement is "prone," i.e., available for sex.

As we saw in 1970s Ireland, consciousness-raising was the method for WLM, and America the inspiration. Betty Friedan's *The Feminine Mystique* (1963) argued that complete female fulfillment in the role of mother/wife was a myth that rewarded women for being passive towards men and shameful about having personal ambitions. The book was so successful (over a million copies sold) that it catapulted Friedan out of her own suburban marriage into the public role of founder of the National Organization for Women (NOW), a liberal-feminist group that fought within legal channels for expansion of women's rights.

Even though domestic sexual politics were a crucial issue of the second wave on both sides of the Atlantic, the origins of the WLM in Britain were socialist rather than liberal. The 1968–70 period saw a rise in women workers' strikes, and the birth of socialist journals published by and about women, such as *Socialist Women* and *Women's Voice*. Female membership rose in New Left groups such as the Revolutionary Socialist Student Federation, the International Marxist Group, and the Communist Party. However, the New Left relied heavily on Marxist analysis, which most feminists disliked, and the Labour Party had a "heavy masculine ambience" (Pugh 318). Historian Olive Banks says the New Left in these years had "a contempt for women that reduced them to servants and camp followers" (Bruley 148). Women needed a new approach to the question of emancipation.

The First National Conference of the WLM met at Ruskin College, Oxford, in 1970. Six hundred women agreed upon four goals: (1) equal pay, (2) equal education and job opportunities, (3) free contraception and abortion on demand, and (4) free twenty-four-hour community-controlled childcare. Within the next seven years, three more demands were added: (5) legal and financial independence of women, (6) an end to discrimination against lesbians, and (7) freedom for all women from intimidation by the threat or use of male violence; an end to the laws, assumptions and institutions which perpetuate male dominance and men's aggression towards women.

The British WLM's methods of pursuing these goals were more radical than NOW's. Civil disobedience and marches were uncommon. Disillusioned by government's ignoring of the peace campaign, WLM was more inclined to bypass the political system of Parliament, Cabinet, and Prime Minister, in favor of local grass-roots consciousness-raising and right living. All-female communes tried to raise their awareness of sexism and its consequences. Leadership was considered hierarchal and patriarchal, so many communes tried to live without a leader. As we see in women's testimonies of the times, such anarchy had both good and bad results. Consensus decision-making was good because women had a voice in how their lives were run, some for the first time in their lives. Yet it was inefficient because it gave voice to so much internal division, making it difficult to take concerted action. One of the most famous communes reveals these tensions in play, while also attesting to the immense courage, patience and wisdom of hundreds of women. I refer to the Greenham Common Peace Camp, described in a later section of this chapter.

Germaine Greer and The Female Eunuch

Exploring the life and writings of the best-known feminist of this period, Germaine Greer, reveals the movement's challenges to patriarchy, as well as the diversity within the movement. Although many disagree with her sexual-liberation feminism and her coarse language, most would agree that Greer provided a face and personality for the British movement, much as Mrs. Pankhurst and Christabel did for first-wave feminism. Although less threatening than many would desire, Greer's challenges to patriarchy made her a household name. She could be called upon to represent a certain kind of sexual-liberation feminism, a similar strand of which would resurge in the third wave under the label "sex-positive feminism." With her good looks and exotic foreignness, sporting a mixed Australian and Cambridge University accent, Greer was in demand as a public speaker in America and Britain. She debated (while flirting) with misogynists such as Norman Mailer, flaunted pornography as a means to empowerment, and popularized the identity of the rock star groupie. In her academic capacity,

Germaine Greer, c. 1971 (Photofest).

she contributed to the stock of feminist analysis with such books as *The Female Eunuch* (1970), about why a woman's revolution was needed; *The Obstacle Race* (1979), about female painters; *Sex and Destiny* (1984), an attack on the nuclear family; *Shakespeare* (1986), a short book of literary criticism informed by her doctoral thesis; *Daddy, We Hardly Knew You* (1989), an exploration of her father's roots and wartime trauma; and *The Change: Women, Aging and the Menopause* (1991), which accuses the medical industry of pathologizing menopause.

In her astute 1998 biography, *Germaine Greer: Untamed Shrew*, Christine Wallace links Greer to the shrewish character in Shakespeare's play, *The Taming of the Shrew*, one of the subjects of Greer's doctoral dissertation. In this play, Petruccio tames Kate, who happily succumbs to his masculine dominance. Greer argues that such a marriage was desirable in dangerous Elizabethan times, since women needed the protection of stronger partners. Shockingly, she also indicates that such an imbalance of power within marriage is ideal for her own times, because women respect men who can better them in argument. This paradox — a feminist claiming that women long for male dominance — reflects Greer's unresolved issues with her family, and causes unpopularity with both equal-rights and radical feminists.

Born in 1939, Germaine suffered the consequences of the Post Traumatic Stress Disorder that her father, Reg, developed during the war. Reg's job required that he live twenty-four meters underground in a bomb shelter, deciphering military code while German and Italian air forces bombed the island of Malta. When he returned home in 1944, he was nervous and distant. To compound matters, he disapproved of Germaine's intelligence, favoring her younger sister and brother. Nor did her mother make up for her father's disdain. Germaine particularly remembers being afraid of her mother's temper. Peggy whipped her daughter for offenses she didn't understand, such as walking with a male friend. Greer found an outlet for her emotions in religion; for a while, she wanted to be a saint, and once, she fasted until she fainted. But by fifteen, frustrated that the nuns at her school could not explain certain dogmas, she lost her faith.

Greer's failure to find love at home resulted in early sexual experimentation when she attended the University of Melbourne. She was sensitive to slights, though often insensitive to the feelings of others. A boyfriend's rejection landed her in the hospital with depression and nervous exhaustion. Later, Greer was raped by a boy she agreed to ride with after a party. Rather than allow her concerned roommates to report the rape, Germaine protested, "they wouldn't believe me; I'm a woman." A few years later, she would again demonstrate this sexual passivity while hitching a ride with an older man in Italy. Though she did not desire it, Germaine suffered his sexual touching for hours, rather than hurt his feelings. Once Greer became atheist at eighteen, she realized that sexual morality was personal, not governed by outside authorities: "I found myself thinking very hard about my virginity" (34–5). Determined to be "honest" about her sexuality, she asked a friend to deflower her. Her newfound sexual permissiveness led her straight to a group of bohemian students called the Drift. Marxist, free-loving, and artsy, this group formed a home for the distressed Greer. Later she would repudiate the value of the experience: "It represented a way of just hanging around. It was full of shit" (Wallace 49). Yet her membership in the Drift prepared her for a more serious commitment to the Push, when she enrolled at the University of Sydney for her Masters in English.

The Push put sexual liberation in front of all others types of liberation, saying it was the first step towards freeing the soul for true living. Anarchist and pessimistic, Push followed the moral instructions of John Anderson, Professor of Philosophy at the University of Sydney. It is worth understanding how central was the practice of permissive sexuality to this philosophy, because this belief remains a key part of Greer's feminist ideology later in her life. In Push, the equation of sexual repression with political authoritarianism meant that anyone unwilling to be sexually free was politically suspect (Wallace 68). It wasn't just a question of accepting sexual encounters; there was an affirmative duty to seek them out. Later, when Greer becomes a spokesperson for the counterculture, and a proponent of group sex, her quasi-religious belief in the spirituality and ethical nature of free sex dates back to her indoctrination by Push. Soon she has sex with Push's leader, Roelof Smilde; throughout her life, she would seek approval by sleeping with leaders. Living with Smilde for several months, Greer suffers quietly from his lack of emotional commitment. As Wallace puts it, "Germaine's commitment was starved slowly by the lack of emotional sustenance he offered in return" (76). In fact, this relationship, strained as it is, seems to be the only sustained love affair in her life.

Greer's choice of a thesis topic aligns with her sexual focus in life. Lord Byron was the eighteenth century's equivalent of a Push man because of his permissive sexuality. Greer's thesis on Byron's satiric mode earned her a scholarship. Determined to go to Oxbridge, she chose Cambridge University over Oxford, because Oxford had sent Percy Shelley away. Under the direction of a prominent, though not feminist literary critic, Muriel Bradbrook, Greer wrote her doctoral dissertation on Shakespeare's comedies. In this work, Greer established that Shakespeare was an early advocate of love-marriages. Because the field was saturated, few doctorates were awarded in Shakespeare after 1950. Greer's pride in receiving hers was clear. This achievement, though not acknowledged by her father, finally gave Greer some of the intellectual authority she had been seeking since childhood.

Although she immediately began tutoring English at University of Warwick, Greer abandoned her literary research and entered the world of entertainment. She acted in a television comedy series called *Nice Time*. She wrote articles for *Oz,* a counterculture magazine similar to *Rolling Stone*, and posed nude for *Suck,* a pornography magazine that she co-founded with three men. She believed that pornography could promote spiritual liberation through sexual liberation. Her pornography career was anti-feminist in the most obvious way (objectifying women), but also because she used her position to sabotage other women. For instance, she wrote that her fellow Australian, Lillian Roxon, was available for fat-girl group sex, and warned that another friend "wouldn't give head." Claiming it as research for *Oz,* Greer slept with rock stars and had group sex. But it was important to her to sleep with only the most successful of rock stars: "I guess I'm a starfucker really. You know it's a name I dig, because all the men who get inside me are stars.... Another thing I dig is balling the greats before the rest of the world knows about them, before they get the big hype" (143). Although it is easy to denigrate the exhibitionism, elitism, and anti-feminism in this statement, it is important to realize that Greer was a product of an unhappy childhood and of a sexual indoctrination during her early twenties. These factors made her regard men's sexual desire as an affirmation of her worth, something she could obtain from neither her father nor her mother. Later in life she would repudiate promiscuity. She felt that her sexual history had made her sterile. In middle age, she longed for the stability and purpose that she thought mothering would afford.

After her graduation in 1968, Greer's agent suggested she write a book celebrating the women's movement fifty years after the first suffrage bill. The result was *The Female Eunuch*, a 330-page rant against patriarchy, but also against women's complicity in their own enslavement. The central idea, that females are castrated by patriarchy and their own internalization of it, is a powerful one. Greer argues convincingly from her own experience that girls are dissuaded from pursuing goals of their own choosing, particularly in the arts. When they reach puberty, their socialization impedes their fulfillment, as they begin to tailor themselves to the demands of the marriage market. But Greer insists that women should not marry. Drawing on her readings in Communism and anarchy, she asserts that marriage is a tool of capitalist society, which makes women second-class citizens, enslaving them to their biological roles as mothers of children and nurturers of men. None of this is new, as the reference to Marxist theory suggests. Also, seven years earlier, Betty Friedan's *The Feminine Mystique* had said the same thing. What was new was Greer's shocking style. She used coarse words, like *cuntpower, fuck,* and *cock,* and was graphic about women's mission: "women must humanize the penis, take the steel out of it and make it flesh again." "The cunt must come into its own" (315, 316).

Greer's sexual radicalism was new for its time. She somewhat disparagingly reduced Freidan's feminist message to "Women just have to get out and make community." Greer took Friedan's message further: women had to get out and make revolution. Women must avoid marriage, but if they are already married, they must "examine the setup." This may or may not entail promiscuity, but they must stop accepting their husbands' ridicule. By sharing their possessions, such as appliances and baby clothes, with other women, they could reject their role as the principal consumers of the capitalist state. They must eschew compulsions like cooking and cleaning, unless these activities give them pleasure. All housekeeping should be fun or else it shouldn't be done. Being realistic, Greer does not claim that one agenda would work for all women, but stresses that finding their creative energy, or libido, will save women's lives. Women must "have something to desire, something to make, something to achieve, and at last something genuine to give." They need to stop bargaining from the underdog position: "stop pretending and dissembling, cajoling and manipulating, and begin to control and sympathize. To claim the masculine virtues of magnanimity and generosity and courage" (328).

Like the essentialism of this final claim, the book has many faults, particularly its frequent blaming of women for their oppressed condition. Greer states that violence against women would stop if women did not champion it. Another painful point is that Greer harshly condemns her mother for, among other things, trying to obtain an education during her middle age. The book is inconsistent in its exhortations. At one point, woman must cut the "Lilliputian ties" that bind her to the service of her husband, father, and children. At another point, woman must find the male-dominated marriage that Greer praises in her doctoral dissertation.

The Female Eunuch enjoyed tremendous commercial success, selling out two editions in five months. Translated into eleven languages, the *Eunuch* became an international hit, making Greer's name famous, and paving the road for future contracts, including book deals, speaking engagements, and even an academic post at the University of Tulsa, which lasted just four years. *The Female Eunuch* launched Greer's career as a celebrity, though it is difficult to label what kind. *Public intellectual* doesn't do justice to her talents, since she was just as creatively oriented as she was intellectual. *Firebrand* is a better description, along the lines of a Bill Maher or Michael Moore. Female firebrands are comparatively rare, but anti-feminists such as Sarah Palin, Ann Coulter, or Camille Paglia fit the bill — women who enjoy shocking others by their reactionary politics. But Greer offers something better than shock value. As Gloria Steinem said, "if the movement is defined as 'women moving' — as women moving 'off our asses,' so to speak, and the movement of ideas, then

Greer is part of the movement" (Wallace 283). According to many women, Greer mobilized them to rebel against patriarchy.

The Women's Peace Movement and Greenham Common, 1981–2000

The nature of the feminist beliefs that created Greenham Common Peace Camp is about as different from Germaine Greer's as one can get. While Greer advocated revolution by free sexual congress with men, the peace women excluded men from their camp because they believed that women would grow in a woman-only environment. In contrast to Greer's isolation from other feminists, the peace women could only achieve their objectives through collective action. Cooperation on the microcosmic level of camp life could serve as a model for the macrocosm of world powers. I choose the Greenham Common Peace Camp (GCPC) as a second focus of my description of British second-wave feminism because it demonstrates some of the variety that feminism entails. Neither feminism nor the WLM are monolithic, but have as many stripes as the rainbow, that entity which the peace women chose to name their individual camps after, such as Green Gate, Blue Gate, and Indigo Gate.

I also choose GCPC because of its uniqueness as a peace movement. On December 12, 1982, when 35,000 women embraced the base by holding hands in a nine-mile circle around it, they were staging the largest women's demonstration in history. On Good Friday of the next year, 70,000 people linked hands across the Nuclear Valley. Over the nineteen-year period of the Camp's existence, thousands of women showed extraordinary moral commitment by jettisoning their jobs and homes to survive in stark camping conditions. Only one motivation was powerful enough to withstand this sacrifice — conscience. As Irish writer Caroline Blackwood describes it, "By their symbolic presence on Greenham Common they hoped to act as the voice of the millions of people all over the world who recognized that they had no voice" (35). Knowing that nuclear holocaust would affect millions of people around the world, women "gave voice" by their presence outside the gates of the Cruise missile site in Berkshire, England. The protest combined various threads—a fitting metaphor since one of their symbols was the spider web, and one of their activities was weaving thread into the fence. The two most prominent threads were the protest against war and the protection of the life and spiritual value of women, children, plants, animals, and Mother Earth. As Christina Welch writes, the GCPC "included a new form of socio-politics, with ordinary women at the forefront, yet it also represented the coming of age of second-wave feminism, especially eco-feminism with its emphasis on spirituality and social change" (63).

The campaign started small-scale in September, 1981, when Ann Pettitt, an Englishwoman living in Wales, decided to organize a 110-mile march from a nuclear weapons factory in Cardiff to a U.S. nuclear base in Berkshire. The purpose of the campaign was to protest both U.S. military presence in Britain and nuclear war in general. The group called themselves Women for Life on Earth. Their intention was to publicize the dangers of radiation, bring public awareness to the existence of U.S. warheads throughout Britain, and give voice to a critique of patriarchy: "Take the Toys from the Boys." Men were welcome to join the march, but women would be in charge. The women felt they had a special responsibility, as women, to offer their children "a future that was not a nuclear wasteland." Women bore the brunt of recent cuts to social services, but rarely took part in governmental processes. A women-led campaign would give them a chance to have a voice (Liddington 227). Consensus was the decision-making method. Upon arrival at Greenham, the peace women requested a public debate between themselves and the Minister of Defense. Although they repeatedly requested it, this audience was never afforded, throughout all the years of their presence at Greenham Common. To raise visibility, four women chained themselves to the wire perimeter fence, and were spelled by others as the weeks wore on. When their request for a debate was repeatedly refused or ignored — reminiscent of the suffragettes' deputations to the Prime Minister — the women decided that they needed to stay until the last warhead was removed. This took nineteen years.

For the first few months, camp life was remarkably low key. Blackwood speaks of its utter boredom. Because of the lack of amenities, the only past times were knitting, painting, reading, or drinking tea. The local Newbury government prohibited tents and trailers, so the women had to construct "benders," polyethylene sheets draped over branches. These were leaky, cold, and small. Frequent rain made the ground a mud bath. Although their supporters were willing to bring the peace women any gear they needed, there was no point in collecting luxuries like lamps, books or blankets, let alone a food supply, since frequent evictions allowed bailiffs to confiscate and destroy all items except those on the camper's person. Because of this rule, women took to hopping around camp in their sleeping bags when an eviction was impending. Outhouses were constructed far from the camps, and water was carted in plastic containers. Supporters brought firewood, the only heat source to sustain the peace women through cold winters.

In February 1982, the peace women decided to exclude men from the camps. Men were permitted to bring supplies, but not to stay overnight. The initial rationale for excluding men was to empower women, but during the campers' tenure, a new reason developed. American and British guards stood watch just inside the perimeter of the fence; only a few feet separated the guards and the women. These guards heckled, cursed, and insulted the women. The peace women's express policy was to ignore all threats and insults. If male supporters were to be present, women feared that the soldiers' violence would escalate to a physical level. The only aggressions the women were permitted were snipping the metal of the fence, painting peace signs on army trucks, and sneaking into the base to dance on silos. The worst transgression of the no-violence rule was when a young woman poured cold custard through the fence at a RAF squaddie for sexually harassing her.

In order to pressure officials to disarm the base, the peace movement needed publicity. Many campers published stories about the experience. Visitors solicited funds and food for the campers back in their hometowns. The media reported on the frequent Newbury court hearings, for offenses such as trespass and obstruction. Women at Main Gate had the greatest responsibility, for they kept watch on the transportation of weaponry. Their mandate was to prevent a warhead from being released for drills. They feared that when Russians saw this exercise on their surveillance equipment, they might mistake it for the beginning of war. They also feared the possibility of plutonium leaks.

The GCPC generated worldwide publicity. Supporters donated funds for the peace women to fly all over the world to speak about the camp and their concerns. Books and articles were written about the movement, and the subject continues to inspire academic interest to this day. Caroline Blackwood's 1984 account of the weeks she spent at the camp documents the hardships suffered in the bleak conditions, as well as the hateful backlash by Newbury residents and press. Particularly entertaining are her interviews with Mr. Learoyd, spokesman for RAGE (Ratepayers Against Greenham Encampments). Learoyd's illogical statements expose a virulence about the peace-loving campers that was typical of the locals: "The Greenham women were all lazy layabouts ... using their protest to do nothing. A lot of them were lesbians and they had only joined the camps in order to indulge in lesbian activity" (65). "They were lawbreakers. They danced naked. They were lesbians. They created health hazards. They smelt" (64). "They were living it up in luxury.... They were taking drugs—they were always drunk. The noise they made was unbearable for the Newbury residents" (66). Blackwood investigated these complaints, and found none of them true. Indeed, Learoyd's self-contradicting statements proved that he hated them for reasons that even he did not understand; he sometimes said they were poor, sometimes rich, and resented them for both. He said that even if the missile were removed, the women would remain in camp because they "loved having no water because they hated washing" (68). Equally puzzling was the attitude of Mrs. Scull, a homeowner whose windows looked out upon one of the Gate camps. Incensed by the rumor that the campers were lesbians, Mrs. Scull blamed their camps for the ugly view from her windows. When asked whether the view of the military base bothered her, with its scrolls of barbed wire atop nine miles of chain link fence, Mrs. Scull said no, it was a pretty view until those women came to destroy it.

Despite the rage it inspired in many locals, the GCPC elicited admiration and even reverence from some quarters. A group of American peace campaigners requested stones from the camp, treating them as tokens imbued with the women's magical spiritual powers. This peace campaign was unique in history in terms of its magnitude and duration, and the permanently peaceful nature of its execution, in the face of constant heckling from soldiers inside the base, and aggressive evictions with bulldozers from bailiffs outside the base. In contrast to the suffragettes' desire for the vote, the peace campers' goal was harder to obtain. They didn't only want the cruise missile removed from Greenham Common; they wanted the world to understand the spiritually destructive nature of armament. It was a moral crusade that couldn't be won, but the women's testimony indicates that their conscience told them to face this ugly truth, and yet to do what small part they could to raise the consciousness of the world.

The backlash the peace women experienced was similar to that experienced by the suffragettes, and by other feminists in the Thatcher years; the backlash demonized women who acted on their conscience. One of Blackwood's interviewees, a Newbury antiques dealer, analyzed the backlash with surprising thoughtfulness: "I think that here in Newbury, we none of us like those women because in our hearts we are all bloody jealous of them. In our hearts we know we haven't got the guts to do what the women are doing" (53). Everybody loves a hero, but not if it's a woman! The fear of being outshone by women has recurred in the history of the women's movement, from Michael Davitt's Land League in nineteenth-century Ireland to RAGE's irrational response to women campers.

The Wave of the Future

Class-Polarization and British Feminism

In her thoughtful book, *Feminist Experiences: The Women's Movement in Four Cultures*, Susan Bassnett paints a dreary picture of British feminism up to 1986. Compared to Italy and other Catholic nations of the south, Protestant Britain never enjoyed the upside of the double-sided image of woman as venerable and contemptible, which Freud popularized as the virgin-whore complex. The absence of any idealized version of women or children resulted in its opposite, a degradation of the qualities of women and children (134). Bassnett gives several examples of downright hostility to women and children in public places, sexist depictions of women in the press, resentment of employed women in times of recession, and astonishment at women's professional abilities. In addition to these social indicators of misogyny, British women lag behind those of Europe and North America in their procurement of government and professional posts. In 1998, 96 percent of British surgeons were men, 93 percent of professors, and 96 percent of company directors. The average woman who works has only half the income of the average working man. In 1997, just over one-fifth of Parliament was female. Married women with full-time jobs still do over two-thirds of domestic work in the homes they share with men (Walters 9).

Besides the absence of Catholic mother-idolatry, Bassnett attributes British misogyny to a class system that has pitted socialism against feminism from the start of both movements. Margaret Thatcher rose from the working class to become Prime Minister, yet shows a singular lack of empathy for women's oppression. Bassnett believes that Thatcher's insecurity about her own place in the class system trumps her care for women as an oppressed class. Thatcher contrives to dress like, speak like, and act like a "lady," that bourgeois identity which feminists have been trying for decades to dismantle, in the interests of exploring the whole range of their human identity. Similarly, Natasha Walter gives an example of the porn magazine editor who anxiously protected his own daughter from the industry, but thought it was acceptable work for working class women, who did not have access to better jobs. A corrective to the class gap would be to create a closer affiliation between women's groups and the organized Left. However, as we have seen in the story of the Pankhurst family, with its dramatic split between socialist and feminist halves, such affiliation is challenging and historically traumatic.

A third source of friction for British feminism is Britain's tradition of anti-intellectualism. According to Bassnett, British intellectuals are often considered a class apart, and "universally despised by all other levels of the pyramid" (163). The association of intellectuals with left-wing politics, especially in the sixties and seventies, increased their stigma, to the point where they have no political representation. Working class hatred of higher classes, middle class hatred of the working class, and aristocratic disdain for them all is prevalent in the culture, and within the women's movement itself, making it difficult to achieve consensus and to grow at the national level. Consequently,

Britain has not seen the number of mass-scale demonstrations common in Europe and North America. Instead, the women's movement operates in smaller, grass-roots organizations, focusing upon local concerns. Since anti-intellectualism and misogyny remain dominant ideologies in Britain, "the position of intellectual feminists has become even more absurd" (163).

It may appear that Bassnett is prejudiced against the country where she is employed as a vice provost and university lecturer in comparative literature, but her depictions of East German, American, and Italian feminisms even the field. For instance, she lauds the solidarity of Italian women in their fight against fascism and for reproductive rights, but notices the same foundering (*dopo-feminismo*) as in Britain, after the brief resurgence of the movement in the early seventies. Her groundbreaking work in comparative feminisms demonstrates some of the founding principles of women's studies. Since history is necessarily a subjective shaping of facts interspersed with opinions, women's studies admits the subjective viewpoint, at the same time validating the observational nature of all social analysis. Because of the clarity and authority of her claims, not to mention her substantial evidence and lived experience in these countries, I trust Bassnett's findings. Citing Margaret Stacey and Marion Price, she summarizes that "in Britain upwardly mobile women have not been closely involved with the post–1968 feminist movement ... [which] has tended to be dominated by younger women uninvolved in public life" (152). Parallel to the relative quiet in political quarters, cultural feminism remains small; there is a paucity of British feminist writers, artists, and philosophers. Some of the fiction writers whom isolated feminist readers want to claim as their own are actually anti-feminist (164). We will see in following chapters that Doris Lessing and Fay Weldon fit this description, although they have contributed in different ways to the women's movement and consciousness-raising.

New Feminism and Old Sexism:
The Changing Face of the Third Wave

As Stacey and Price noted, the third wave in British feminism has tended to be dominated by young women uninvolved in public life; it takes as its focus the "empowerment" that young women derive from sexual display, promiscuity, and the sex industry. Natasha Walter's recent book, *Living Dolls: The Return to Sexism* (2010), is notable not only for its intelligent dissection of the pornography debate, but also for the fact that her views have changed 180 degrees since the time of her previous book, *The New Feminism* (1998). This about-face has less to do with the rate of growth of sexism in the first decade of the twenty-first century, than with Walter's maturing as a person (between the two books, she had two children and turned forty-three). Many women follow this pattern of resisting feminism in their twenties and becoming more sympathetic to it as they mature and encounter the sexism in their culture. In the earlier book, Walter argued that the work of feminists over the decades had given women a sufficient amount of control over their personal lives. Therefore, women should drop the motto, "the personal is the political," and free themselves from "the straitjacket of political correctness" (5). Feminism had "enunciated too many critiques of dress and pornography, of poetry and filmmaking, of language and physical behavior" (5). Now, feminists must "free up the personal realm," focusing instead on "the material reality of inequality" (6).

Within the next twelve years, Walter would come to realize that sexism, as exhibited in bed, bar, or boardroom, *is* the material reality of inequality. The ways in which young women use their bodies is intricately connected to the material realities of their class position as well as their gender. Commenting on the mainstreaming of pornography and sexual display of all kinds, which starts at a very young age, Walter notes, "the rise of a hypersexual culture is not proof that we have reached full equality; rather, it has reflected and exaggerated the deeper imbalances of power in our society" (8). Walter's second book, *Living Dolls*, encapsulates some of the most critical problems in the recent phase of British feminism. In the last ten years, Britain has seen the return of sexism and the return to a belief in the theory of biological determinism as an explanation for essential differences between males and females. Most feminists whose consciousness was formed in the second wave consider this kind of essentialism dangerous, because it stereotypes women and men, hardening gender roles and preventing full empowerment of women.

The sex industry has mushroomed within the past few years. From a handful of clubs in the 1990s, the number grew to over 300 lap-dancing clubs in Britain in 2008. Due to lax licensing laws, it is no harder to get a permit for lap dancing than for selling liquor, resulting in a proliferation of the clubs in town centers. Their visibility and increasing acceptability among men of all ages and occupations have changed cultural attitudes to the objectification of women, by familiarizing and normalizing the practice (47). In addition to lap dancing, pole dancing and stripping, even prostitution has come to the mainstream, thanks to a number of best-selling memoirs by prostitutes. In these books, prostitutes pretend to like having sex with johns. They treat the selling of their bodies with nonchalance. Of all three types of sex industry — lap-dancing, prostitution, and pornography — porn has become most normalized by its ubiquity and the apparent consent of most people to its presence in their lives.

While the sex industries are mainstreamed in British culture, the actual participants continue to suffer the consequences of their participation. Walter interviews men and women who are either in the sex industry or use its services. She also talks with boys and girls, because they are exposed to the sex industry at an increasingly early age (as early as four for girls, whose dolls, movies, and video heroines are highly sexualized). Adults and teens tend to justify the sex industry with two terms, "choice" and "empowerment." Since women have the choice whether or not to engage in sex work or sexual display, they are not being forced to become sex objects by a patriarchal society. Since they can potentially earn a lot of money by displaying themselves and offering sex, then they are empowered by the industry. Digging deeper, most of Walter's subjects debunked both myths. One ex-stripper says that women feel constrained to go along with objectification because we live in a hypersexual culture: "Women get told they are prudes if they say they don't want their boyfriend to go to a club where he gets to stick his fingers in someone else's vagina, or if they say they don't want to watch porn with their boyfriend.... But being sexually liberated [doesn't] mean that we have to enjoy and accept the forms of sexual entertainment that were invented by men for their own pleasure" (49). Nor does she think there's anything empowering in the business: "We hear a lot about choice or liberation, but it just isn't equal ... you just look at the lap-dancing club, and it says so much about our culture. The men in there are respectable, they are in suits, they have bank accounts, the women are not respectable, they are naked, they have debts" (49).

Interviews with prostitutes revealed one of the costs of selling oneself—the psychological dead end. One of them said, "It's very disempowering. It's harmful. It narrows how you value yourself, how you define yourself. It's very dangerous to define yourself through the eyes of these men who are buying your body" (60). She also talked about how dangerous the trade had become. Her johns were requesting to "experiment with stuff they'd seen on the internet," including tying up and gagging their prostitute, and having threesomes. She remarks, "I get the feeling that some of the men get off on the fact that the woman doesn't want it. Basically you've consented to being raped sometimes for money" (61). In these circumstances, the idea that men's sexual desire empowers women is ludicrous. In one survey, 75 percent of johns thought prostitutes were "dirty and inferior." Their "desire" for these women is the desire to hurt them.

Interviews with pornography users and partners of users revealed similar psychopathology. One problem is that the Internet gives such easy access to pornography that the violence of the practice has increased in order to sell in a saturated market. One pornography addict, Jim, who has been using for thirty years, says he finds recent internet pornography more demeaning to women than in the past: "The stuff I saw as a kid was what we called hardcore, but the idea in the text alongside was that it was based on mutual consent — mutual pleasure — but what I see now is more male domination" (115). Having lost his seven-year relationship with his girlfriend due to his pornography addiction, Jim is aware of porn's devastating effect on his ability to attain intimacy. He fears for a whole generation of boys who are viewing porn before they have any relationship: "I think that kind of violence associated with sex lodges in your mind and you never forget it, however much you want to" (115). Female partners of users are aware of this objectification too; they wonder whether their partner is seeing them or an image remembered from the screen or page.

Because the voice of feminist dissent to pornography has largely died down in this decade, young people, both male and female, feel isolated if they hold an alternative viewpoint to the general acceptance of porn and the sex industries. Usually, they do not dare to express such unpopular views. Therefore, they express relief when they read a book such as Walter's, or encounter any other critique of the hyper-sexualization of western culture. The dirty secret that brings home the critical nature of this problem is that pornography use is widespread among children. One Canadian study showed that 90 percent of 13- and 14-year-old boys and 70 percent of girls the same age had viewed porn, most of it over the Internet; one-third of those used it regularly. One of the problems of such early exposure is that when children view pornography before their first experience of sexual intercourse, it effectively loses their innocence for them, making it difficult to understand what human intimacy is about.

Alongside this popular trend to hypersexualize our culture there exists a companion trend in the academy. This is the return of biological determinism to define differences between the sexes and justify different treatment of men and women. When a Newcastle University psychologist tested the color preferences of women and men, he found that women preferred pink and men blue. Professor Hurlbert decided that the difference was due to "sex-specific functions in the evolutionary division of labor." Men had once associated blue skies with better hunting days, while women food-gatherers liked pinks and red because they were the colors of ripe berries and other fruits (145). This speculation ignores the fact that, fifty years ago, the gendered color preferences were in reverse, with boys being dressed in pink. In a far more serious example of essentialist thinking, in 2005, Lawrence Summers, President of Harvard University, justified female under-representation in the science and engineering faculty on the basis of "intrinsic aptitude" (174). Undertaking an extensive review of science test scores, Walter learned that there is only one science test in which females consistently underperform males, which is the mental rotation of a 3-D object. After being trained for a few hours, however, women showed no difference from men in their ability to mentally rotate the object.

For fifty years, cultural determinism was the dominant explanation of male-female difference; the recent return to biological determinism marks a shift in attitudes towards men and women's place in society. If we believe that women are hardwired to enjoy nurturing and communicating, while men are hardwired to appreciate systems like math and science, then there is no reason to stretch society, to accommodate and encourage female engineers and male social workers. But essentialized difference does more than rigidify gender role boundaries; it rationalizes patriarchy, in which better jobs and better pay are men's natural right, where abuse of women continues without critique, and girls are taught that they are inferior and that submission to authority will bring them the greatest satisfaction.

In this chapter, we have seen British women fight long and hard for a voice in their society and home. In 1908, after nearly forty years of steady protest, certain suffragettes changed their game plan, launching a militant campaign that gradually weakened the government's resolve. These women sacrificed their safety, reputation, and peace for the attainment of the right to vote, yet many were vilified in their time for atrocious behavior unbecoming of ladies. Within two years of their participation in Britain's war campaign, the Prime Minister consented to the suffrage bill, raising the question whether the suffrage campaign itself was successful, or whether the Pankhursts' new-found patriotism won the vote. The interwar years saw a return to separate spheres for men and women. Even though there were more women in the workforce, the type of job available to women was inferior, and their pay level reflected gender bias. In World War II, millions of women gave assistance to wounded soldiers, to the munitions industry, and to evacuees. The women's liberation movement of the early 1970s raised consciousness about social inequalities in domestic relationships, but was less successful in expanding work opportunities for women to an appreciable degree. Britain's patterns of social change tend to stem from grass-roots efforts, but it remains difficult to mobilize these efforts across class boundaries. The WLM split into multiple interest groups such as eco-feminism, lesbian-separatist feminism, and equal rights feminism. Germaine Greer represents a particular strand of sexual-liberation feminism, which was popular for a brief period, but by no means monolithic. The peace camps represent a quite different strand of feminism; the purpose of women-only groups was to make a spiritual protest against a male-dominated war industry, and a masculine way of looking at life. In third-wave British, as in American and other feminisms, young women want to believe that equal rights have already been achieved, and that sexual liberty means sexual equality. But these beliefs are tested once young women encounter sexism in marriage and employment. The willingness of many young people to be sex objects or to use others as sex objects drives the sex industry and the ideology of a hypersexualized culture, making it difficult to separate patriarchy and women's complicity with their oppression. In the following chapters, we will revisit many of the historical moments of the century, examining how British and Irish women writers interrogate the terms of patriarchy and create new choices, or survive the choices they have made.

CHAPTER THREE

The 1920s: Androgyny and Gender Performance in Virginia Woolf's *Mrs. Dalloway* and Elizabeth Bowen's *The Last September*

Abbreviations: ROO A Room of One's Own; MT Mulberry Tree; PPT People, Places, Things; and TG Three Guineas.

Synopsis: The political unconscious of these two novels gives voice to gender and class oppressions. The two protagonists, one young, the other old, experience isolation. Their false feminine voices belie those authentic interior voices that modernist novels excel at representing through stream of consciousness and symbolism. The feminist impulse of both authors resides in their anatomy of melancholy. Woolf and Bowen stage the psychic costs of the performance of gender.

Historical Backgrounds

The 1920s brought tremendous social and economic upheaval to Britain and Ireland. In Britain, the demobilization of millions of troops caused crises of employment, since women assumed many of the jobs formerly held by men. Women workers were not the only phenomenon contributing to a breakdown of the family. The suffragettes' campaign challenged people's notions of propriety. What was the proper role of men and women in society, and how did gender performance relate to other problems facing Britain, including the threat of another war, and increasing demands for social responsibility on the part of government? In the twenties, the Labour Party developed a mass membership that elected a Prime Minister in 1924 and 1929. Minister of Labour Margaret Bondfield was the first-ever woman cabinet minister of any party. Although short-lived, the Labour government brought class issues to the parliamentary table, and to public view through the media. On the other side of the Irish Sea, the decade begins with the Anglo-Irish treaty that affords Ireland a Commonwealth status, but divides the nation in two, followed by traumatic civil war and Eamon de Valera's conservative government. Unlike the party changes in English government during the early twentieth century, de Valera's *Fianna Fail* party was to remain in office for 33 years, from 1926 till 1959. Ireland was nominally free, but not flush, and both countries were in mourning for their war dead for decades to come.

Literature of the era reflects these traumas, posing the classic questions of modernity, such as the problem of isolation, the breakdown of communication, the discomfort of gender roles, the fluidity of identity, and the challenge of meaninglessness in a world where war and government had eroded faith in abstract notions like justice, freedom, nation, and democracy. To compare Irish and British feminist awareness in this decade, I have chosen two novels that highlight the pains of modernity. Both novels employ modernist literary methods that value the representation of consciousness over traditional elements of plot and social detail. Interior monologue, stream of consciousness, free indirect discourse and lyricism are styles that prioritize consciousness and symbolism over realist details. In "Mr. Bennett and Mrs. Brown" (1924), Virginia Woolf claims that the best way to get readers interested in fictional characters is by fully representing their consciousness. She maintains that Victorian writers (especially Austen, Charlotte Brontë and George Eliot) made believable characters, but that Edwardian writers (especially H.G. Wells, John Galsworthy and Arnold Bennett) failed to create real characters, thus failing to capture our imagination.

In *Mrs. Dalloway* (1925), Woolf shows how to revitalize the novel. The narrative uses free indirect discourse, a third-person narration that approximates first-person speech by leaving out the "He said, she said(s)." Its effect is to bring us straight into the character's mind. Woolf uses it to extraordinary effect in comparing her two main characters' feelings. Although they are divided by chasms of gender, class, and age, Mrs. Dalloway and Septimus Smith become linked by their similar perceptions of life's terrors. Elizabeth Bowen's *The Last September* (1929) also uses free indirect discourse, but more frequently uses dialogue to make its point about the breakdown in communication among her characters, especially those of different classes, ethnicities and genders.

I choose these two novels to investigate feminist consciousness in the 1920s for several reasons. Both novels foreground a female protagonist whose personal anxieties about gender performance are set against a backdrop of war and shell-shocked men returning from war. The protagonists identify with these men, in part because their own traumatized selves are mirrored in these Others (Mrs. Dalloway mirrors Septimus; Lois Farquar mirrors Mr. Daventry). Both novels demonstrate the inextricability of class and gender issues, insofar as the protagonists take on the politics of their male protectors. Mrs. Dalloway is married to a Conservative MP, thereby limiting her awareness of, and ability to relate to, the lower classes. Similarly, *The Last September*'s Lois Farquar, abandoned by parents and cared for by Anglo-Irish Ascendancy relatives, must play by their political rules, which include not talking about socialism or republicanism in their house. Bowen satirizes the Irish landed gentry and the English middle classes, while at the same time sympathetically illustrating the difficulty of belonging to a hybrid, Anglo-Irish class. Similarly, Woolf's novel foregrounds class isolation in several unusual relationships. The two main characters never meet, being separated by the abyss of their class, gender and age. In addition, upper-middle-class Peter Walsh can never know the Otherness of the singing beggar woman; the middle-class Miss Kilman and higher-class Mrs. Dalloway indulge in murderous fantasies about each other; and the middle class is the object of numerous barbs from Mrs. Dalloway, whose own status as upper-middle class is too close for comfort.

Although neither protagonist could be called a feminist (very broadly defined as believing that women are equal, and should be treated as equal to men), we can trace feminist sensibilities in their authors. Indeed, the free indirect discourse method of narration lends itself particularly well to such a representation, because it captures the private thoughts of women who are reacting, often violently, against the expectations of others for proper female behavior. Yet the sensibilities of these protagonists, like those of their creators, are very different. It is in this difference that we can explore relations of class to feminism; questions of separatism, androgyny, and equity; and finally, the relations of literary genre to questions of gender. *Mrs. Dalloway* is a novel of sensibility that explores a middle-aged woman's affective life during the course of one day, while *The Last September* uses a full cast to satirize Anglo-Irish complacency, while stressing the one woman's difficulty in finding an identity in a world constrained by class and gender expectations. While *The Last September* delineates the pain of gender performance without attempting to show any alternative, *Mrs. Dalloway* critiques patriarchy, but also attempts to cross class and gender boundaries by forming an identification between Mrs. Dalloway and Septimus Smith. The distinction may seem slight, but it points to very different beliefs and values on the part of the writers.

Feminisms of Elizabeth Bowen and Virginia Woolf

What makes such a comparison more interesting is the fact that neither author consistently called herself a feminist, showing dread at the word much as many young women do today. College students often begin their contributions to class with the disclaimer, "I am not a feminist, but ..." As late as 1961, Elizabeth Bowen writes: "I am not, and never shall be, a feminist. I should be sorry to think that women's achievement, their soaring prestige, their present central position, was due to men's inadequacy or failure, or, even, to lessening masculine self-confidence" (PPT 379). Yet her editor notes: "Bowen's declaration should be read in context of her war work, her journalism, her service on the Royal Commission on Capital Punishment, and numerous other activities that took her outside the *domus*" (PPT 458). In other words, Bowen achieved much recognition in the "man's world" of the public sphere, but she ignored the fact that most other women of her time did not share the same access, regardless of their merit. Likewise, Woolf derided the word *feminist*, once even staging a mock public cremation to celebrate its obsoleteness after suffrage: *feminism* "was a vicious and corrupt word that has done much harm in its day and is now obsolete" (TG 102).

In contrast to Bowen, Woolf did briefly join up with a feminist organization. For a few weeks in 1910, she addressed envelopes for the People's Suffrage Organization. During the First World War, she even called herself feminist, seeing it as a way to oppose the patriarchy that created militarism and war: "I became steadily more feminist, owing to the Times, which I read at breakfast and wonder how this preposterous masculine fiction keeps going a day longer — without some vigorous young woman pulling us together and marching through it" (quoted in Briggs 89). After suffrage was achieved and the war over, Woolf's attitude changed, in part because she felt that the vote was only a peripheral part of the reform that was needed. In order for radical change to occur, she believed that the movement (and writers) must excavate and unveil the deep psychology of male dominance, which she begins to do in *Three Guineas*, and in novels like *To the Lighthouse*, where Mr. Ramsay's narcissism is satirized, particularly in his rages and his obsession with philosophical prestige.

Although she was extremely capable in her search for the roots of patriarchy in male psychology, Woolf felt she must leave activism for feminists, believing herself incapable (probably correctly) of the stamina such work required, and defining her own area of human rights work as writing. In reference to her reluctance to join anti-fascist organizations, she writes: "The army is the body: I am the brain. Thinking is my fighting" (Black 49). Woolf was opposed to the word *feminist* because it produced hostile reactions in others. Furthermore, she believed that she could not be a feminist because she hoped to serve all humans, not just women. Feminism was not good for literature either; she faults the suffrage campaign for having made novelists too conscious of sex, blaming the movement for male writers' bad novels. The feminist campaign made men too needful of asserting their superiority, and their writing too egocentric (AROO 99). After suffrage, Woolf pinned her hopes for rejuvenating the writers' craft upon writers' ability to cultivate an androgynous mind. Only when male and female parts of one's mind are "spiritually cooperating," can the mind be "fully fertilized" (AROO 98).

Revisionist critics have worked to change our perceptions of Bowen's and Woolf's avowed anti-feminism, looking beyond their disparagement of the term *feminism*. Naomi Black calls Woolf's "a deeply radical sort of feminism" (7). With her book-length essay *Three Guineas* (1938), Woolf envisioned a completely changed society, in which women, under the aegis of an Outsider Society, would work to curtail the production of war by entering the professions and educating young people to believe that war is wrong. Far from being genteel or anti-feminist, Woolf's argument is "tough and sophisticated, [with] transformative implications that are quite staggering" (7). Part of the reason that Woolf did not participate in the mainstream feminism of her period is that her peers were liberal feminists, who believed that achieving equal legal rights for men and women would solve the problem of discrimination. Woolf, on the other hand, was a "social feminist," meaning she believed that men and women are essentially different, and must evaluate and protect these differences as a means to transform social and political institutions.[1]

Marxist critic Alex Zwerdling traces Woolf's reluctance to call herself a feminist to her quite open preference for dealing with the concerns of her own class, whom she addresses as "daughters of educated men" in *Three Guineas*. In other words, she was not equally concerned about the welfare of all women. Another individualistic factor about Woolf's feminism was its separatist strain. In *Three Guineas* she says that since they have different values, women must work separately from men. Although the WSPU was a woman-only membership, many other suffrage societies did not believe in gender separation. In general, equal-rights feminists argued that they could "pacify" public institutions by entering them, not by staying in separate spheres from men.

In line with Naomi Black, Anne Fernald calls Woolf's feminism "resistant and revisionist"; it "makes room for herself at its center" (5). Woolf's contribution is particularly strong in feminist literary history, as we owe to her the idea of "thinking back through our mothers" (considering female authors as our role models). Rachel Bowlby also insists that Woolf's feminism is pervasive, as she "sexually inflects all questions of historical understanding" (70). Like Zwerdling, Bowlby suggests that Woolf's resistance to feminism had much to do with her social class. Woolf's fictional suffragettes are always working women whose political zeal is the butt of satire.

Unlike Woolf, Elizabeth Bowen did not contribute to the suffrage campaign. Born in Ireland but resident in Britain from age seven onwards, Bowen attended high school at Downe House in Kent from 1914 to 1917, so she certainly had exposure to the cause of suffrage. A social and political conservative, she married a civil servant and attended the Anglican Church. When she worries that men's self-confidence is lessened by feminism, her anti-feminism is at its clearest. Yet, revisionist critics have interpreted her fiction in ways that show committed feminist thinking. For instance, Neil Corcoran sees in *Bowen's Court* (1942), her book about the history of her family's estate, a "subliminally corrective and revisionist feminism" (23–4). And Renee Hoogland, who believes she is a "truly radical, innovative and critically practicing feminist," accuses other critics of "virtual gender blindness and unwillingness to engage in the destabilizing sexual subtexts which constitute Elizabeth Bowen's radical edge" (20). I agree with Hoogland's strong assertion; by adopting Judith Butler's theory of gender-as-performance[2] I am able to connect Bowen's characteristic gender-melancholy with her radical, though unacknowledged, feminism. By showing the absurdities and constraints imposed by gender expectations, Bowen powerfully critiques patriarchy for compelling heterosexuality and placing people according to their gender. Several features of Bowen's life enabled her to "fly by the nets" (in James Joyce's famous formulation) of Ireland, family and class that would otherwise have captured her and possibly have made her an avowed feminist.[3] Avoiding many of the oppressions of patriarchy because of her unusual life, Bowen felt she did not need feminism to solve her own problems. On the other hand, the melancholy of her characters, and their repressed homosexual desires, speak to the presence of a highly developed consciousness of patriarchy and its costs.

Lives of the Writers

Virginia Woolf (1882–1941)

Born in Hyde Park, to Leslie Stephen and Julia Duckworth Stephen, Virginia Woolf's first blessing was her timing. She was born into the age of high modernism. She and her literary peers revolutionized the British novel, turning from Edwardian social realism to modernist experimental forms. Her contemporaries were the well-known writers E.M. Forster (b. 1879), Lytton Strachey (1880), James Joyce (1882), and D.H. Lawrence (1885). Her father was an eminent Victorian. He attended the right schools and became a parson at Cambridge, but later resigned because of his lack of faith. Staunchly abolitionist, Stephen's first important work condemned biased reporting about the American Civil War. He is best known for his editorship of the massive, 63-volume *Dictionary of National Biography*, and for essays on freethinking and intellectual history. Like all Victorian upper-middle-class fathers, he provided for his two sons' educations at Trinity College, Cambridge, but not for his daughters, except for giving them tutors and the run of his library. His and Virginia's ambivalent relationship is well documented in her writing. Although she respected his moral standards and his success, she scorned his dominance over her mother. Leslie Stephen's irascibility and emotional demands are accurately represented in *To the Lighthouse*'s Mr. Ramsay.

When her mother died, thirteen-year-old Virginia suffered the first of roughly half a dozen mental breakdowns in her lifetime. While still mourning her mother, she was the victim of sexual molestation by her half-brothers, George and Gerald Duckworth. The causes of her illness were cumulative: the death of her mother (when Virginia was 13), the death of her half-sister Stella (when Virginia was 15), the death of her father (when she was 22), of her beloved older brother Thoby (when she was 25), and sexual abuse by her stepbrothers. These traumas, plus her perfectionism and fear of criticism, caused breakdowns which biographers diagnose variously.[4] Whether manic-depression, schizophrenia, hysteria, anorexia, or some combination thereof, Woolf's breakdowns are as much a part of her legacy as her literature. Such scrutiny of a writer's personal life, not to mention questioning of sanity, is not as prevalent in critical estimation of men's writing.

In 1912, Virginia married Leonard Woolf, who had recently retired from the Colonial Service in Ceylon. She warned Leonard that she was not attracted to him physically, and the marriage soon became one of friendship rather than romance. Together they established their own Hogarth Press, living on its proceeds, their writing, and Leonard's editing jobs for the *International Review* and *Nation*. Before their marriage, Leonard consulted Virginia's doctors about whether Virginia could handle the stress of a pregnancy and child rearing. While the doctors' votes were tied, her sister Vanessa tipped the scale to the side of "no." Virginia obeyed Leonard's decision, but later regretted that choice. She would always envy Vanessa her motherhood, her femininity and domesticity, even though Vanessa's was a companionate marriage. Vanessa did, however, maintain a long extramarital sexual relationship with artist Duncan Grant.

The Woolfs enjoyed their Bloomsbury Group and Cambridge Apostles friendships, most of which carried on for life. Lytton Strachey remained a close friend and reader of Woolf's work; E. M. Forster was one of her foremost critics. Roger Fry (Vanessa's lover) and Clive Bell (Vanessa's husband) were art critics whose esthetic views influenced Virginia's writing. Duncan Grant was Vanessa's partner from 1916 until her death in 1961; his fame in the circle was as much for his good looks, charming personality and bisexuality as for his art. John Maynard Keynes was the political oddball of the Group (unabashedly capitalist), yet his work as a world-famous economist (*The Economic Consequences of the Peace* predicted World War II), and his ardor for history rounded out the interests of the primarily artistic circle.

Virginia Woolf, early 1900s (Photofest).

Biographers radically disagree on the nature of the Woolfs' marriage, yet when Virginia committed suicide in 1941, she left a suicide note assuring Leonard that she owed all the happiness of her life to him. Some believe Virginia's madness is exacerbated by Leonard's complicity with doctors in enforcing the rest cure. Like the protagonist of Charlotte Perkins Gilman's novel, *The Yellow Wallpaper* (1892), Virginia rebelled inwardly at the imposed isolation of this cure. Her stated reason for suicide was that she could feel another breakdown approaching and could not face another convalescence. Yet Leonard was acting in accordance with the best medical advice of his time. Leonard was also her first reader and the protector of her free time and space for writing. After the publication of *Jacob's Room* (1922), Virginia's success was such that she could have provided a Room of Her Own, but she needed the security of marriage to feel fulfilled, and never regretted hers.

Elizabeth Bowen (1899–1973)

In contrast to Virginia Woolf's, Elizabeth Bowen's life was uprooted, even peripatetic, yet she was equally successful, achieving marriage, fame, public appointments, and friendships. Born in Dublin to Henry and Florence

Elizabeth Bowen, left, with students (Photofest).

Colley Bowen, Elizabeth grew up at Bowen's Court in County Cork. By becoming a barrister, her father had broken the mold that required first-born Bowen sons to manage the family estate. His father's extreme anger about Henry's career decision, combined with Henry's guilt about his mother dying from smallpox she had caught from him, were the precipitating causes of Henry's mental breakdown in 1905, when Elizabeth was seven. One day, instead of filing his legal briefs, Henry dramatically threw them out the window. Diagnosed with anemia of the brain, Henry checked himself into an institution, while Elizabeth left with her mother Florence to live in a small town called Hythe, on the Kent coastline in Britain.

From the trauma of her father's sickness, Elizabeth developed a life-long stammer that was particularly prominent on pronunciation of the word "mother." These childhood years spent in her mother's exclusive company may have given Elizabeth the interest in woman-to-woman relationships that pervades her novels. Her mother's love was intense, though her notions of mothering were slightly unusual. To prevent the insanity that ran in Henry's family, Florence prohibited her daughter from learning to read until the age of seven. Their relationship was playful, as when they visited every villa for sale in Kent in order to indulge fantasies of possible lives. Unfortunately, the idyll was to end in 1912, when her mother died of cancer. Her aunts sent Elizabeth away to school.

Downe House upheld high standards for its students, who were made aware of their privileges during wartime. During food rationing, they were required to clean their plates. They were told that soldiers were sacrificing their lives for their country. One of the characteristics bred at Downe served Elizabeth well in her future role as diplomatic hostess. The girls competed for "best table," a contest won by out-charming others at dinner conversation. Despite youthful spirits, a certain doom prevailed at the aptly named Downe House: "They did not discuss men much — perhaps because of the war, and people's brothers at the front, which gave the whole sex a morbid, quasi-religious association. The war cast a moral seriousness on all their undertakings" (Glendinning 42). Early exposure to feminism in this school included being called "person" instead of "girl," and the cultivation of "gentleman's honor" by the young ladies, meaning that rules were strictly obeyed. Bowen recalls that all of her friends wanted to marry early because this "appeared an achievement." Yet none of them anticipated maternity with interest, and when some friends did later become mothers, to Bowen it "seemed inappropriate," perhaps because Bowen herself remained childless (MT 17). The school, in short, was an excellent place for Bowen to cultivate detachment and repression of feelings. "Life with the lid on" was how she named her pose. Her reserve was a response to the mental illness of her father and early loss of her mother.

After graduation, Bowen spent two terms in a London art school, where she learned that painting was not her métier. Switching to writing in 1923, she found success both in her career (*Encounters*, her first story collection, was published) and in marriage to Alan Cameron. An ex-soldier who had been wounded and gassed in the War, Cameron was Assistant Secretary for Education in Northampton. Curious about his sexual preference, biographers make much of the fact that at the time of meeting Bowen, thirty-year-old Cameron was living in an odd ménage with his mother and a gay clergyman. Most agree it is unlikely that Bowen's marriage was consummated — one clue is that her first lover, Humphrey House, believed she was a virgin at thirty-four. Yet the marriage lasted a lifetime, and by all accounts Elizabeth and Alan were a devoted pair who cared about each other's success. To the best of their ability they shared a social life, though Elizabeth's literary friends were not Alan's cup of tea. In response to rumors of Alan's stupidity, biographer Glendinning describes the very different types of intelligence of the spouses:

> He was cleverer [than he seemed]. He was a very shrewd man and a very good man. He did not pander to Elizabeth, in private not at all; in private her dependence on him for all things practical and administrative, but not only for these things, came to the fore. He was extremely protective of her.... He was not above a gentle dig.... He loved his work. He was a very good administrator [132].

Cameron's administrative skills were rewarded by a promotion to Secretary of Education in Oxford in 1925. After another ten years, he moved on to the educational division of the British Broadcasting Corporation in London. It was in Oxford that Elizabeth became a successful writer, hostess, and friend to several university dons who provided literary critiques and professional connections.

Upon her father's death in 1930, Elizabeth inherited Bowen's Court. Although costly to maintain and distant from their first home, the big stone mansion was a perfect retreat during their holidays. Unable to afford the upkeep after Alan's death, she finally sold Bowen's Court in 1959. The family home had meant more to her than a symbol of the brief period of tranquility before her chaotic girlhood. Bowen's Court signified the dignity of Ascendancy culture, which her 450-page history of the house and her ancestors memorialized. *Bowen's Court* is rare among Bowen's works for its critique of colonization, coming closest of all of her writing to admitting the colonial guilt that plagued the Bowen family for generations. Reading the history book as a background to *The Last September* reveals the complex relationship Bowen had to her past, and humanizes the otherwise stereotypical Sir and Lady Naylor, characters in that novel.

Since her husband was apparently unavailable for sex, Elizabeth had a few romantic affairs. Her most important and long-lasting liaison was with Charles Ritchie, a Canadian diplomat who admired her intelligence, humor, looks, originality and strength. The relationship might have accelerated her interest in political affairs; during World War II, she became an active citizen. As air raid warden, her charge was to make sure that Londoners observed blackout. Hired by the Ministry of Information, Bowen collected information about Irish attitudes towards their country's neutrality. Ireland was afraid that Churchill's plan to lease Irish ports would open Ireland to bombing by the Nazis. Ireland, Bowen discovered, was desperately afraid of being involved in the war. On the strength of her helpful government report, the British Council requested Bowen to deliver a series of literary lectures in Eastern Europe between 1948 and 1950. One diplomat commented that her lectures had "a classic perfection" (Glendinning 218). Later, one of her Oxford friends lamented that she had not become head of one of the women's colleges—suggesting that there was academic and administrative potential in Bowen that she did not explore. The year after the British Council commission, she was appointed a member of the Royal Commission on Capital Punishment, which published its opinion to abolish the practice in 1953. Bowen was lenient in her opinion, believing, for instance, that verbal provocation should constitute sufficient cause to reduce murder charges to manslaughter. As these projects show, Bowen accepted civic responsibilities of diverse kinds, managing to execute them with efficiency and pleasure. At the same time, she produced 28 books and numerous articles for periodicals.

"Maimed" was how Bowen described herself after Alan's death in 1952. Seeking diversion, she moved to Oxford, but found that her Oxford friends were too busy to socialize. Her American sojourns involved lectureships at Bryn Mawr, Vassar, and Princeton. But Bowen did not wish to settle down as an academic: "novelists find it easier to imagine than to learn," she wrote (Glendinning 266). After selling Bowen's Court in 1959, Bowen no longer wished to live in her native country. Buying a small house on the Hythe cliffs overlooking the English Channel, she returned to the site of her happiest years. At age 74, Bowen died of lung cancer, having been an avid smoker all of her adult life. In her last days she was assisted by her editor and friend, Spencer Curtis Brown, who spoke of Bowen's strong self image: "She was unswayed by others in any sense, being strong and aware of herself emotionally and mentally. While she was in no way arrogant, it did not occur to her to pretend to herself or to others to underrate herself" (*Pictures* xviii). Writing for the *New York Times*, Howard Moss mentions characteristics that one might attribute to her Irishness: "It would be hard to imagine anyone kinder ... She could be acerbic, was one of the wits of her time, and could detect, from a great distance, the faintest whiff of the false. With the pretentious, she could be devastating" (*Pictures* xii–iii). Of her strength, Brown notes: "She had so much intrinsic power that I don't think the idea of acquiring any ever crossed her mind.... She was the least snobbish person I knew" (*Pictures* xv).

Comparing Woolf and Bowen's lives, I am struck by similarities. Both lost their cherished mothers at the vulnerable age of thirteen. Both had successful, close, companionate marriages. Mental illness touched both lives. Bowen, like her mother, adopted a motto of "life with the lid on" in order to guard against the mental frailties passed down through her father. Both were childless, which, combined with being an only child in Bowen's case, gave her a sense of perpetual longing and impermanence. As her biographer puts it, "A psychoanalyst, in the unlikely event of his ever getting anywhere near Elizabeth, might have exposed, but perhaps not illuminated, the connections she preferred not to explore except obliquely and imaginatively in her writing: connections between her parents' history, her ambiguous situation as a child, her own childlessness and the child she might have had, her dislocations" (Glendinning 283). Both were fascinated by women-to-women relationships, Woolf openly in her lesbian relationship with Vita Sackville-West, Bowen, again obliquely, in her fictional explorations. Bowen proclaimed her impatience with lesbian relationships, which she called "claggy, muffish, and squashy"— interpreted by Glendinning to mean "over-analytical, sentimental, sublimated, mawkish and maudlin" (quoted in Walshe, 9). Patricia Coughlan asserts, "there can be no doubt of [her] taste, under the highly polished surfaces, for the monstrous, the perverse, the necessarily antithetical," which is often code-speak for homosexuality (111). Her fascination with same-sex desire does not mean she indulged in it, but that she found it real and compelling. Finally, both Woolf and Bowen publicly denounced feminism at points in their careers, while at the same time writing works replete with feminist consciousness.

Contrasting the two writers' lives, we see a difference in the social stability of each woman. Woolf surrounded herself with like-minded people from the beginning to the end of her life, whereas Bowen came from a dispossessed class, was orphaned early, and created her own ambiance from scratch. Woolf had not only her intellectual family, but also friends whose mission was to revolutionize art and literature. Woolf was grounded; Bowen was uprooted. Living an uprooted life limits the extent to which any woman can cultivate feminism or a stable class identity. Woolf's politics, again influenced by her marriage and Bloomsbury Group, were socialist at least in name, while Bowen's were avowedly conservative. Woolf inherited her father's atheism, while Bowen must have clung to her Anglican religion as the only bulwark in a peripatetic existence. Elizabeth had affairs with men, while Woolf had them with women. Finally, their chosen literary genres illustrate their social beliefs: Bowen's satire belongs to a conservative ethos, while Woolf's lyricism attests to a more romantic and radical desire to change the ways in which we live, write, and think. Bowen's cultural inheritance and difficult childhood made it unlikely that she would adopt the progressive politics of feminism or become an overtly political person at all.

Mrs. Dalloway and *The Last September* Synopses

Mrs. Dalloway

Woolf's fourth novel is similar to Joyce's *Ulysses* in being set on a single day in a capital city that symbolizes its country's identity (Dublin for Joyce;

London for Woolf). Each author uses a central consciousness, supplemented by several minor ones, to reflect the *Zeitgeist* of a particular place and time. In *Mrs. Dalloway*, the title character prepares for and hosts a party for colleagues of her husband Richard, who is a Member of Parliament for the Conservative Party. On a beautiful June day in 1923, reminders of the war abound, both in concrete images such as Septimus Warren Smith's talking to hallucinations, and Lady Bexborough receiving news of her son's death; and in abstract feeling-states, such as Clarissa's sense of terror, that accompanies her everyday life ("she always had the feeling that it was very, very dangerous to live even one day," 11). Septimus and Clarissa never cross paths, but symbolically, their consciousness is shared, though not identical. Both are death-haunted; they seriously question the meaning of life, since their own experiences have so dazed them. By comparing Septimus' clear case of post-traumatic stress with Clarissa's ambiguous one, Woolf brilliantly unifies diverse lives through common suffering.

Even without knowledge of Woolf's mental anguish, we can detect Clarissa's vulnerability to sadness. Critics have different ideas about what causes Clarissa's anxiety. For instance, Karen DeMeester pinpoints the cause in an easy-to-miss detail that is mentioned only once — her father accidentally killed her sister by felling a tree that landed on her. On the other hand, John Clayton locates Clarissa's terror in the repression and loss of her younger self, in particular her attachment to two friends, Peter Walsh and Sally Seton, who were wilder and freer than her eventual husband, Richard Dalloway. Peter had wanted desperately to marry her, but was refused on the grounds that he was too intense. To these causes for Clarissa's terror, I would add that Clarissa's age — 52 — signals menopause, a time in which women take stock of their lives and have to reckon with the loss of their youth and femininity. With the loss of the ability to create life comes the necessity to anticipate death. To symbolize Clarissa's loss of sexual power, Woolf uses the apt metaphor "Narrower and narrower would her bed be" (45). Richard relegates his wife to a single bed in the attic for a long convalescence. The narrow bed prefigures the coffin in which she will lie. In this context, Clarissa's unexpected reunion with Peter and Sally is an important benchmark. They haven't seen each other for thirty years, and notice acutely the marks of age.

Woolf cleverly connects Septimus' story to Clarissa's by several threads. For instance, they hear the same street noises (the backfiring of the Prime Minister's car engine), see the same sights (the sky-writing advertisements), have the same refrains in their heads ("fear no more the heat o' the sun," from Shakespeare's *Cymbeline*), and share the same feelings about Sir William Bradshaw (to Clarissa, "obscurely evil, capable of some indescribable outrage — forcing your soul," 281). To both of them, Bradshaw represents the power to make life intolerable. Septimus' day begins with hallucinating in Regent's Park and ends with suicide; in between, he travels back in time to the killing fields, particularly to his Commander Evans' death. Septimus believes that he has anesthetized himself and feels no pain. However, his interior monologue proves the opposite — he feels *too much* to be able to cope. Schizophrenic, he believes he is Christ, come to tell the world: "There is a God. There is no crime. Do not cut trees. Change the world. No one kills from hatred" (35). Alternating with his delusions of grandeur is his intolerable misanthropy. Shakespeare's plays appear to contain coded messages of doom: "The secret signal which one generation passes, under disguise, to the next is loathing, hatred, despair. Dante the same. Aeschylus (translated) the same" (134). Particularly despicable are bodily functions: "the business of copulation was filth." Above all, men are greedy, selfish, and bestial: "They hunt in packs.... They desert the fallen. They are plastered over with grimaces" (135). These images derive from recollections of battle that his psyche is unable to assimilate. According to trauma theory, returned veterans need to make meaning of their suffering in order to recover from Post-Traumatic Stress Disorder. But Septimus cannot achieve the catharsis of his confessions, because his wife and doctors are not willing to hear, or to understand his disease. His PTSD is aggravated by his community's refusal to hear, "by a culturally sanctioned process of postwar reintegration that silences and marginalizes war veterans" (De Meester 77).

When Septimus threatens suicide, his wife takes him to two doctors, Holmes and Sir William Bradshaw. The first is a fool, who tells him there is nothing wrong with him that a hobby won't cure. The second is a narcissist, who orders the rest cure in a mental institution. In her descriptions of Dr. Bradshaw, Woolf assumes a narrator's voice; there is no way that Septimus would know all of the background that is provided about this evil figure. This narrator's intrusion breaks the narrative flow, a fault that Woolf accused Brontë of committing when Jane Eyre rants about the restricted lives of women. That she would violate her own stylistic preferences suggests the intensity with which Woolf hated the medical establishment. In *Three Guineas*, she also rants about doctors' love of power, linking their authority over vulnerable lives to the tyranny of the military-industrial complex. Nothing less than the entire class structure and patriarchy of Britain are implicated in Woolf's tirade about the doctor that kills Septimus. Sir Bradshaw's two "goddesses" are Proportion and Conversion. Proportion requires that patients stifle their emotions in order to fulfill their particular class-based destiny, while Conversion requires that doctors quash all rebels and disbelievers. Conversion is a hypocrite, who "offers help, but desires power" (151). Bradshaw's dominating will operates in the home as well as the examining room; his wife is his marionette. To avoid succumbing to Bradshaw and all he represents, Septimus jumps to his death.

Later that evening, Clarissa hears of his death from Lady Bradshaw. Initially peeved that anyone should talk of death at her party, Clarissa retires from the crowd to sort her feelings. Although she does not know him, she understands why Septimus chose suicide. She sees it as an act of defiance, which in effect it is— Septimus exclaims, "I'll give it you!" to Bradshaw as he flings himself onto spiked railings below (226). Clarissa understands that fear of Bradshaw was the cause of Septimus' death, because Sir William's "power" would make life intolerable. Relating to Septimus' emotion, she recalls her own terror that same morning, which she was able to push aside only because she had a secure marriage. Contrasting Septimus' terror ("she felt somehow very like him," 283) and her own delight in beauty (the sky, books on a shelf, the old lady across the way), she feels glad that he jumped. Somehow, it enhanced her own perceptions: "He made her feel the beauty; made her feel the fun" (284). After soul-searching, Clarissa is free to enjoy her reunion with Sally and Peter. The last paragraphs of the novel show the "terror and ecstasy" alternating in Peter's mind at the vision of Clarissa, whom he still loves. For Peter, the terror consists in the inability — still, at age 53 — to find a love that lasts. By adumbrating the terrors of three very different characters, Woolf conveys the *Zeitgeist* of postwar London.

The Last September *(1929)*

Unlike Clarissa's Westminster, where war is peripheral and in the past tense, the County Cork of Elizabeth Bowen's second novel hears, sees, and feels the tremors of war. The main Anglo-Irish characters inhabit a large country estate called Danielstown, at the time of the War of Independence. The urgency of the rebels' cause contrasts starkly to the frivolity of the Anglo-Irish household. Sir Richard and Lady Myra Naylor host tennis parties and entertain houseguests, their attitude one of nonchalance to the troubles around them. This insouciance is a defensive pose that masks an underlying desperation. Anxiety is more pronounced in the younger generation — Laurence and Lois— the nephew and niece of the Naylors. No matter how practiced their genteel pose, the Naylors cannot help but realize that their days are numbered. When the novel opens in September 1920, the centuries-old Anglo-Irish Ascendancy has only a few months left to live.

The novel's protagonist is nineteen-year-old Lois Farquar, who has come to stay with her Uncle Richard and his wife, Lady Naylor, after completing school. Her mother Laura died during Lois' youth; her father had already left the marriage and abandoned Lois. Bowen doesn't develop a characterization of him, except for Richard's remark that he is "one of the meanest men of the north." While Lois looks sweet like her mother, Lady Naylor claims she is more like her father. Although Lois is not mean, her aunt's uncharitable opinion does foreshadow the fact that Lois is incapable of loving her first suitor. Laurence, her slightly older cousin-by-marriage, does not provide much companionship. Staying with the Naylors between Oxford terms, Laurence lazes around, reads, eats as much as he can, has Republican sympathies, and wishes the IRA would attack the house. In many ways Laurence's opposite, Gerald Lesworth, a subaltern in the British army and unthinking proponent of its colonial policy, loves Lois and wishes to marry her. Lady Naylor disapproves of the marriage because Lesworth is of a lower class and "hasn't any money." Lois is uncertain of her feelings for Gerald. She is not physically attracted, though she enjoys his attention. Desperate to marry her first suitor, Lois' friend Livvy Thompson is Lois's foil. She represents normative heterosexual femininity, a role that Lois rejects.

Three Danielstown guests—Hugo and Francie Montmorency and Marda Norton—enliven Lois's September. The Montmorencys are old friends of the Naylors who have sold their own Big House and wander aimlessly between friends' houses while Hugo tries to decide how to make a living. Hugo represents one kind of (ineffectual) masculinity that Lois tries on for size, and rejects. His long-suffering wife Francie lives vicariously through her fantasies about Lois' love life, which turn out to be far from the truth. Lois' boredom with the Montmorencys is contrasted with the dramatic arrival of Marda Norton. Marda is a thirty-year-old woman of independent character with a couple of broken engagements in her past. Now engaged to a stockbroker, Marda doesn't seem to admire him, speaking of him as a stereotype. Falling immediately for Marda, Lois is attracted to her mild rebelliousness against patriarchy. Hugo also falls for Marda, perhaps because she has a self-esteem that his wife lacks. With her marriage-breaking aura, Marda becomes a disruptive element that Lady Naylor would like to evict. Marda causes "catastrophes," in the hyperbolic language of her class, such as wounding her hand and losing her engagement ring. This walking-accident-of-a-female symbolizes the threat that feminist thinking poses to a traditional community like the Naylors.'

In the course of dances and tennis parties, we meet the Naylors' neighbors and other soldiers. Daventry is a shell-shocked World War I veteran, whose cynicism both scares and attracts Lois. Mrs. Betty Vermont is the wife of a British officer who, like Gerald, can't see past the rhetoric of British colonial pride. Of the uprisings, she says, "who would ever have thought of the Irish turning out so disloyal" (62). Offstage lurks the sinister figure of Peter Connor, an IRA man captured by Gerald. Peter's death incites the retaliatory raid that causes Gerald's own death. When adapting the novel for a screenplay, John Banville brings Connor onstage. As the film medium seems to require violent action, Banville turns Connor into a central character that rapes Lois and kills Gerald. In the novel, Gerald's death occurs offstage.

Rather than processing its protagonist's reaction to her suitor's death, the narration jumps ahead to the final scene a few weeks later. Perhaps Lois' disinterest in Gerald is already so firmly established that Bowen does not need to examine the process of her mourning. In the final scene, we learn only that Lois has gone to Tours to study French. On the final page the narrator tells us that the rebels burned Danielstown in February, while Sir Richard and Lady Naylor silently watched. Unlike *Mrs. Dalloway*'s ending, this one does not afford any unifying vision, hope for the future, or resolution of Marda or Lois' man problems. *The Last September* aims instead to expose Anglo-Irish complacencies, British colonial obtuseness, and the angst of each main character — Lois, Marda, Laurence, Hugo and Francie — who sees through the social fabric into the sheer loneliness of human existence.

Relationship of Gender and Class in the Authors' Lives

The importance of social class to one's status, employment, and social possibilities has lessened somewhat in twentieth-century Britain, but is still, and certainly was during Bowen and Woolf's lives, a major determinant of the quality and nature of one's life. Although both are similarly well-educated, cultured women, Bowen and Woolf are in fact from different social classes. Owning their country estate from 1653 till 1959, the Bowens were *landed gentry*, giving them upper-class status. Peerage titles were not required for membership in this class. Ironically, Virginia Woolf's father's family had the title, the public education, and the colonial service, but not the country estate, making him upper-middle-class instead of upper. Alex Zwerdling further characterizes Virginia's segment of the upper-middle-class as the "intellectual aristocracy, that stratum of the middle class associated with higher education and professional life" (91). Although this stratum appears to be based on the merit of one's professional achievements, Noel Annan shows that, in practice, "certain families gain position and influence through persistent endogamy," turning it into a hereditary caste (quoted in Zwerdling 91). The club was exclusive: "Like any other powerful class, it soon developed a private network of communication and influence, of nepotism, of early training for success in the competitive sweepstakes that effectively excluded all but the most exceptional interlopers" (92). This funneling of talent explains how it is possible for a group as small as Bloomsbury (13 people) to represent the intelligentsia of an entire country. These young thinkers inherited the right to be Britain's top intellects. Woolf's father was considered second only to Matthew Arnold in late Victorian literary status. Her intellectual inheritance put substantial pressure on Woolf to excel in literature, and explains her vulnerability to criticism. The circle is tight, making the competition fierce, even among family members. When her father dies, Woolf comments, to her diary: "his life would have entirely ended mine [if he had not died in 1928]" (Hussey 271). She also felt a distinct rivalry with other female modernists. Upon Katherine Mansfield's death, she wrote: "At that one feels—what? A shock of relief?—a rival the less?"

Bowen is also aware of the privileges and perils of her class. In *Bowen's Court*, she writes a detailed history of her family, starting from the Welsh soldier in Cromwell's army who received land in lieu of pay. *Bowen's Court* contains two different interpretations of the prestige of land ownership. On the one hand, Bowen's ancestral piety renders a "sympathetic, imaginative family elegy" (Corcoran 23). On the other hand, her sympathy is tempered by criticisms of her family's "vanity, fantasy, opportunism, and general abuse of power." Elements of *Bowen's Court* rival Maria Edgeworth's *Castle Rackrent* (1800) for their exposure of Ascendancy landlords' vice. Bowen alternates praise and critique of her family's behavior as landlords. She is aware that maintaining their position of dominance requires repression of her ancestors' humanity: "The structure of the great Anglo-Irish society was raised over a country in martyrdom. To enjoy prosperity one had to exclude feeling" (248). This last sentence could be the motto for Bowen's personal life "with the lid on." Awareness of her own defense mechanism helps her to understand the stoicism of her ancestors. However, in this passage describing the house's isolation, she buries her political awareness beneath her pride:

> Inside and about the house and in the demesne woods you feel transfixed by the surrounding emptiness; it gives depth to the silence, quality to the light. The land round Bowen's Court, even under its windows, has an unhumanized air the house does nothing to change. Here are, even, no natural features, view or valley, to which the house may be felt to relate itself. It has set, simply, its pattern of trees and avenues on the virgin, anonymous countryside. Like Flaubert's ideal book about nothing, it sustains itself on itself by the inner force of its style [21].

Choosing "unhumanized," rather than the more common "dehumanized" suggests her suppression of the fact that her ancestors *de*populated the terrain of its original inhabitants. By personifying the house, the passage projects the author's loneliness onto the physical space. At the same time, it ignores the truth: the house doesn't sustain itself on "style," but on servant labor, and the countryside is neither virgin nor anonymous. Its original inhabitants were colonized; their anonymity is only in the eyes of the beholder.

Bowen began writing *Bowen's Court* in 1939, but her participation in wartime defense activities over the next two years changed her mind about her social class. These ruminations appear in a 1941 Afterword to her book. I quote at length because she develops the argument gradually. The first part reveals a guilty awareness that Hitler's megalomania resembles the will-to-power in her own ancestors.

> Possibly, the judgments of war-time have affected my view of my family ... so I examine them as we now re-examine major historic figures, in the light of a present psychology [Hitler's campaign]. I have stressed as dominant in the Bowens factors we see dominant in the world now—for instance, subjection to fantasy and infatuation with the idea of power. While I have studied fantasy in the Bowens, we have seen it impassion race after race. Fantasy is toxic: the private cruelty and the world war both have their start in the heated brain [this shows Bowen's characteristic fear of insanity]. Showing fantasy, in one form or another, do its unhappy work in the lives of my ancestors, I have been conscious at almost every moment of the nightmarish big analogies of today. Also, the idea of power has governed my analysis of the Bowens and of the means *they* took—these being, in some cases, emotional—to enforce themselves on their world.... That few Bowens looked beyond Bowen's Court makes the place a fair microcosm, a representative if miniature theatre [454, brackets mine].

Bowen thinks that isolation is an Anglo-Irish trait, one that made her family dependent on property ownership to retain their sanity in a sea of Otherness. When they lose land, the Anglo-Irish lose all their power: "Without putting up any plea for property ... I submit that the power-loving temperament is more dangerous when it either prefers or is forced to operate in what is materially a void. We have everything to dread from the dispossessed.... The outsize will is not necessarily an evil: it is a phenomenon" (455). In a surprising comparison of the Bowens to the Nazis, Elizabeth describes people who, when physically dispossessed, try to possess themselves of an idea of power that is more dangerous than actual power over real estate and local economies. Being so general, the passage could refer to several of Bowen's personal anxieties: fear of her future without Bowen's Court, fear of the local peasantry coming after her, and fear of her ancestors' mental instabilities, especially at junctures when their ownership was threatened.

Insanity and will-to-power aside, Bowen also considers positive characteristics of her class, including honor, energy, discipline, independence, toughness, style, and courage. This list helps explain her attachment to the fictional Naylors and Montmorencys:

> They honoured, if they did not justify, their own class, its traditions, its
> rule of life. If they formed a too-grand idea of themselves, they did at
> least exert themselves to live up to this: even vanity involves one kind of
> discipline. If their difficulties were of their own making, they combated
> these with an energy I must praise. They found no facile solutions; they
> were not guilty of cant. Isolation, egotism and, on the whole, lack of cul-
> ture made in them for an independence one has to notice because it
> becomes, in these days, rare. Independence was the first quality of a class
> now, I am told, becoming extinct. To my mind, they are tougher than
> they appear. To live as though living gave them no trouble has been the
> first imperative of their make-up: to do this has taken a virtuosity into
> which courage enters more than has been allowed [456].

"To live as though living gave them no trouble" is a perfect description
of the dandy. In the 1890s, Oscar Wilde popularized dandyism by his writing
and lifestyle. Declan Kiberd calls the dandy "the darling of Anglo-Irish literature." Male or female, the dandy maintains an aristocratic hauteur "in the
absence of any court in which to rehearse and play out such gestures" (144).
In the case of the Anglo-Irish, the court is missing because the whole tribe is
declining. The dandy's *modus operandi* is self-control, a suppression of feeling.
Bowen's motto, to live life with the lid on, is like a dandy's. Her tribe shares
the attitude:

> Like others of her kind she lived at a certain remove from her own emo-
> tions, some part of her always held in reserve and able to monitor an
> experience, even as she submitted to it, with a cold, clinical precision.
> This observant detachment had long been a feature of Anglo-Irish writ-
> ing, which achieved an almost anthropological status, seeking to view
> man as if he were a foreign, even non-human witness of himself [Kiberd
> 137].

The field of psychology has a name for this mechanism. It is "splitting-off,"
a coping strategy used to survive trauma. Like all repressed fears, colonial
guilt continually resurfaces in the form of terrors and feelings of isolation.
Elizabeth Bowen's awareness of death and dispossession are always just under
the surface of her polished upper-class characters, like dark fish seen darting
underneath the glassy surface of a pool.

Bowen and Woolf's class affiliations limit the extent to which they developed their feminist consciousness. Bowen's class identity was more precarious
than Woolf's because her class was reviled by Irish people of the new Free
State, and misunderstood or unknown by many of her British acquaintances.
The Anglo-Irish Ascendancy would essentially cease to exist after 1922. Those
Anglo-Irish who returned to their properties after the War of Independence
would occupy a different and debased status. In contrast, Woolf's class affiliation, passed down by her highly successful father, was a mark of pride, even

in the post-war climate of democratization. In Bowen's life span, she sees the dissolution of her sub-class, the Anglo-Irish, while Woolf's sub-class, the "intellectual aristocracy," is thriving. Bowen even attributes the rise of fascism in Europe to an outgrowth of attitudes held by her own class, whereas Woolf's class was trying to avert the spread of fascism by popularizing socialism. R. H. Tawney was one example of a Bloomsbury member who espoused Fabian socialism. In his book *Equality* (1929), he proposed a radical improvement to British society by means of making education available to those from all social classes.

On the other hand, Bowen's conservatism does not arise from a sense of class superiority, but from the instability caused in her personal life by the loss of father, mother and home at an early age, combined with the instability of her entire class, as it was being dispossessed of its property and status. Because of these traumas, Bowen found social attachments difficult. She said that she made stronger attachment to places than to people, and Bowen's Court was a very strong attachment. Bowen's Court was spared from IRA arson because the Bowens were kinder to their servants and neighbors than most (Corcoran 25). Without overt sentimentality, Bowen cherished the estate as a reminder of her identity, keeping it for as long as she could. To some, this attachment to property in itself would make her a political and social conservative. But to an artist, having a port in the storm can be vital, even if it is a house instead of a family: "This house was built for a family," she writes, "so it makes one" (*People* 149). She imbues the house with the qualities she desires: "Bowen's Court seems to me like a ship that has steadily, forwardly voyaged through time.... From having forged through storms, sheered its way past reefs and pulled clear of whirlpools, it has accumulated organic confidence" (149). She draws strength from the conviction that her people were brave and independent; the house reifies these qualities and reminds her of their existence. Childless and an only child, she is the last of the Bowen line.

Especially for women, whose economic and social position depended on the men in their family, class and gender identities were inextricable. Virginia's secure class and family positions, in both her family of origin and her family by marriage, enable a feminism that becomes, by the time of *Three Guineas* (1938), outright and unmitigated. In contrast, Bowen's insecure class and family positions send her feminism underground, not exactly to an unconscious level, but to an expression in her writing that may be spoken of, according to Fredric Jameson, as the political unconscious of the text.[5] Similarly, Woolf's strong identification with her own class made her unsympathetic to the gender and economic oppressions of the working class. More precisely, she believed that it was impossible for someone of her class to understand the underclass. In "The Leaning Tower," she envies nineteenth-century writers for living in a time when there were clearer class demarcations: "[they] did not seek to change those divisions; [they] accepted them" (quoted in Zwerdling 99). By the twentieth century, Marxist theory and the depredations of war made class privilege the focus of struggle. For her writing's sake, Woolf tried to learn about the individual experiences of working class people by walking around London, observing and talking to them. Ultimately she found such understanding impossible. Wanting to know what a certain beggar thinks (perhaps to create the singing beggar woman of *Mrs. Dalloway*), Woolf writes: "How she came to be there, what scenes she can go through, I can't imagine. O damn it all, I say, why can't I know that too?" (quoted in Zwerdling 112). When the Russian Revolution brought class struggle to the forefront of British attention, Woolf felt hampered by middle-class guilt. At this time, she wrote: "I'm one of those who are hampered by the psychological hindrance of owning capital" (Zwerdling 104).

Gender and Class Oppression as the Political Unconscious of the Two Novels

The Last September is haunted by lacks and lacunae that are characteristic of modernism. For instance, communication between Danielstown's inhabitants is severely attenuated, and Lois's isolation is her most prominent feature. Death lurks everywhere, not just in the skirmishes outside Danielstown's boundaries, but also within Lois's consciousness. Every new social experience, such as kissing Gerald or meeting Marda, brings fears of death, often symbolized by the figure of Laura, her dead mother. Lois believes that her gender, like her class, is "superfluous." For a sheltered nineteen-year-old, Lois is extremely aware of the expectations of her class. She does not challenge patriarchy, but registers its defeating rules and regulations. This resignation to gender expectations is mirrored in her acceptance of the destruction of her class. Lois is so unmoored that she says of Gerald's marriage proposal: "After an anxious glance at the possible, a pain so sharp that it seemed to her like her own forbade recantation. It was inevitable that she should marry Gerald" (243). This indirect language captures Lois' disassociation from her own feeling. She can only tell that pain is hers and not someone else's if it is acute — "a pain so sharp it seemed like her own," recalling Kiberd's characterization of the Anglo-Irish as a self-anesthetizing people.

Like many teenagers, especially orphans, Lois is more aware of others' expectations than she is of her own inclinations. Bowen emphasizes that Lois is more attracted to women than men, yet Lois herself does not recognize this. Marda is Lois' real first love, and her androgynous qualities are pronounced:

she looks like a man from behind, and homosexual Laurence calls her manly. When they meet an armed IRA man hiding in the mill, Lois gains courage from Marda. She also perceives that Hugo is weaker than Marda. Lois experiences a "revelation" when she perceives Hugo's cowardice (185). As a modernist, Bowen does not define the revelation, but lets the reader discover that Hugo symbolizes male cowardice, and that the moment of revelation switches Lois' erotic orientation to Marda. Lois realizes that Hugo loves Marda, but that his love is "no good.... It doesn't make anything" (186). In this scenario, she perceives a fundamental futility about the nature of all man-woman relations. During her visit to Marda's bedroom, Lois concludes, "I must be a woman's woman" (145); her changing impressions of Hugo confirm that impression. She is unable to regard possibilities of marriage without painful anguish, and when Gerald kisses her, she wishes he were a woman (253). On their final meeting, Lois wants Gerald to convince her that she loves him. In "desolation at not being compelled," Lois makes a beseeching movement, which Gerald ignores, because he had promised her aunt not to kiss her (280). Even before Myra's interventions, Gerald resisted touching Lois. In short, Lois expected to be carried away by passion, and to understand marriage through her experience of passion, but passion never occurred for her. The first kiss of her life was "just an impact with inside blankness," that left her feeling lonely (127).

Half-heartedly, Lois plays the roles prescribed for her gender: "She had never refused a role. She could not forgo that intensification, that kindling of her personality at being considered very happy and reckless even if she were not" (40). Yet Lois wants to be a person, not a woman: "she did not mind being noticed because she was a female, she was tired of being not noticed because she was a lady," she complains to Marda. This statement suggests that her class is a heavier burden than her gender, yet in a startling bit of misogyny, she tells Gerald that women are as superfluous to culture as the Anglo-Irish are to Ireland: "Can you wonder this country gets irritated? [about not being able to control the rebels] It's as bad for it as being a woman. I never can see why women shouldn't be hit, or should be saved from wrecks when everybody is complaining they're so superfluous" (66). Impotence to solve the troubles makes Ireland feminine in Lois' estimation (an equation shared by many postcolonial critics). From her anger at being stuck in her gendered position, Lois lashes out at women, though clearly the subtext of the complaint is that patriarchy creates a helpless subclass in order to bolster men's chivalry. Gerald, the perfect manifestation of chivalry, concurs: "it would be ghastly if those things went" (66).

Like Woolf, Bowen describes women's identities as fluid, and men's as absolute. Gerald sounds like a simpleton in the narrator's description:

> He did not conceive of love as a nervous interchange but as something
> absolute, out of the scope of thought, beyond himself, matter for a confi-
> dent outward rather than anxious inward looking. He had sought and
> was satisfied with a few repositories for his emotions: his mother, coun-
> try, dog, school, a friend or two, now — crowningly — Lois. Of these he
> asked only that they should be quiet and positive, not impinged upon,
> not breaking boundaries from their generous allotment [53].

Julia Kristeva's portrayal of the human psyche as a vigilant policer of its own
staged boundaries is very helpful in understanding the rigid boundaries of
Gerald's psyche.[6] The horrors that we cannot admit within ourselves are collectively known as *the abject*, which has to be evicted from the Self in order
to survive. Kristeva suggests that maturity and sanity consist in relaxing these
boundaries to some degree — making Gerald look immature more than
insane. For Gerald fills the role of unthinking imperialist as much as bad
boyfriend. When Laurence asks what England thinks it is protecting, Gerald
answers that the British side is right, from the point of view of civilization:
"looking back on history — we do seem the only people" (133). Gerald's
obtuseness rests as much on his imperial arrogance as it does on his inability
to communicate with Lois to her satisfaction. Yet these class and gender roles
are inseparable; while Lady Naylor may disapprove of Gerald marrying Lois
because of his class status, Lois feels it is his male cowardice that makes him
"impossible," and it is likely that both categories combine to make him unacceptable to either woman. Marda has led Lois to believe that "men are cow-
ards" — a line in Banville's screenplay that does not appear in Bowen's novel,
but is inferable from its characters' thoughts and actions. After Marda, Lois
thinks "honeymoons are wastes of travel" (143).

In rereading *The Last September*, I am continually reminded of Virginia
Woolf's dictum: "As a woman, I have no country" (TG 109). Woolf meant
that because women do not contribute to public affairs, their interests are
not represented in the public sphere, and they cannot be benefited by war in
the same ways that men can. Since men fight wars to gratify a sex instinct
unshared by women, women should not be made to feel guilty or otherwise
compelled by men who are fighting for "our country" (TG 108–9). As a young
Anglo-Irishwoman in the time of that race's extinction, Lois feels unmoored
from her country. When she sees an IRA man patrolling the edge of her property, Lois imagines he is impassioned by his political motive, something she
could not share: "She could not conceive of her country emotionally: it was
a way of living, abstract of several countrysides, or an oblique, frayed island
moored at the north but with an air of being detached and drawn out west
from the British coast" (42). She is detached from the rebels, but equally
detached from the British, who are only a distant reality. The best comedy of

the novel stems from the fact that both the military and the rebels think that the Anglo-Irish are British, but the Anglo-Irish consider themselves Irish. Yet the Anglo-Irish do not identify with their neighbors because of their class difference. In such isolation, they have to create their own moral standards, which are strikingly solipsistic.

Bowen recognizes the tragedy of Anglo-Irish ignorance, writing in *Bowen's Court*: "If Ireland did not accept them, they did not know it — and it is in that unawareness of final rejection, unawareness of being looked out at from some secretive, opposed life, that the Anglo-Irish naïve dignity and, even, tragedy, seems to me to stand. Themselves, they felt Irish, and acted as Irishmen" (117). In the movie, Banville adds a scene to express this confusing lack of national identity. Trying to explain why Gerald and Lois are an inappropriate couple, Marda tells Gerald that the Anglo-Irish are a tribe, and that tribes always prefer their own, even if "their own" don't recognize them as such. Marda knows that Lois would be more capable of loving an IRA rebel than a British soldier.

Lois is a heroine who could conceivably break the mold of Anglo-Irish naïve. She interrogates the men in her life about the meaning of the rebellion. She tries to understand the war, but knows that women aren't meant to do so. She tells Marda she "hates women" (142), but clearly means she hates the role that women are expected to play. Yet her isolation and lack of role models leave no prospect for Lois' maturation (Bowen speaks often of Irish immaturity, and of the "infantile" characteristics of her male ancestors). There is no model, for Lois, of right-thinking political activist, nor is there anyone to bend the gender rules enough to become a self-actualized woman. Briefly, Marda appears to be this model, but since she is growing old (in her thirties), she has given up, telling Lois, "I need Leslie [her fiancé].... If you never need anyone as much you will be fortunate" (146). Although feeling that her brief stay at Danielstown changed her, Marda still succumbs to Leslie: "So much of herself that was fluid must, too, be moulded by his idea of her. Essentials were fixed and localized by her being with him — to become as the bricks and wallpaper of a home" (187). Despite her youthful independence, it seems that Lois will become bricks and wallpaper too. She tells Marda she likes "to be in a pattern. I like to be related; to have to be what I am. Just to *be* is so intransitive, so lonely" (142).

Loneliness is also Clarissa Dalloway's problem. Watching an old lady pace her room across the street, Clarissa feels her isolation. She thinks of Peter Walsh's solution to isolation (love) and Doris Kilman's (religion). In Clarissa's view, neither love nor religion could solve the problem of human isolation: "here was one room; there another" (193). Woolf's novel expresses loneliness quite differently than Bowen's. It is not that she believes that words or passion can bridge the gap any more than Bowen does. Instead, imaginative connections allow people to realize a common humanity. Clarissa and Septimus' connection is the prototype of such consciousness; but Peter Walsh has the same kind of desire to connect, and Septimus even tries to communicate with his doctors.

In the novels, Woolf does not make gender such a confining trap as Bowen does. Although she does recognize basic sex antagonism (for instance, Peter Walsh found women's rights "antediluvian"), she finds men's minds as interesting as women's, especially those that are more androgynous, like Septimus and Peter's. Extremes of gender performance elicit satire. For instance, when Lady Bruton wants to send "respectable" young people to Canada to solve population explosion, Rachel Bowlby describes this emigration project as a masculine aggression quite incompatible with her female lack of confidence: "The disparity between Lady Bruton's ruthless projects and her feminine failings makes a comic exaggeration for the novel's suggestion of the incompatibility of masculine and feminine identities in the present form of their distinction" (82). Elizabeth Dalloway has a chance to transcend rigid gender roles if she steers between her father's hyper-masculinity and her mother's super-femininity. But the novel does not gesture towards a future of gender or class equality. Characteristic of Woolf's feminism is that she does not know where feminism will lead. Instead, she "keeps open many lines, as a response to what she always acknowledges as the impossibly complex network of the determinations of women's difference ... and the difficulty of knowing which questions to put in order to understand that difference" (Bowlby 70).

The novel's structure reflects this complexity. The narrator enters the minds of the three main characters, Clarissa, Septimus, and Peter, as well as dozens of others who happen to be in their vicinity. The narration also shows the multiple mood swings to which all three main characters are prone. This multiplicity of experience, the shifting nature of consciousness and the contingent nature of happenings, are all reflected in the fluidity of gender identifications. Woolf's desire for androgyny makes her connect people beyond their gender containers. The singing beggar woman, whose voice "was of no sex or age," symbolizes the transcendence that Peter is trying to accomplish (122). She cannot remember what her lover "a million years ago" looks like, but it did not matter—"he was a man who had loved her." For Peter, her ballad unifies humanity by its appeal to the common experience of love. For Clarissa, the trauma of the war unifies Londoners: "This late age of the world's experience had bred in them all, all men and women, a well of tears" (13).

Woolf's desire for androgyny does not mean that she excludes sexist thinking in her characters, just as their desire for the well-being of strangers does not rid Clarissa or Peter of their class prejudice. When feeling rebuffed by Clarissa, Peter takes refuge in stereotypes: "women do not know what passion is" (121). And Lucrezia thinks Septimus is selfish because "so men are" (34). Each time that Woolf mentions gender, she is questioning stereotypes. In detailing what men and women think of each other, she is experimenting with her androgynous mind. Clarissa resents the fact that she (femininely) performs acts so that others will think her *nice,* unlike her husband, who does things for their own sake (13). When remembering how it felt to love young Sally Seton, Clarissa says she "felt what men felt." Like Bowen, Woolf uses the word "revelation" to describe homosexual desire, perhaps as a code for the forbidden. The revelation that Clarissa loved Sally is described like an orgasm, "as it spread, one yielded to its expansion, and rushed to the farthest verge and there quivered and felt the world come closer, swollen with some astonishing significance, some pressure of rapture, which split its thin skin and gushed and poured with an extraordinary alleviation over the cracks and sores!" (47). Connecting such pleasure to "what men felt" is a compliment rather than a putdown.

Peter and Clarissa revert to several gender stereotypes during the course of their June day, but Septimus's visions are surprisingly gender neutral. Even in his tirade against copulation, it is an act in which men and women are equally engaged. It is not women, but "human beings," who "have neither kindness, nor faith, nor charity" (135). In contrast, his idol Shakespeare gives some of the most misogynistic lines in literature to his heroes Lear and Hamlet. Obviously, Woolf does not intend Septimus's broken mind to be exemplary, yet perhaps his transcendence of gender differentiations near the end of his life is meant to affirm that tragedy itself is gender-blind.

Clarissa is less egalitarian when it comes to questions of class. The rigid boundary between the nearest classes is not something that the wife of a Conservative MP questions. Clarissa uses the term "middle class" disparagingly, showing pride in her upper-middle-class status. When buses block the Queen's progress through the streets, Clarissa blames the middle class: "The British middle classes sitting sideways on the tops of omnibuses with parcels and umbrellas ... were, she thought, more ridiculous, more unlike anything there has ever been than one could conceive; and the Queen herself held up" (24).

Peter's class identity is more troubled, and perhaps more fluid than Clarissa's. He is both class-proud and anti-imperialist: "Coming as he did from a respectable Anglo-Indian family which for at least three generations had administered the affairs of a continent (it's strange, he thought, what a sentiment I have about that, disliking India, and empire, and army as he did), there were moments when civilization, even of this sort, seemed dear to him as a personal possession" (82).

The central class conflict of the book, however, involves Miss Doris Kilman, Elizabeth's history tutor and an evangelical Christian. To some extent, Clarissa's emotional intensity is due to jealousy about being replaced by Kilman in her daughter's affections. But Clarissa is savvy enough to know that she hates not so much the person as what Kilman stands for, a certain kind of middle-class person with strong morals and political causes, which "always make a person callous" (16). Aware that she is stereotyping, Clarissa fears that the feeling is mutual: "Year in year out she wore that coat; she perspired; she was never in the room five minutes without making you feel her superiority, your inferiority; how poor she was; how rich you were; how she lived in a slum without a cushion or a bed or a rug or whatever it might be, all her soul rusted with that grievance sticking in it" (16). Christine Froula remarks that ethnic prejudice is also at play. She explains the Kilman-Clarissa conflict as a representation of the prevalent English-German animosities of the period. Of German descent, Doris Kilman is fired from her teaching post because she refuses to express anti–German feelings. In Clarissa's mind, Kilman stands for "those specters ... who stand astride us and suck up half our life-blood, dominators and tyrants" (12)— Nazis in the making! Kilman in turn places Clarissa firmly in her class, "the most worthless of all classes— the rich, with a smattering of culture" (123). Their mutual hatred is an intentional reference to the "competition, envy, hatred, and aggression between classes and nations that had already engulfed Europe in war and would slowly rise to a boil again in the 1920s and 1930s" (Froula 104).

Clarissa's unthinking class pride doesn't bode well for a nuanced understanding of the coming national conflict (World War II). As Peter says, her marriage to a prominent Conservative increased her natural-born hauteur: "The obvious thing to say of her was that she was worldly; cared too much for rank and society and getting on in the world" (115). She liked Duchesses and Countesses because they "had courage." Peter believes that she learned these preferences from Richard: "a great deal of the public-spirited, British Empire, tariff-reform, governing-class spirit ... had grown on her.... With twice his wits, she had to see things through his eyes— one of the tragedies of married life" (116). Peter's insight links the bondage of class and gender into one colossal tragedy, called marriage. Although he cannot solve his own romantic problems, Peter does have good insight into Clarissa's social entrapment. Peter perceives the social changes brewing since the war more clearly than Clarissa does. When he hears a housemaid's laugh, for instance, he suspects "that shift in the whole pyramidal accumulation which in his youth had seemed immovable" (246). In this one objective correlative of a laughing housemaid, Peter apprehends the loosening of patriarchal hegemony, containing in one image — the maid — both its gendered and class elements.

In *The Political Unconscious*, Frederic Jameson theorizes that literature is like a cultural utopian dream, in which individuals experience the contradictions and conflicts of society. In literature, unlike life, these unresolved elements are mediated or solved. Both novels exhibit powerful unconscious elements, with emphatic resolutions, such as Danieltown's destruction and Septimus' suicide. Just as Bowen's guilt about her colonial past leads her to burn Danielstown, so too does Woolf's attraction to death (as an end to anxiety) find expression in Septimus's suicide. As Neil Corcoran points out, *The Last September* uses ellipses and dashes in characters' speech and thought, to elide the unconscious colonial guilt that Danielstown residents repress. I maintain that the political unconscious of the text also contains its gender anxiety. Many of the ellipses in this novel refer to unspeakable truths about what Judith Butler calls the melancholy of performing gender. When Lois hears her aunt and Francie discussing her character and options, she literally blocks them from assigning her an identity. When she hears, "Lois is so very — ," Lois breaks her water jug to avoid learning what they think she is, because "knowledge of this would stop, seal, finish one. Was she now to be clapped down under an adjective, to crawl round life-long inside some quality like a fly in a tumbler?" (83). Like T. S. Eliot's Prufrock, Lois' captured insect denotes the pain of definition by gender and class, for it is of marriage to the right class that the two women are talking. Although she tells Marda that she "likes to be in a pattern, to have to be what I am," Lois would rather define her role for herself than have it imposed upon her.

While Lois is at the beginning of her romantic life, Clarissa is at the end of her reproductive years. What patriarchy has defined as her *raison d'etre* is gone. Whereas Lois has fears about becoming a woman, Clarissa fears aging and the hardening that goes with it, marveling at "how little the margin that remained was capable of stretching" (44). Yet the old woman across the street is the quiet heroine of Clarissa's day, suggesting that acceptance of one's aloneness is the final dignity. In contrast, the ending of *The Last September* does not afford its protagonist any dignity or vision. In the final segment, she does not speak, but is only spoken of by her aunt and another gossip. We do not know how she feels about moving to Tours. Where Lois will end up is even less certain than the vague aspirations of Elizabeth Dalloway, that other nineteen-year-old who, to spite her mother, might take up farming or medicine. What does the political unconscious of *The Last September* suggest for Lois' future? If Marda is the most powerful female figure, then her fate — marriage to a man she doesn't love, for the sake of security — seems to be the best that Lois might hope for. There is little hope that Lois' death-haunted world will lighten. To the degree that the novel has autobiographical elements, we might compare Lois's imaginary future with Bowen's life story. Bowen grows from a dark childhood into becoming a successful novelist, but reports the same haunting by the ghosts of her past as Lois suffers in adolescence.

While both novels expose limitations placed by gender and class upon their protagonists' opportunities, *The Last September* delineates the pains of gender performance, while *Mrs. Dalloway* attempts to cross class and gender boundaries by forming a bond between Mrs. Dalloway and Septimus Smith. If we take their bond literally, several problems emerge: for one thing, it is only Clarissa, not Septimus, who makes the connection. This imbalance perpetuates the age-old gender distinction that says that women can imagine men's lives, but men cannot imagine women's. Another problem is that Clarissa's bridge to the Other is sheer imagination, never actualized. But if we use Jameson's model of the text as a cultural utopian dream that mediates conflict, we begin to appreciate the novel as Woolf's act of meliorating society — not by activism, but by imagination ("thinking is my fighting"). Although one writer's attempt to make her mind androgynous may be a drop in the bucket of feminism, it is nonetheless a radical alternative to status quo patriarchy. In contrast, Bowen's conservatism lends itself to the satiric mode, which anatomizes patriarchy and class isolation without attempts to ameliorate them.

CHAPTER FOUR

The 1960s: Hegemonies and the Abject in Doris Lessing's *The Golden Notebook* and Edna O'Brien's *The Country Girls Trilogy*

Synopsis: The novels explore what happens to authentic female voices when dominant national and political ideologies indoctrinate women. Catholicism and Communism utilize femaleness as a debased category that threatens to corrupt the purity of Church and State. Just three or four years before second-wave feminism produces strong, public female voices, Lessing and O'Brien's characters feel such shame at their own female sensibilities that they drive themselves to insanity. The feminist impulse of these authors manifests in their subversive denigration of patriarchal institutions, in which women cannot survive without quashing their authentic voices.

Historical Backgrounds

The 1960s are commonly known as the decade of revolution and sexual experimentation. Linking the women's movement with the American civil rights movement and the British Campaign for Nuclear Disarmament, it is convenient to place sexual permissiveness alongside them. Yet, Doris Lessing reminds us that, in many parts of the world, sexual experimentation started in the 1940s and 1950s. In the late 1940s, her Rhodesian circle of communists did not frown on extramarital sex; they advocated a free sexuality, unbounded by the "reactionary confines of bourgeois marriage," reminiscent of the Push anarchist philosophy described in the previous chapter. On the other hand, Lessing's comrades told her to downplay sex, since a focus on the pleasures of the body "could prevent her growth as a socially responsible person" (Klein

76). When Lessing moved to London in 1949, she found the same atmosphere of sexual permissiveness in her British and American comrades. Many American Communists in London were former Hollywood actors, writers, and producers who had been blacklisted by Senator McCarthy and the House Un-American Activities Committee. In Lessing's opinion, communist males were sexually liberated, although the *mensch* type (that she preferred) used sex as a weapon, hardly a way to liberate self or other.

The two novels I take as exemplary of early 1960s consciousness deal openly with sex and gender conflict. Catholic Ireland was unlike Britain in that sexual permissiveness was never a possibility. However, Irish art was a forum for otherwise unexpressed material, even if publication often meant censorship. Joyce's *Ulysses* (1922) was censored for its obscenity in numerous scenes, including Bloom and Dedalus's visit to the brothel, Leopold and Gerty McDowell's voyeurism and exhibitionism, and Molly's sexual fantasies. In 1960, O'Brien's *Country Girls* was banned as obscene for its mere depiction of fourteen-year-old girls who drew a dirty picture. The dawning awareness that sex was something women might speak about was finding its way into literature.

While first-wave feminism concentrated on suffrage more than sexuality, the second wave shifted direction. I choose Doris Lessing's *The Golden Notebook* (1962) and Edna O'Brien's *The Country Girls Trilogy* (1964) to represent the early sixties because they treat questions of gender and sex roles in unprecedented and passionate ways. They are similar in subject matter and scope. Lessing's text explores the struggles of its protagonist Anna over the course of a year, with lengthy flashbacks to her youth and twenties. O'Brien's novel treats protagonist Kate from the age of fourteen to twenty-five, with a flash-forward to her suicide. Both novels feature important secondary characters that are best friends and alter egos of the protagonists. Each text incorporates the spirit of place — Anna's Rhodesia and Kate's western Ireland — as a shaping characteristic of the women's psyches. Each narrative moves the protagonist from rural to urban environment, which increases her isolation and contributes to her breakdown over the loss of her relationships. The authors share a cynicism about heterosexual relationships, though Lessing's character strives to overcome her gender hostility, while the experience of O'Brien's protagonist hardens her perceptions of irreconcilable differences between all men and women.

Other differences between Lessing and O'Brien reveal distinctions between mid-century British versus Irish sensibilities. The characters in both novels suffer, as females, from the cultural hegemony exerted by patriarchal institutions; for Kate, this is the Irish Catholic Church, for Anna, the Communist Party. (Communism was the milieu that formed Lessing's identity from her mid-teens to mid-forties.) Each writer acknowledges the profound and lasting influence of these institutions, both of which are strongly patriarchal in structure and ideology. Lessing says Communism fulfilled her religious and emotional needs, while O'Brien claims she was afraid to confront religion because, "like a woman, I flee my persecutors" (Guppy).

Irish Catholicism is openly opposed to the beliefs of feminism. It teaches that a woman must serve her husband, her family, and the Church. In 1940s Ireland, thoughts about self-fulfillment were selfish and unworthy of a Catholic woman. Scripture and the Credo stereotype men and women's roles in binaries, as follows: Man is maker; woman is lover. Man is rational; woman is intuitive. Man makes theory; woman puts it into practice. Man thinks abstractly, woman concretely. Man is initiator, woman responder. Man is ruler, woman follower. Man asserts self; woman surrenders self. Man originates projects; woman nurtures man (Kalven 37–8). In Sandra Gilbert's words, the institutional structures of Catholicism, such as the solemn liturgy of the mass and the brilliant argumentation of the Church fathers, "nakedly embodied and perpetuated the assumptions and oppressions of a patriarchal culture that defines women as secondary and inferior, indeed as basically vessels for the transmission of physical life" (xi). Mary Kenney believes that frequent repetition of the Hail Mary ("Blessed is the fruit of thy womb, Jesus"), sends deeply into the Catholic subconscious a symbolic affirmation that women's most cherished role is to be a vessel for life (154).

Communism is less transparent about its misogyny, but nonetheless culpable. Marx and Engels were so convinced that abolition of capitalism would result in a fair society that they overlooked historical gender discriminations as a contributing factor to human injustice. In their abstractions of human behavior, they neglected to consider whether the abolition of capitalism would magically erase patriarchy's stronghold. In the *Communist Manifesto*, they had little to say about women, their desire to abolish the family having more to do with children's wellbeing than women's. In Chapter II, they use the concept of marriage to deride bourgeois customs of adultery and prostitution, not to interrogate women's role in patriarchy. Asserting that it is "self-evident" that abolition of capitalism would end prostitution, Marx begs the question of how this would happen. More revealing of Marx's misogyny than the *Manifesto* is his personal correspondence. He wrote jokingly to Ludwig Kugelmann about his wife's political activities, assuring him that "social revolutions are impossible without the feminine ferment. Social progress may be measured precisely by the social position of the fair sex (plain ones included)" (KM to Kugelmann 12 Dec 1868). Although Engels recognizes that marriage is a system of exchange that treats women as chattel, he does not extend his analysis to the repercussions of such objectification upon women's wellbeing. Nor does he explain why he predicts that patriarchy will wither in the ideal State. Idealizing workers, he forgets that they are men. In practice, most 1960s communist organizations relegated their women members to secondary roles. The necessary "feminine ferment" extolled by Marx usually manifested in women supporting men's endeavors, like yeast enabling the rise of bread! An example of this "feminine ferment" quality is captured in Marx's joking postscript to his December 5, 1868, letter to Kugelmann about his wife: "I think that German women should begin by driving their husbands to self-emancipation." It is not clear whether he means that Mrs. Kugelmann is annoying to live with, or whether women (tongue-in-cheek) may be the instigators of communism due to their energetic moral natures.

Communist aesthetic proscriptions (writing about personal life is "petty bourgeois") may have affected women artists more than men. Communism teaches that to focus on one's individuality impedes the collective goal of the movement, which is to free the proletariat. Alan Woods describes Communist objection to personal art in this way: "The chief weakness of bourgeois aesthetics is that it rejects *a priori* the social influences that shape the development of art. Thus, the development of art is reduced to an essentially personal, i.e., psychological phenomenon." All artists have an effect on society: "Despite all the prejudices about the lonely artist communicating with himself, in practice, no writer writes a novel just for their personal consumption." A novel is not just about an individual struggle, but stands for a social condition: "In order that characters be interesting to us, they must stand for something more than just themselves" ("Marxism and Art"). Marxist critic Teodor Adorno's famous pronouncement, that to write poetry after the Holocaust was barbaric, may or may not have been known to Lessing. But the requirement in her social circle that art be "committed" to the aims of communism was strong enough to give her character Anna a guilt complex leading to a nervous breakdown.

Indoctrinated by Communism and Catholicism, Lessing and O'Brien experienced a repressive double bind. First, the culture of early 1960s Britain and Ireland had not yet produced a foremother to show women how to emancipate themselves. *The Feminine Mystique* came out in 1963, three years after O'Brien's first book, and a year after Lessing's. Second, the institutions that indoctrinated Lessing and O'Brien preached against the personal liberation that each woman desired. Both writers internalized the vision of goodness handed down by these institutions. But another internal force — the desire to write —clashed with their training. In giving outlet to this internal force, they experienced conflict between the role of writer, for whom authenticity is key, and the role of woman as inherited from these institutions, which wasn't "authentic" for a thinking woman. Communism and Catholicism taught women the same morals: to be kind, one must put others before self. To be good, one must obey authorities. To be accepted, one must adopt prevailing mores. Neither institution values individuality; both command obedience. In turn, the penalties for disobedience are dire: excommunication and social ostracism by the Church; ostracism, condemnation, torture, and death by the Party.

From the perspective of the early twenty-first century, it is easy to underestimate these pressures upon mid-twentieth-century writers. Lessing traveled to Russia at a time when being executed for a misstep was a distinct possibility. Working with Soviet presses, Lessing reviewed fiction that was either approved by Communist authorities or rejected for failing to regurgitate the Party line. While creating *The Golden Notebook*, the Communist directive to avoid a bourgeois focus on the self was a nagging constant; it shows up in Anna's guilt about the proper role of a female Communist writer. This guilt impels her to want to universalize human experience. Anna consistently tries to overlook gender difference, while negotiating some of the most grueling relationship battles ever written. On one level, Anna's breakdown is a generous attempt to overcome the boundaries between female and male, using herself and Saul Green as cases in point. She consistently identifies with others as oppressed beings needing her compassion, a mental habit instilled by the Party. Moral imperatives undermine her ability to analyze gender relations as an institutionalized system of patriarchy. Contemporary readers wonder why she cannot apply to patriarchy the same sophisticated analysis she uses on capitalism. Similarly, O'Brien writes convincingly of Kate and Baba's stresses as a result of constantly being devalued in their relationships. Except for Baba's occasional cynical remarks, however, O'Brien avoids describing the larger picture of a patriarchy that inscribes these attitudes into its citizens.

On the one hand, this failure to theorize is historical. Lessing and O'Brien are born too early in feminist history to benefit from feminists' theorization of patriarchy as hegemony. Although Simone de Beauvoir's *The Second Sex* becomes available in English in 1953, its philosophical jargon prevents its easy assimilation by non-philosophers. On the other hand, Lessing and O'Brien's failure to theorize is a question of individual temperament. Paradoxically, Catholic O'Brien and Communist Lessing are extremely individualistic women, so that the prospect of joining with other women for collective action may have been unappealing. To use Adrienne Rich's terminology, Lessing and O'Brien are not *woman-identified women*[1] but instead they find role models in prominent men. Lessing identified with male Communist leaders, O'Brien with male writers such as James Joyce, Anton Chekhov, and Leo Tolstoy.

Identification with males is common to women writers of their time. This phenomenon raises questions about Elaine Showalter's theory of the progression of the last three centuries of women's writing. If women writers moved from imitation of male writers in the nineteenth century to *écriture feminine* in the twentieth,[2] then Lessing and O'Brien should be writing in a mode that consciously seeks to interrogate what it means to be a female writer. Lessing's protagonist is tantalizingly close, as she questions the very genre of the novel in its incapacity to represent Anna's female consciousness. However, Anna stops short of identifying her consciousness as female (unless insulting her femaleness), always seeking to heal the pain of her existence by identifying with her male partners and Communist colleagues.

O'Brien is much more explicit than Lessing about choosing male writers as models, citing James Joyce as the first writer who was "writing about her own life," and Hemingway as the first author who taught her to scale down her prose. In Lessing's case, the models are political rather than literary; the Communist colleagues who were critiquing her manuscripts act as internalized moral critics. This rest of this chapter investigates the tensions between Communism, Catholicism, and feminism; between art and social advocacy; between goodness and individuality; and between Lessing and O'Brien's style, content, and personal background.

Comparative Feminisms of O'Brien and Lessing

Lessing strongly disavowed feminism. "Everything I dislike about politics is enshrined in the women's movement. It's just petty and stupid" (Klein 192). Prior to second-wave feminism, the *personal* was not yet considered the *political*.[3] Lessing's long affiliation with Communist politics prevented her from politicizing the personal realm of male-female relationships. To write about one's love relationships was *petit bourgeois* (conventional and conservative), unserious, and self-indulgent. The only proper objective of artistic endeavor was to implement world revolution by the proletariat. Publishing lyrical prose or poetry was seditious and heretical, or even barbaric, à la Teodor Adorno. Although she *does* write about relationships, Lessing's virulent rejection of feminism and the women's movement is traceable to her indoctrination in Communist ideology. As we have seen in earlier chapters, most Communist, Labour, and New Left organizations were skeptical or hostile to women's participation as equals. Women were recruited as helpmates to men, to serve food, carry messages, distribute pamphlets, create networks, and provide sex, a clean home, and companionship. But in terms of real political contributions, such as policy-making, international representation, speech writing or intellectual analysis, women were not considered equal to men.

In contrast to Lessing's, Edna O'Brien's early life and writing is characterized by her detachment from political subjects (using *political* in its pre-second-wave sense). O'Brien's interest in Kate and Baba is restricted to their romantic loves and losses. Her avoidance of political topics causes many feminists to disown her, yet her depiction of heterosexual relations makes her a strong feminist of a certain type. Although O'Brien doesn't theorize her feminism, her books express it by exposing power relations between men and women. There is no sugar coating to the tragedy of Kate's life.

In interviews, O'Brien frequently expresses her biological-difference feminism, meaning she believes there is a defining biological difference between men and women. "Women are more discontent than men [because] ... there must be in every man and every woman the desire, the deep primeval desire to go back to the womb.... A man partly and symbolically achieves this when he goes into a woman.... A woman never, ever approaches that kind of security" (Eckley 30). Women writers are doubly damned: "A woman writer has a double dose of masochism: that of the woman and that of the artist. Men are better at escaping their psyches and their consciences" (Guppy). In a 1984 interview, Shusha Guppy asked O'Brien whether she believed that gender is a cultural construct. O'Brien replied that she didn't, because gender difference is "fundamentally biological and therefore psychological." Along with repudiating the constructionist argument, O'Brien does not believe that conditions of inequality can be changed: "I would like women to have a better time, but I don't see it happening: people are pretty savage towards each other, be they men or women" (Guppy). Because advocacy for change has long been a key element in definitions of feminism, many creative writers don't seem feminist, because their contribution is one of artistic expression. Yet writing reaches numerous readers, opening their minds to conditions of patriarchy. Art is its own kind of political work, involving struggle. As Woolf said when she declined advocacy work, "thinking is my fighting."[4]

A revaluation of the feminist awareness of formerly dismissed writers has occupied many literary critics of the 1990s and 2000s. In some ways, the honesty and courage of a writer like Edna O'Brien, who unflinchingly represents gender wars in their most intimate manifestation (romantic relationships), exceed the courage of those who theorize exclusively. One of the prime tenets of women's studies is that the personal voice of experience matters. All knowledge is a combination of the subjective material of experience and the supposedly objective material of scholarship. Good writers reach a large audience, contributing to knowledge that leads to social change.

Lives of the Authors

Doris Lessing

Born in 1919 to British expatriates in Persia, Lessing started life far from what her parents knew as home; a sense of not belonging would follow her throughout life. Her mother Emily McVeagh may have passed on her rebellious streak. Emily rejected her father's plan for her to attend university and chose nursing instead. If Lessing inherited her mother's stubbornness, from her father she got her indignation at social injustice. His anger at the British government gave young Doris a clear picture of how war can damage a sensitive psyche. Before enlisting for World War I, Alfred Tayler was a high-spirited, sensual clerk, who thought nothing of walking fifteen miles to a country dance. The war embittered him, exposing the social injustices that put well-born men in offices and places of relative safety, while working-class soldiers experienced the squalor and danger of the trenches. As Britain's World War I poets[5] expressed, the war came to seem absurd, tragic, and unfair to Alfred, who lost his leg as the result of shrapnel wounds. Nursing him, Emily McVeagh fell in love, or at least accepted his marriage proposal! Marriage must have seemed urgent at the age of thirty-five, well past the average age for a 1920s marriage.

After the war, Alfred accepted a bank job in rural Persia, a welcome escape from the pettiness of England, which he felt had betrayed him. Doris remembered their first home being like a prison. Emily and Alfred didn't bother to name their newborn because they were disappointed she wasn't a boy. It was the doctor who named her. Doris cried a lot during her first year; later, Emily found it was because Persian cows' milk was too thin. Emily might have learned to love her firstborn had she not produced a son two years later. Seeing her mother lavish affections upon Harry confirmed Doris' sense of being

Doris Lessing, 1990s (Photofest).

unlovable. Her mother told her that she must love Harry because "he is your baby." Protesting her parents' injustice, Doris began having tantrums, a pattern that would continue to her maturity (and might underlie her radical pronouncements to this day).

During Alfred's leave of absence in 1924, he made a fateful visit to the Wembley Empire Exhibition. Like many restless Europeans, Alfred made an impulsive decision based on the allures of advertising.[6] Marveling at the foot-and-a-half-long corn cobs displayed in the Rhodesia booth, Alfred fell for false government promises of easy wealth, using his veteran's discounts to buy 1500 acres of land in Southern Rhodesia. What the government concealed were the tough conditions of drought, blights, locusts, the decreasing value of corn, and the always-difficult relations with native employees. Within the first year, Emily was so depressed that she simply went to bed. Alfred dealt with his own depression in different ways. Inefficient at both farming and people-management, he dreamed of striking gold. During the next ten years he invented unsuccessful gold-divining devices, while his diabetes, hypochondria, bitterness and depression got steadily worse. Without servants, Emily eventually had to get out of bed to raise her children and run the house. Although she regretted that she would never again enjoy the cultured life of London or Tehran, she did not despair of educating her children for that kind of life. She sent them away to school in Salisbury. This early separation proved traumatic for seven-year-old Doris.

At school, Lessing was bullied until she discovered her alter ego, Tigger. Tigger was a confident, cheerful character in *Winnie-the-Pooh*, which Doris' family enjoyed acting out. As Tigger, Doris became a favorite among teachers and pupils. When Lessing later underwent Jungian therapy, she analyzed the various roles that she played in search of identity. She saw that her childish Tigger had morphed into her Hostess role when she was grown up. Lessing felt ambivalently about the Hostess's propensity to please others. Her biographer believes that playing Tigger deflected people's ability to perceive her dark side, and sometimes convinced her of her own invulnerability. When she contracted pinkeye, Doris pretended that she couldn't see so that she didn't have to return to school. She was fourteen when she quit school for good.

Although not yet planning to be a career writer, Lessing began writing articles and stories at this time. Olive Schreiner was her role model and inspiration. Reading *The Story of an African Farm* (1883), Doris found her first, and perhaps only, intellectual sister. Schreiner's novel chronicles the life of a white girl growing up on a small, struggling farm in the South African *veldt*. Raised by a selfish, judgmental mother and a saintly, impractical father, Lyndall has to create her own future. She educates herself, but can find no satisfactory work. Returning to the farm after a discouraging affair, Lyndall refuses to marry a man she does not respect. After giving birth to a stillborn infant, Lyndall dies.

Like Lessing, Schreiner grew up in colonial Africa to parents whose conservative views felt constricting, though Lessing was at an advantage in having a mother who believed in her creative abilities. Like Schreiner, Lessing was shocked to learn of the color bar. Schreiner's firm conviction that women have to educate themselves and resist traditional roles strikes a chord with Lessing. Perhaps the most striking of their commonalities is the supreme individuality that Schreiner expresses in *African Farm*. Rather than following a single genre, she interpolates lectures, satire, symbolism, magic realism and social realism. This pastiche of different voices represents a solitary woman, literally crying out in the wilderness in her attempt to write a female coming-of-age that cannot be expressed in the traditional, male *bildungsroman* form.[7] Lessing would also create a uniquely-structured novel that represented a female sense of disintegration in a hostile environment. Her intense identification with Schreiner was the most positive experience of Lessing's young adulthood. "The book became part of me," she said, "I had only to hear the title or 'Olive Schreiner,' and my deepest self was touched" (Klein 51).

Noticing her restlessness at home, Alfred recommended that Doris become an *au pair* in Salisbury. Although not particularly progressive, the *paterfamilias* at her new situation shared his books on Marxist theory. Newly aware of her womanly attractiveness, Doris tried to sleep with her boss' brother. With shapely legs and a pixie face, she was appealing, confident, and motivated to find love. Leaving the *au pair* situation for a job as telephone operator and a room in a boarding house freed Doris for a social life. During the rounds of tennis, drinking and dancing, she found Frank Wisdom. Given her "biological drive," Lessing finds it "natural" that she entered a young marriage with Frank Wisdom and had two children: "nature wants women to have babies" (Klein 63). Although she wished to abort her first child, she believes that "nature" caused her to deny the existence of her first pregnancy until it was too late to have an abortion. In an effort to repress guilt, especially over abandoning the children of this marriage, Lessing attributes many of her actions to fate, nature, or the *Zeitgeist* (Klein 63).

Wisdom, despite his name, was not a man to hold Lessing's respect for very long. He was only tepid in his endorsement of Communism. Lessing blames the divorce on herself, saying marriage was not for her, because "men want to dominate, and women lose any position of autonomy and strength" (Klein 67). At the time of her divorce, Lessing threw herself headlong into communist activities. The Rhodesian Communists, though not accepted by the Soviet headquarters, used the Party platform as a method of dismantling the color bar. Their cell was made up of Royal Air Force working-class men and European refugees, many Jewish. Lessing distributed leaflets, attended meetings, and absorbed Marxist philosophy. In return, the group provided the emotional support that she needed to leave her marriage. When asked whether it had been a mistake to abandon her children, Lessing replied, "If I hadn't, I would have had a very bad breakdown or become an alcoholic" (Klein 70). There were other caretakers in her absence: her mother, Frank's sister, and a neighbor. She told her son John that she had to leave in order to make the world a better place for him and his sister Jean (Klein 75).

Her next liaison was a "political marriage." A political refugee, Gottfried Lessing needed to obtain Rhodesian citizenship in order to avoid deportation to Germany. Intellectual leader of the Rhodesian Communists, Gottfried is the basis for *The Golden Notebook's* Willi Rodde, whose liaison with Anna is also one of convenience. Cold, dogmatic, and committed, Willi's ironic demeanor and emotional detachment capture some of Gottfried's less flattering traits. In the first flush of romance, Lessing describes her lover as considerate and gentle, but later, he becomes "a cold, sarcastic, authoritarian man who lived by emotionless logic" (Klein 81). Despite this, Doris appeared to love their son Peter, this time taking full responsibility for her child's upbringing.

In 1949, Lessing departs with Peter for London. Two books record her first impressions of the English: *Walking in the Shade* chronicles her impressions on arriving at the center of Empire, and *In Pursuit of the English* analyzes what it means to be English. Intent on defining the elusive Englishness that her father always revered, Lessing risks her safety to study a conman, wondering how London "spivs" differ from the African type. Lessing made haste to join the Communist Party and find a job. Postwar London is difficult aesthetically and economically. Her description of its squalid bombed neighborhoods fills *In Pursuit of the English* with a Dickensian appreciation of poverty. During the next ten years, Lessing would live in these slums and study their inhabitants. In the Party, doing time in the slums made her commitment more credible.

Shortly after her arrival, Lessing finds a sympathetic agent and publisher for *The Grass Is Singing* (1950). This novel draws on Lessing's childhood, touching on the loaded theme of race relations in southern Rhodesia. The protagonist is a woman like her mother, who marries an inefficient dreamer who fails at farming. After many years, she suffers a mental breakdown, and allows a black man to cross the rigid boundaries set up by colonials to establish their authority over natives. In this plot appear both influences of Schreiner (the rural setting, despair at the rigidity of social forms, entrapment in marriage) and the seeds of *The Golden Notebook* (the idea of experiencing different identities while breaking down, deep involvement with an extreme Other, female depression and sensation of entrapment).

The Golden Notebook reflects Lessing's preoccupations during her first ten years in London. Rescued from the boardinghouse by Joan Rodker, an intellectual refugee with her own apartment, Lessing fictionalizes her as Molly, Anna's best friend in the novel. Lessing's next boyfriend is a disturbed Czech refugee, who has seen eleven of his friends hanged for supposed betrayals of the Communist Party. Jack would turn into both Paul and Michael of *The Golden Notebook*. Although Jack never suggests that he will leave his wife, Lessing believes he will. After a five-year affair, he leaves. Her numbness, alcoholism, and despair are well rendered in the novel.

After Jack leaves, she takes her own flat, renting a room to a working-class Jewish-American writer, Clancy Sigal, who becomes Saul Green in the novel. Knowing Sigal is like living in the working-class boardinghouse — it expands her Communist résumé. Yet there is nothing opportunistic in Lessing's commitment to the relationship. A schizophrenic and promiscuous *mensch*, Sigal is more of a burden than a pleasure. According to Lessing, the role of *mensch* was a manifestation of American 1950s cultural angst. Unlike the usual Yiddish meaning of *mensch* (a man with noble characteristics), the sexual *mensch* was out for his own pleasure: "A real man [is one who] fucks them and leaves them" (Klein 378).

Lessing's attraction to hyper-masculine men, whose promiscuity she does not regard as sexist, is part of her non-feminist belief system. Yet the personal trauma caused by her relationships with Jack and Clancy taught Lessing that she had to change her lifestyle: "I was a falling-in-love junkie ... addicted to the condition of being in love." The realization was "a shock to me ... truly the end of something" (Klein 325). "I was determined my emotional life would be different" (Klein 334). After Clancy, she had no more serious relationships. Eventually, she stops wearing makeup and coloring her hair, taking pride in her role as intellectual spokesperson, although she would not like this label (one journalist called her "the angriest woman in London"). When she had passed sixty, Lessing told a friend that she envied her for being in love, since love had been absent from her own life for many years. On the other hand, she also felt freed "from the clutches of a demon" (Klein 227). Interestingly, Edna O'Brien expresses a similar sentiment, which I will discuss in the next section.

After *The Golden Notebook*, Lessing radically changes direction. Like Anna Wulf, she regretfully says goodbye to the Communist Party. In 1956, Khrushchev publicizes Stalin's brutalities in 1956. Like many other Communists, Lessing can no longer ignore the party's hypocrisies. She briefly turns her political energies to the Campaign for Nuclear Disarmament (CND), which invites her to be their spokesperson. But the infighting between factions remind her too much of the lies and pettiness of the Communist Party. Also, after years of marches protesting nuclear armament, Lessing felt that nothing was achieved. From politics, she turns wholeheartedly to spiritualism, following the Sufi guru, Idries Shah. "From the end of the fifties onwards there was a main current in my life, deeper than any other, my real preoccupation" (Klein 354). Sufism is a combination of secular and religious philosophies that sees nothing wrong with earning profits while following mystic principles. Sufi parables are similar to Zen koans; their dry humor must appeal to a person of Lessing's ironic temperament. One koan says: a man is a prisoner on an island, but he does not know he is a prisoner. When offered an escape, the man says: "Oh thank you, I'll come, but I must bring my ton of cabbage with me" (Klein 354). Like Plato's Allegory of the Cave, this Sufi koan teaches that most humans never realize that their perceptions are illusions. It is possible that the literary qualities of the teachings constitute their strongest appeal to a person of Lessing's profession and temperament.

While channeling her spiritual fervor from Communism to Sufism, Lessing also switched the genre in which she wrote. Her social realism gave way to what she called "inner space fiction." She believes that fantasy worlds are the perfect way to describe social problems. Responding to criticism, she says that fantasy and science fiction do not place any limitations on character development. Much of Lessing's oeuvre after *The Golden Notebook* is science fiction, including *Canopus in Argos: Archives, The Four-Gated City*, and the operas, *The Making of the Representative for Planet 8* and *The Marriages Between Zones Three, Four and Five*. Lessing complains of readers' desire for realism: "Can't they see that there are more important things to write about than men and women marrying or having sex? This stuff that I'm writing about now is where it really is" (Klein 232).

Although she jettisons Communism in her early forties, she retains its central belief that the individual pursuit of romantic happiness through personal relationships is bourgeois and unworthy of a true social progressive. Her experience of Communism as a polarizing, judgmental simplification of moral complexities makes Lessing cautious of *all* binary values. She denigrates feminism, which she treats as monolithic instead of various. Calling them Cruel Sisters, she scorns what she perceives as feminists' double standards of judgment for male and female behavior. She thinks that feminists have created a culture of reverse sexism, in which it is socially acceptable to bash males.

Lessing is not alone in being a strong public figure that contributes feminist material, yet disowns basic tenets of feminism. Germaine Greer's *The Female Eunuch* anatomized western culture's subjugation of females to undesirable roles, yet she played such roles herself, such as pornography model, rock-band groupie, and tamed shrew. More self-analytical than Greer, Lessing named this trait (playing second to men) *masochism*. Yet she did not choose to theorize it as *female* masochism, a phenomenon that is predicated on women's subordinate role in patriarchy. The remarkable absence of the word "patriarchy" in Lessing's writing signals her failure to place women's sexual roles within an explanatory socioeconomic framework of patriarchy (Anna uses the word just once in the novel). Much like Greer, Lessing tends to blame the victim: "Lessing made it clear that intelligent women must fight repressive aspects of their sexual submission" (Klein 190). Such a response to the inequities of sexual relationships is remarkably individualistic, as opposed to collective. Lessing's Communist training said that social change can only be achieved through collective endeavor, but Lessing insists on the individual fight, for women.

These teasing inconsistencies make Lessing a fascinating biographical study. *The Golden Notebook's* coincidence with the early days of the Women's Movement offered her the opportunity to become its primary intellectual leader. But feminism never appealed to her. The soul-battle she waged over Communism, and to a lesser extent, the CND, depleted her of faith in other social movements. To understand why she did not choose women's liberation over people's liberation in the first place, we need to appreciate her early history.

Like many would-be feminists, Lessing wanted to create an identity absolutely different from her mother's. Perceiving Emily's depression, isolation, and subjugation, Lessing strove to find her own identity outside of marriage bonds. When both of her marriages became difficult after a few years, Lessing divorced. By writing parts of her mother's temperament and situation into the protagonist of *The Grass Is Singing*, Lessing begins to exorcise her mother-in-herself. Not only will she refuse to be trapped in provincial southern Africa, she will not bind herself to the economic and emotional contingencies of a bad marriage. When the Communist Party became Lessing's substitute family, first in Rhodesia, then in London, she held herself to very high standards of moral integrity. Yet these standards came from a masculinist ideology, which denigrated the "personal," as a mere distraction from the collective. The leaders of the movement were male; female members identified with these leaders. Thanks to later theory, we now understand that in patriarchy, most young women feel compelled, if unconsciously, to identify with males. Adrienne Rich names "compulsory heterosexuality" as a tool of patriarchy that keeps women identified with men, because they rely on men as sources of their own identity and power. In this case, Lessing identified with male Party leaders, combining her sexual orientation with her political affiliations by having relationships with members who treated her as a second-class citizen. Lessing's adolescent search for a role model led her to male choices, with the sole exception of Olive Schreiner. The replacement of her biological family with a Communist one — a male-dominated organization — resulted in her male-identification and denigration of female solidarity.

At the end of *The Golden Notebook*, Anna calls her illness a "sadistic-masochistic cycle" that she was sharing with Saul Green (584). When Green tells her he is *proud to be sexist*, Anna describes patriarchy, without ever naming it: "Good, because in a society where not one man in ten thousand begins to understand the ways in which women are second-class citizens, we have to rely for company on the men who are at least not hypocrites" (583). Were she to rely instead on women, she would be making a feminist choice, becoming a woman-identified woman on Rich's *lesbian continuum*. Such orientation is not necessarily sexual. The term expresses women's need to develop satisfying relationships with each other, to explore the lives of their sisters and mothers throughout history, and to value their own femaleness. Instead, Anna vows to begin life afresh as a marriage counselor in a welfare center. She will join the Labour Party (also sexist), and teach night classes for social delinquents. All three choices are noble and believable, based on Anna's former commitment to the Communist Party. But as Molly remarks, they are an attempt to "integrate with British life at its roots," in other words, inherently conservative rather than revolutionary (GN 638). The lessons that Anna learned during her breakdown are not articulated in feminist terms, where feminism is defined as an attitude of concern (at least) and advocacy (at best) for the reparation of gender inequities in society. Ultimately, Lessing's novel compels respect by its deep honesty about one woman's experience, yet also frustrates by its refusal to frame this experience in feminist terms, with feminism's ameliorative intentions. Like O'Brien, she exposes power imbalances in personal relationships, but seems to blame female masochism for women's pain.

Edna O'Brien

There is no full-length biography of Edna O'Brien. The following information comes from her 1976 memoir *Mother Ireland*, several published interviews, and two monographs on her life and work. Born December 15, 1930, to a family of fallen gentry in County Clare, O'Brien grows up with struggling farmers. Because of her father's drinking, the family has had to move from the Big House into a cottage. O'Brien calls her father the "archetypal Irishman: a gambler, drinker, and totally unequipped to be a husband or father" (Guppy).[8] Both of her parents are "superstitious, fanatical, and engulfing." Although talented themselves, they are afraid of what it means to be a writer in Ireland. In their Irish Catholicism, the Word was God's.

O'Brien describes her family heritage as one of "talent, despair, and permanent fury." Both parents were staunchly Catholic; they forbade Edna to study English literature because the artistic side of life invited heretical thoughts. After five years at the Convent of Mercy at Loughrea, County Galway, she matriculated in Dublin's Pharmaceutical College of Ireland. Like Lessing, O'Brien wrote stories as a young girl, but never thought of herself as a writer. In 1948, O'Brien begins writing articles for the *Irish Press*. In 1950, Ernest Gébler walks into her pharmacy, beginning a courtship that leads to their marriage in 1951, when they relocate to London.

Born in 1914 to a Dublin usherette and an Austro-Hungarian musician, Gébler had a successful novel under his belt when he met O'Brien, but soon became jealous of her greater success. Their first son's memoir, *Father & I*, confirms what O'Brien has said about her husband. Gébler scorned her Irish provincialism, insulted her intelligence and moral character, and blamed their son Carlo's faults (such as asthma) on her "degenerate Irish genes." He especially resented the ease with which O'Brien entered the writing field. A publishing firm offered her twenty-five pounds to write a novel. She wrote *The Country Girls* (1960) in three weeks, achieving immediate popular success in America and Britain. This infuriated Gébler, and he told her to sign over her royalties to him.

Edna O'Brien, c. 1972 (Photofest).

In 1964, she left her husband, attaining custody of the boys with difficulty. Besides Carlo, who became a writer, they had a second son, Sacha, who became an architect. O'Brien now began the difficult life of a single mother living on a writing income. To protect her sons, she tried to keep her romantic activities outside of their home: "They had been through enough trauma without — knowing my taste — some new putative monster around." O'Brien knew that she was attracted to frightening men because of her father: "I have a very strong pull toward god and the devil and I used to be drawn towards men with elements of both, and who would exert power over one — over one's mind and body" (quoted in Eckley 39). An involvement with a high-level, married politician ended badly. The pain of the relationship was so great that it stopped her from writing. Like Lessing, O'Brien took stock of the high emotional cost of her style of engagement: "Some people have a predilection, when they fall in love, for life to be very heightened. There's a lunacy in it" (*Guardian*). She attributes her subsequent productivity to her state of being single. Keeping a certain amount of privacy about her personal life, she admits to having had "one or two affairs," and reveals her tendency to break down when involved with a man. Describing women as either givers or takers, she believes she is the former. Takers are "more clever at negotiating the dance of their lives. I'm not clever" (*Guardian*). In therapy with R. D. Laing in the 1960s, she sought some explanation of her melancholic temperament, but he could not help her, because "he was too mad himself."

The *Country Girls* (1960) was a huge success in America and Britain, but the Irish Censorship Board banned it for sexual content. The parish priest of O'Brien's small village staged a public burning of the few copies that parishioners had bought, while O'Brien's mother stood by approvingly. Like so many books banned in the early twentieth century, the avowed reason for censorship covered other, unstated ones. For instance, in Lawrence's *The Rainbow*, there are several challenges to British propriety: a brief lesbian interlude between a girl and her gym teacher; the anti-military, anti-imperialistic portrait of Anton Skrebensky; and extramarital sex that the author clearly condones. In *The Country Girls*, the ostensible offense is that Kate and Baba engage in sexual acts. However, there are other, political reasons for censorship. Like Synge's *Playboy of the Western World*, Kate's story reveals unsavory aspects of west Ireland life that censors wished to hide from outsiders, including her drunken father, her long-suffering mother, adulterous affairs, child-abuse and molestation, the uncomprehending priest, and the hopelessness of such an environment. Clearly, O'Brien did not allow censorship to stop her, for the next two volumes of the trilogy are more "scandalous" than the first.

Apart from the popular outrage about her portrayals of real Irish life, critics also expressed difficulty in categorizing her rank and genre. Some feminists felt that her heroines weren't authentic or exemplary because they failed to resist the romantic relationships that destroyed them. Others said she was not a serious novelist because her subject matter, "women's emotional problems," left out vast areas of public interest, such as poverty and war. Others said that she relied entirely on autobiography. According to one critic, "O'Brien's persona is not particularly endearing" because she has "manipulated the physical presence to a level of often living out the role of heroine ... to a notion of nostalgic romanticism perceived as being typically Irish" (quoted in Greenwood 19). Another critic says "too much posing as a tragedy queen has turned O'Brien deaf to her own bathetic efforts" (Greenwood 2). As mentioned in the section on Virginia Woolf, ad hominem attacks of this nature are more commonly directed at women writers than men. A woman's life tends to be, or to seem, more connected to the value of her writing than for men.

Despite such hostile reception, O'Brien manages to maintain a social life in London, mixing with Hollywood actors and producers. Three of her novels have successful screen adaptations. Upon learning how much she loved *Catcher in the Rye*, one actor introduced her to J. D. Salinger, with whom she enjoyed a short friendship. After 1967, O'Brien responded to the criticism that she had ignored Irish social problems, by writing a state-of-the-nation trilogy. These three novels dramatize the topical events of IRA terrorist attacks, the Miss X abortion case, and a famous murder. Researching the first novel, she interviewed an Irish National Liberation Army convict named Dominic "Mad Dog" McGlinchey, who had reportedly shot thirty people. She also interviewed IRA leader Gerry Adams for the *New York Times* and attended the 1996 *Sinn Fein* conference. For her efforts, the press accused her of falling in love with hardened criminals.

O'Brien excels at lyrical prose, but like Joyce, she believes that the dramatic form can better express the emotions. She wrote four plays, *A Cheap Bunch of Nice Flowers* (1963) about a mother dying of cancer and her daughter stealing her boyfriend; *A Pagan Place* (1973) about her childhood; *Virginia* (1981) about Virginia Woolf; and *Zee and Co.* (1971) about a woman's love affairs. *Virginia* is the best known of these; it debuted in Canada, and played at the Theatre Royal Haymarket and New York's Public Theater. Her adapted novels were good enough to attract stars to play the screen roles, including Maggie Smith, Elizabeth Taylor, Michael Caine, Susannah York, Rod Steiger, Claire Bloom, and Peter Finch. Her biographies of Lord Byron and James Joyce manage to retain her lyrical style without sacrificing accuracy and authority. Joyce and Chekhov are her strongest influences, and the Joycean influence is easily recognized in her poetic prose style.

At eighty years old, O'Brien was writing her memoir. The first memoir, *Mother Ireland* (1976), covers her life from childhood to marriage. Written like fiction, it only describes significant moments, rather than providing linear narrative. Recently, novelist Andrew O'Hagan countered criticisms of O'Brien's work, saying: "She changed the nature of Irish fiction; she brought the woman's experience and sex and internal lives of those people on to the page and she did it with style, and she made these concerns international" (*Guardian*). I think we can make even greater claims for O'Brien's achievement, by evaluating the feminist urge behind her work.

Synopses of the Novels

The Golden Notebook

Much to Doris Lessing's displeasure, *The Golden Notebook* was acclaimed as the first feminist novel. More than its exposé of sex wars, she wanted readers to appreciate its innovative structure, whose complexity reflected the multiplicity of human identity: "my major aim was to shape a book which would make its own comment: to talk through the way it was shaped" (Preface). By inserting raw materials inside the frame of a conventional novel, she illustrated her dissatisfaction with the novel as form: "how little I have caught of all that complexity; how can this small neat thing be true when what I experienced was so rough and apparently formless and unshaped" (Preface). The source materials are always richer than the completed product; a novel is only a partial representation of what an author wants to say. In 1962, such an innovative structure was radical for a woman writer. Writing an epic, putting a woman's consciousness front and center, contesting a writer's ability to represent consciousness at all — these were new ground. Proust and Joyce are the closest male equivalents, but their modernist concerns are different from Lessing's postmodernist angst, which she symbolizes as the Atom Bomb. *The Golden Notebook* compares Anna's individual consciousness to the collective consciousness, with its terrors of war, holocaust, and nuclear destruction.

The Golden Notebook consists of Anna Wulf's entries into four notebooks, plus the frame story, "Free Women." The fifth chapter, "The Golden Notebook," relates a period of several weeks in which Anna and Saul Green go mad. The novel finishes with a final installment of "Free Women." The careful separations between the notebooks and the outer frame represent the disintegrated self, which the writer of "Golden Notebook" tries to heal. Part of the healing involves Anna owning her Shadow, in Jungian terms. Because of its negative nature, the psyche disowns the Shadow, and projects it on others. In Anna's case, her projection is a Dwarf who represents joy-in-destruction. By experiencing herself as this creature, Anna acknowledges that destruction is a necessary part of the artist's existence. In Nietzschean terms, destruction of the existing norms is necessary for the revaluation of all values, a process that constitutes the artist's role in modernity. One by one, her ideals reveal themselves as delusions, and Anna has to learn to accept this chaos as potentially productive. Without such disillusionment, an artist has not truly lived. Living is letting herself feel deeply, not shutting down in self-protection. Since the breakdown is productive, she prefers to call it a breakthrough. The multi-part structure of the novel is meant to reflect the psychic reality of fragmentation.

The frame story, "Free Women," depicts Anna and Molly's relationship, one that is constructed around their duties towards their children, Molly's ex-husband Richard, and Richard's second wife, Marion. The frame story is linear, and uses the conventional components of protagonist, antagonist, conflict, and resolution. Long-term friends whose principal affinity is their status as bitter divorced women, Molly and Anna help Marion leave Richard. Immediately after reading Anna's notebooks, Molly's son Tommy attempts suicide. Instead of dying, he blinds himself. This prompts his conversion into a radical-looking-for-a-cause, just the type of person that he had previously despised. Her desire to help her stepson immerses Marion in his causes, which has the positive effect of curbing her drinking. From exposure to the "free women" Anna and Molly, Marion finally acknowledges her repressed hatred of Richard. She leaves him, which enables him to marry his much younger secretary.

By the end of the book, the radicals have modified their course. Tommy grabs the economic opportunity provided by his tycoon father, training to become a progressive businessman. Molly finds another progressive business-man to marry. During the course of "Free Women," Anna has half a dozen affairs with men who cannot commit to her. Anna's journey through schiz-ophrenia with Saul enables her to write *The Golden Notebook*. Her mental breakthrough enables the "real" Anna to finish "Free Women," but Lessing has the fictional Anna give up writing and return to social work, because "I am too diffused" (61SS). Experiencing herself as multiple personalities, Anna loses the unifying voice needed to create fiction. In addition, the breakdown has made her aware that she needs to keep herself sane for her daughter, Janet.

Parallel to Anna's exploration of sexual relationships is her troubled involvement with the Communist Party, as told in the Red Notebook. Having been a committed Communist before Stalin's atrocities were revealed, Anna has great difficulty giving up her affiliation. To do so would force her to admit her despair of achieving a better world. The Party afforded her a sense of belonging to a collective, and a set of values that gave meaning to life. Yet the vagaries of the British Communist Party teach Anna that she must not tolerate its hypocrisy. The ironic pose of her fellow Communists, in which they tol-erated corruption for the sake of a noble goal, eventually lost its validity for Anna. As with the roles she plays in her personal life, Anna must learn to reject the political roles provided by her culture. It is a revelation to her that none of her peers dare say in a public meeting what they confide in private, that is, that the Stalinist regime is corrupt to the core. Learning to be truer to her knowledge of politics helps Anna to question the roles she plays in her romantic life. However, she is not as successful in giving up romance as she is the Communist Party; she repeats her pattern of choosing unavailable men, falling deeply in love, experiencing conflict, repressing her sense of self, and being left.

There are three parallel realms in which Anna questions her identity: romantic love, party politics, and writing. What is the truest way to represent reality, or can a writer ever represent reality, she asks? As Anna embarks on her journey of self-exploration, she becomes increasingly wary of the falsity of her nostalgic tone, but equally wary of its opposite, irony. In her revaluation of her highly successful novel, *The Frontiers of War*, Anna now perceives in its tone an embarrassing nostalgia for the innocence of her past as a twenty-three-year-old in Rhodesia, who was committed to Communist dogma, and ostensibly helping native Africans gain control of their lives, but actually only perpetuating colonialist stereotypes. Parallel to the simple, deceiving myths of Communist dogma, Anna finds that her five-year Jungian analysis with Mother Sugar is based upon monolithic myths and outdated archetypes that do not speak to Anna's time. Although Anna does not say it, Jungian myths focus on men, and do not provide an equivalent hero quest for women. The Blue Notebook contains Anna's attempts to write a truer voice. She uses a realist, documentary tone to straightforwardly report the events of her days. Paradoxically, she finds this style less truthful than one that includes her interpretation of events.

The second insincere pose that Anna wants to drop is irony, her "natural disposition towards the grimmest understanding of life and events" (*Walking* 43). Irony was an ego-defense against despair; all intellectual communists used it to survive. It helped them to deny the fact that Communist practices were corrupt. The ironic smile exchanged by two men in Anna's nightmare "cancels all creative emotion" by its insistence on status quo (345 SS). While proselytizing about the noble goals of the proletarian revolution, Russian officials use lying, torture, repression and murder to attain and keep their power. Anna's fellow members of the British Communist Party desperately seek to hold mutually contradicting narratives in their brains without cracking up. On the one hand, they know of the Party's corruption; on the other, they desperately need ideals, meaning, and order. Similarly, Anna uses irony to cover her depression about male-female relationships, her ability to write truthfully, and her faith in humanity. The Black Notebook contains notes about her Rhodesia days that became the romantic novel, *The Frontiers of War*, and her self-criticism about the falsity of her voice.

The Yellow Notebook tries to separate sexual politics from communist and artistic politics. It focuses on the novel Anna is writing, called *The Shadow of the Third*. In this novel, the protagonist Ella has much in common with Anna, as Anna does with Lessing. She is a writer involved with a disillusioned activist, a married psychoanalyst named Paul. The "shadow" of the title encompasses various archetypes that plague Ella: Paul's silently suffering wife; Anna's projection of an ideal wife; the ghost of Anna's previous lover; and Paul's negative side, which is critical, cold and cruel. As in "Free Women," it takes a man in *The Shadow of the Third* to pull the woman out of her despair, raising the question whether or not women are capable of healing themselves. By informing her that social workers are genetically programmed to care for others, Paul assures Ella that she is not alone. There is some universal force that gives social workers their roles in the universe. Though they cannot change the world, working for others is their "soul's necessity." Paul gives Ella the Myth of Sisyphus: "We are boulder-pushers. All our lives, you and I, we'll put all our energies, all our talents, into pushing a great boulder up a mountain. The boulder is the truth that the great men know by instinct, and the mountain is the stupidity of mankind" (182 SS). His certainty that boulder-pushers must do their work in spite of their knowledge of futility is like Anna's final revelation in the Golden Notebook section. Knowing that life is unfair, people unspeakably cruel, and pain the very condition of life, she must still value that "small seed of courage" that is the spark of life.

The Country Girls Trilogy *(1960, 1962, 1964;*
Epilogue, 1986), by Edna O'Brien

The trilogy opens in almost the same way as it ends. Its protagonist, Caithleen Brady (Kate), awakes with a jolt, terrified because her father has not come home. This can only mean he is on a bender; he will spend all their money, then come home and beat her and her mother. At the end of the book, Kate drowns herself, out of dread that her latest lover will never come home. After four troubling love relationships, Kate's life has lost meaning. If lovers can be as cruel as these four (and she believes their cruelty is her fault), then she must be doomed. Her best friend, Bridget Brennan (Baba), believes that Kate imbibed her Irish melancholy from her sad family and poor farm. Kate also believes that west Ireland defines her: "the swamp fields, the dun treeless bogs, the dead deserted miles of country with a gray ruin on the horizon: the places from which she derived her sense of doom" (494).

Growing up in 1950s County Clare, twenty miles outside Limerick, Baba and Kate demonstrate different ways of coping with rural isolation, poverty, family dysfunction, Catholic teaching, and the gender wars. While Kate thinks that love will solve everything, Baba is more calculating. Having a good time, nice things, and security are her goals. As far as Baba or the narrator let on, love is never expected. Baba's parents lack affection; her mother is a lush who likes to flirt with traveling salesmen, while her gentle father is often on call, wearing himself out in his duties as country veterinarian. O'Brien understands that daughters tend to repeat their mother's patterns, even when they mean to rebel. She makes both Kate and Baba's adaptations psychologically believable in the context of their family dramas. Kate's mother never stood up to her father; she drowned in an accident with a man who *might* have been her lover.

The Country Girls, Part One, develops Kate's dependent relationships with friends and family. Sure of her primacy, Baba treats Kate cruelly. Signaling her future behavior with lovers, Kate passively accepts Baba's cruelty and remains loyal to her. But Baba is not loyal to Kate; she tries to steal Kate's suitors. When their neighbor Mr. Gentleman pays court to Kate, Baba tries to wrest him away with lies. Fourteen-year-old Kate has also attracted the attention of sixty-year-old Jack Holland, publican and journalist, whose sexual games are predatory.

While pretending to visit her brother, Kate's mother drowns in the Shannon with another man, leaving Kate stunned. Rather than suffer her father's rage, Kate moves to Baba's house. Soon afterwards, she and Baba enroll in a convent school in another county. Relieved to be away from her father, Kate has to confront the reality that the Sisters are also cruel and narrow-minded. The food is disgusting, rules are hard, and unfair punishments abound; it is not long before Baba concocts an escape. Although Kate's scholarship is valid at any other convent, she rejects this avenue to independence because Baba wants to quit school and move to Dublin. Once the girls arrive in Dublin, Mr. Gentleman returns to court Kate. Mr. Gentleman shares many of the narcissistic traits of Kate's future husband. Gentleman is French and superior to the native Irish, while Eugene is Jewish and supercilious towards the locals. Both are older than Kate, reserved, withdrawn and melancholic. Gentleman begins to teach Kate about sexuality, but Kate romanticizes her affair. She is sure that sex means love, and that Gentleman will leave his wife. Instead, he jilts her on the banks of the Liffey, never showing up for a holiday he had promised.

The second book in the trilogy, *The Lonely Girl*, opens two years later, with Kate working the same job in a small grocery in north Dublin. She and Baba share the same room at the same rooming house. Only lovers have changed. Crashing a party, they meet Eugene Gaillard, documentary filmmaker. A leftwing liberal who produces films about squalor in the Third World, Eugene is using his profession to meet nubile actresses. He enjoys cynical American friends, who share his putdowns of the Irish. Not until they are several weeks into their affair does Kate find out that he is married. By then, she has spent chaste weekends at his country home, chaperoned only by the housemaid Anna. Convinced that his wife's departure for America makes him a free man, Kate determines to overcome her sexual fears. Catholicism has taught her to fear the sexual act, perhaps because it carries the possibility of unwed pregnancy. Kate does not experience physical desire. Never is Eugene presented as a kind man, but as a lover, he is gentle enough to gain her trust. She assumes that he is faithful, though she knows he loves less than she does. In the presence of his American friends, he mocks and then ignores her.

On New Year's Eve, Kate's drunken father shows up at her shop to rescue her and save the family honor. He kidnaps her and takes her back to Clare. Hoping for haven in Baba's house, Kate is chagrined to find that Baba's party-loving mother has converted to Catholicism. The village priest attempts to shame Kate into giving up Eugene. Her only friend, Jack Holland, concocts an escape. Arrived in Dublin, she runs to her lover's arms, only to find that her father is behind her. He and his three friends beat up Eugene until his housemaid fires a gun. Eugene blames the incident on Kate's rough Irish background, and she is not able to deny this fact. Soon, her emotional dependence becomes more than he can handle. Kate threatens to leave if he visits his American wife. He calls her bluff. Baba "saves" Kate from herself, making plans for them to start life over in London.

The third book, *Girls in Their Married Bliss*, takes place a few years later, in London. O'Brien shifts the viewpoint to Baba's voice, which has none of Kate's sentiment or sensitivity. Baba talks and thinks like a sailor. On the surface, she has not softened at all towards her friend since the days of playground taunts. Beneath her rough surface, Baba conveys the importance of having a sister in the gender wars. When Baba mocks Kate's romantic aspirations, we wonder whether she is trying to control her own, so that she will never get as hurt as Kate does in every relationship.

A year after their arrival, Eugene had followed the girls to London. He married Kate because she was pregnant. They had a son and lived unhappily in the suburbs. The condescension of the courting Eugene ("you have a fat bottom" ... "Do I love you? Ask me in ten years' time") gets even worse when he is married: "I must say it took me quite a time to get to know you. I must congratulate you on your simpleton's cunning, and your simpleton's servile ways" (404). Seeing his role as a Pygmalion, he despises the creature he created. Desperate for love, Kate begins to see another man, a local politician called Duncan. Although their affair is platonic, Eugene finds their love letters and increases his hostile attacks. Kate tries to leave him, but returns, begging for mercy. Abasing herself before him, she only succeeds in eliciting ever more hostile criticism. Baba thinks they are both insane, Kate with possessiveness, and Eugene with self-righteousness.

Baba is not immune to the fate of the Irish. Her husband is impotent, so Baba has sex with strange men. One is a pervert, who wants her to wear boots and cellophane while he singes her hair with a cigarette and kisses her teeth. Afterwards, Baba stalks him, to see if he will switch to normal sex. Kate finds a house to rent, but her son is so terrified by its drafts and leaks that he refuses to stay the night. Kate forces herself to socialize, but a disastrous one-night stand worsens her depression. The stranger takes her home, but leaves the room to be with another woman. When he returns, he accuses her of not loving him, but only wanting an orgasm. Kate is beginning to understand more about male psychology and her own reaction to male sexual behavior, but her new understanding cannot save her. One last affair is so hurtful that she gets sterilized so she'll never make the mistake of loving again. Of her operation, Baba remarks that "too much had been cut away, some important region that they both knew nothing about" (508). Neither had known love.

The *Epilogue* takes place twenty years later. Kate's son Cash is a "genius" at Harvard University. Kate works in a bookshop in a London suburb, until one last love affair unbalances her. Shortly before her suicide, she tells Baba of her apocalyptic dreams, in which Christians and Muslims fight with pools of blood as weapons. If she could get through "this last big breach," she feels she could make a change: do social work, read poems to prisoners, read Rilke (530). Not knowing exactly what precipitated the suicide, Baba imagines that Kate tried to go back to the man who had jilted her. Receiving one last rejection, she signed into a health farm and drowned herself. Meantime, Baba seduces a black man whom she calls Old Snowie. She offers him money for sex, which offends him. She is called home to care for Frank, who has had a stroke. Baba has no wisdom about Kate's demise, saying only "there are some things in this world you cannot answer" (532).

Communist and Catholic Hegemonies, the Abject Female, and Feminism

Under patriarchy, women tend to internalize the negative projections of femininity made by individual men and by cultural institutions such as church, state, and family. As Antonio Gramsci describes it, *cultural hegemony* is a process of consensus formation that shapes "the way things look, what they mean, and therefore what reality is for the majority of people within a given culture."[9] Starting at birth, humans absorb ideologies, taking them for truth. It requires effort and courage to untangle these belief systems. Our survival instinct tells us to obey, instead of to question. Adrienne Rich's term, *compulsory heterosexuality*, is a good example of this survival instinct in action. Individuals feel compelled by society to enact heterosexuality without questioning whether it is their true orientation.

I believe that the process of psychological *abjection* dramatizes this compulsory ideological formation (hegemony) in infants. The *abject* is "that which is cast off or away; refuse, scum, dregs. Figuratively, of persons" (OED). In theorizing the *abject*, psychoanalyst Julia Kristeva describes some of the most basic and universal activities of the psyche. The abject is both material and ideological. As material, it consists of objects, fluids, or smells that one's culture terms "disgusting," such as feces, blood, vomit, sweat, pus, menstrual blood or urine. As an activity, abjection is a means by which the psyche casts off unwanted otherness, whether otherness is defined as a series of human traits, or a person or group that embodies them. Abjection is a conscious psychological state of feeling abased, and wishing to fuse with others, which in turn is related to the death drive. It is also an *un*conscious psychological process by which the psyche tries to rid itself of unclean, debilitating things (certain thoughts, relationships, feelings, objects). This process of self-cleansing begins in infancy, and continues through life. An *abject* is a person who fails to form "active, ego-based, external objects of desire," and who persists as a "fascinated victim of abjection." An *inability* to perform abjection makes the *abject* person desire "to fuse with the Other rather than sustain a painful state of subjectivity and difference from the Other.... The other is projected as of one substance with the ego, that is, as maternal" (quoted in Coughlan 178).

It is interesting to note that infants see the mother, upon whom they depend, as harmful. In infancy, the self's first object-relation is with its mother. Before birth, it is attached to her body; after birth, it is attached through the process of nurturance. Psychologically, it is utterly dependent on her care for its survival. The mother is the agent of the baby's abjection process, for she is responsible for cleaning abject substances (feces, dirt, urine, vomit) from its body. The baby learns from the mother the importance of such abjection. As the baby grows, however, the mother becomes one of the objects *to be abjected*, so that the self can attain its own identity. In both Freudian (Oedipal) and Lacanian (mirror stage) individuation, the infant must break its identification with the mother in order to resolve the Oedipal complex (Freud) and enter the Symbolic Order (Lacan).[10] The father's role is to help the child separate from the mother, resulting in the formation of a superego, which is the internalization of parental and cultural rules and taboos. The abjection process is neither linear nor capable of completion, because the abjected material returns throughout life, in both conscious and unconscious manifestations.

In cultural life, the abjection process occurs on a collective level. In the 1930s, Georges Bataille described the abjection of the poor by richer classes. Class prejudice entails *abjecting* that which it perceives as literally unclean, and metaphorically contaminated. To the middle class, the working class is vulgar, immoral, and unstable; Communism reverses this order, projecting negative values on the bourgeoisie. The patriarchal institutions of Communism and Catholicism perform this hegemonic function of abjection. Catholicism has defined sex in terms of abjection, as that which is unclean, immoral, base, and threatening. It also draws rigid boundaries between male and female gender roles, so that the woman's role is to serve men, and her qualities are inferior to male ones. Communism's most abjected class is the *bourgeoisie*, so that bourgeois persons, attitudes, literature, religion, individualism and capitalism are undesirable. Communism ideology pathologizes these entities, making them into negative components of human experience, expelling them from its group-identity, and projecting them onto the Other.

Like individual abjection, socio-cultural abjection is an ongoing process. Privileged groups are always threatened and haunted by the categories they exclude. In Bataille's reading, an ideology requires the presence of the abject in order to sustain, by exclusion, the constructs of the symbolic order (Coughlan 179). Just as language is a system of meaning-making that operates by negations (*cat* is *cat* because it is not *dog*), so too do classes define themselves by what they are not. The middle class defines itself as *not* poor, *not* uncultured, *not* promiscuous, and so on. Gender is another construct that operates by opposition and negation. *Male* is privileged insofar as it defines itself as *not female*. The male infant attains a masculine identity by affiliating with the father, abjecting the mother, and abjecting its own feminine qualities. The female infant under patriarchy does the same, clearly with damaging results.

In her 2006 essay, "Killing the Bats: O'Brien, Abjection, and the Question of Agency," Patricia Coughlan describes O'Brien's internalization of Catholic misogyny. I am indebted to this brilliant essay for a fuller understanding of Kate's psychic processes. During O'Brien's childhood, Irish society prohibited women from acknowledging or experiencing desire, from questioning authority, from molding their own lives and identities. In *The Country Girls Trilogy*, Kate Brady imbibes Catholic-nationalist ideologies. In addition to the particular instance of her family dysfunction, Kate's psychic limitations are a product of Ireland's hegemonic constructs.

Ireland's repressive view of female subjectivity became entrenched over several centuries. Heather Ingman describes the process. As early as the seventeenth century, writers of *aislings* (poems) constructed Ireland as a woman victimized by an English male colonizer. In literature and propaganda, Ireland was personified as female: Mother Ireland, Cathleen ni Houlihan, the Poor Old Woman and the Dark Rosaleen were popular icons. After the Famine, religious iconography was added to the picture. The Virgin Mary became an important role model for Irish women, while men were to serve nation and religion by sacrificing their lives for pure, Irish womanhood. Standards of female behavior, particularly chastity, were linked to national identity. This gave women an important, albeit passive and prescriptive role as protectors of Ireland's reputation: "Ireland authenticated its Catholic identity largely through its women, and nationalism in Ireland became the language through which sexual control and repression of women were justified" (Ingman 254).

Kate Brady's difficulty in establishing her self-worth is directly related to the process by which women's sexuality and agency become abject in Irish social constructions of gender and nationhood. Compared to her girlfriend Baba, Kate takes Irish female abjection to a deeper level. She is what Kristeva calls a *deject*, a "borderline personality who dwells in abjection" (quoted in Coughlan 190). Masochistic sexuality is one aspect of a deject personality; a masochist performs sexually what she thinks is expected of her. "I felt no pleasure, only some strange satisfaction that I had done what I was born to do," says Kate of sex (316). Kate was "born" to serve men's needs. The Catholic-nationalist ideology imbibed at the mother's breast determined her behavior to such an extent that her only fulfillment was in obedience to these norms. As Patricia Coughlan cogently argues, Kate's adult sexual behavior can be traced to her failure to abject the maternal object in infancy. Instead of healthy individuation, Kate experiences an exceptionally strong longing to fuse with the Mother, combined with the conflicting desire to abject the maternal in order to construct her own subjectivity.

Kate's bond with her mother is stronger than any she experiences with a male. She seeks to replace her mother's love with a boyfriend's, yet her choices condemn her to dissatisfaction. Her object choices are cold men who resemble her father: old, cynical, melancholy, and dominant. Kate's desperate identification with her mother appears in the first pages of the novel: "I was always afraid my mother would die when I was at school" (9). "She was the best mama in the world ... she held me very close for a minute as if she would never let me go" (6). "My two greatest fears were that Mama would die of cancer and that Hickey would leave" (29). Cementing their bond, they would sleep in the same bed when her father didn't "need" his mother for himself. When her mother drowns, Kate has great difficulty processing her grief. "Somehow she was more dead than anyone I had ever heard of" (45) suggests that something of Kate's self dies along with her mother.[11] Like many children of alcoholics, Kate adopted an adult role of protecting her mother at an early age.

Reenacting her mother's submission to her father, Kate chooses sadistic love objects that enable her to enact her own death wish and self-abjection. Characteristic of her object choice is the distant man whom she can invest with divinity. Thus, she describes both Gentleman and Gaillard's faces as divine. Gentleman became "my new god, with a face carved out of pale marble and eyes that made me sad for every woman who hadn't known him" (57). Eugene's face "reminded me of a saint's face carved out of grey stone" (185). The need for abjection to a higher being is part of Kate's Catholic indoctrination. Like many Catholic girls, Kate thought of becoming a nun. When grown up, she transferred that need for self-sacrifice to her romantic relationships, always choosing men who would thrive upon her self-abasement.

Kate's relationships with Gentleman, Eugene, and Baba are sadomasochistic. Instead of being attracted to warmth and generosity, Kate chooses lovers and friends whom she fears. In childhood, Baba was the person she feared most, next to her father. Yet she continues to let Baba make her choices: "I had never made decisions in my life. My clothes had always been bought for me, my food decided on, even my outings were decided by Baba" (232). Even after she leaves the abusive Eugene, Kate still seeks to reunite with him, confusing fear for love: "She was still joined by fear, by sexual necessity, by what she knew as love" (454). Even though Kate knows of her own delusions, she is nonetheless compelled to seek her own destruction.

Although Kate displays a strong awareness of male and female differences, she lacks the feminist power to resist her temptations to debase herself before male authority. When Kate defines the feminine, it sounds like a mockery of patriarchy. She thinks, "Women care mostly for themselves or for their children, who are extensions of themselves, or for their husbands, who fill their days and their thoughts and their bodies" (349), implying that men are more compassionate than women (and turning the more common stereotype on its head). Kate laments being female: "I hate being a woman. Vain and shallow and superficial" (161). Yet her self-abjection, and her abjection of the maternal, forces her to adopt patriarchy's devaluation of female qualities. Kate critiques womanhood without understanding that it is socially and psychologically constructed. The novel demonstrates the magnitude of the obstacle that Irish Catholic constructions of womanhood present to feminist awareness and action in the most repressive decades of the century, the 1930s through the 1960s.

Despite her character's psychological limitations, Edna O'Brien activates feminist awareness by transmuting it into art. As a writer of female abjection, O'Brien creates characters that founder till they drown in their own abject. Yet these characters also experience moments of vision. Because of the unstable ego boundaries of the *deject*, she can become a "vessel for visions which creatively unfix and decenter the symbolic order" (Coughlan 190). *The Country Girls Trilogy* is the first product of O'Brien's writing career, and Kate is no visionary. In her later novels, Coughlan believes that O'Brien arrived at a point in which she could transcend abjection by staging it. The writer confronts her own abjection; the act of representing the abject in her work makes her both sane and feminist. Even though O'Brien disavows the feminist label, her texts do the work of unsettling patriarchy through a sustained examination of its deep psychological damages.

In contrast to O'Brien's childhood indoctrination, Doris Lessing finds her moral compass later in life, becoming Communist at seventeen. Psychologists believe that a person's fundamental temperament is developed much earlier than adolescence, and it is likely that Lessing's early childhood exposure to race discrimination primed her for her later espousal of Communism. Of the several groups who fought colonial racism in Rhodesia, including churches and the Labour Party, the Communist Party was the most active. Lessing had grown up with racial discrimination. Although her father was a kind man, Lessing would have known of the degraded conditions of his Black employees: "Their living conditions were patently abysmal. They were given only a day to build a makeshift hut and they were given meager foodstuffs in comparison to the white farmers. There was actually an ethnocentric assumption that the Africans' nutritional needs were less than the Europeans'" (Klein 43). Beating the workers was standard practice. When she moved to Salisbury, Lessing witnessed apartheid. The color bar denied blacks the vote. They could not join unions, be employed in commercial establishments, or enter restaurants and hotels. Lessing's early sense of her community's hypocrisy must have made Communist rhetoric particularly refreshing. "I can't remember any time in my life where I wasn't sitting looking at the grown-up scene and thinking, this must be some great charade they've all agreed to play" (Klein 43).

Her biographer believes that Lessing's early attachment to the Party stems from a need to escape her own family. Lessing herself believes that her attraction to Rhodesian Communism was emotional rather than intellectual. Klein writes of Lessing's psychological attachment to this new group:

> That Doris passionately agreed with the group's convictions enabled her to reconcile the conflicting pulls that had caused so many years of torment: the need to preserve her individuality, and the longing for connection. As a Communist she remained outside the social and political conformity of Rhodesian society that she had found impossible to accept. But now there were others standing beside her. Similarly, her double fears of dependency and isolation had lost their threatening power. Here she would not be isolated, here dependency was comradeship, built on strength, not weakness [74].

Lessing's political indoctrination came later than O'Brien's religious one, and was chosen instead of assigned. Nevertheless, Lessing's absorption of Communist ideologies predisposed her to reject feminism. When Communist politics exposed her to masculinist ideology and sexist practices, she identified with them, instead of critiquing them.

Anna Wulf's love affair with Communism and Communist men in *The Golden Notebook* dramatizes Lessing's complex psychological relationship with Communism and feminism. The parallel that Anna fails to draw between Communism and patriarchy is supplied by the text itself, which traces her conflicted gender roles alongside her conflicted party affiliation. It is up to the reader to apply the knowledge that Anna gains in the political arena to the personal one. Anna is highly conscious that the British Communist Party members only pretend to believe in the Russian Party's integrity. Privately, they confess their disenchantment. Anna is fascinated by Arthur Koestler's dictum, that any communist in the West who stayed in the Party after a certain date (probably in 1956, after Russia's suppression of the Hungarian Revolution and Khrushchev's denunciation of Stalin) "did so on the basis of a private myth" (169). Asking herself what her own private myth is, Anna decides she "must" believe that there is a body of people in the Soviet Union who are "biding their time" until they can "reverse the present process back to real socialism" (170). Although she would like to ask her friends what their myth is, she is convinced that they would lie. The togetherness that she had hoped to find in joining this noble cause is just another of its myths. Instead of joining her with other people, she realizes that her affiliation actually increases her isolation. "I joined the Party [with] a need for wholeness, for an end to the split, divided, unsatisfactory way we all live. Yet joining the Party intensified the split — not the business of belonging to an organization whose every tenet, on paper, anyway, contradicts the idea of the society we live in; but something much deeper than that" (171).

At the end of this passage, she doesn't define her inner "split." She drops the inquiry because her boyfriend is laughing at her efforts to understand the human soul. Neither one frames the split in terms of gender. Yet the reader easily sees that the "split, unsatisfactory way" in which she lives includes her repeated involvements with men who can give her no satisfaction. When Michael chides her, she feels both guilty and relieved that she can quit thinking. This passage is like many others in combining spoken debates about the problems of Communism with an unspoken exposure of the problems of man-woman relationships in patriarchy, without ever making an explicit link. In this particular instance, Michael mocks Anna for thinking so hard about an existential problem. While he may have joked with a male Party member about the same thing, he would not have condescended in the way he does with his female lover, whom he frequently addresses as "dear Anna." Anna never links the hypocrisies that she notices every day in her Communist friends, with the hypocrisies inherent in her relationships with men, or with those men's double standards towards women.

Anna's ability to analyze her psychological need for the Communist Party does not carry over to the sexual realm. She cannot productively analyze her need to submit to abusive relationships with men, or the ways in such submission is sanctioned by patriarchy. Although her breakdown gives her a clear realization of her masochistic sexuality, she still does not see female masochism as a problem of patriarchy. At one point, she even jokes that it is "megalomaniac" to think her problem might represent "the position of women in our time" (559). Doing so would be the beginnings of a feminist analysis, in which she could accept that her problems are not hers alone, but shared by many women. Instead, her main objective in this scene is to keep the differences between herself and Saul at a minimum, so that they can enjoy a night's sleep. If Anna gains one thing from her breakdown, it is the resolve to write the book, *Free Women*. This novel rewrites her affair with Saul, condensing it to six days, and giving Anna the power to end the affair. In the novel, Saul rescues Anna by breaking her obsession with global brutalities, and she rescues him by sleeping with him and empathizing with his schizophrenia.

Dream work is one powerful way in which Lessing adds psychoanalytic dimensions to the novel. One constant in the many dreams that constitute Anna's schizophrenia is the experience of men as stronger than women, a stereotype that feminisms seek to dispel. In one series of dreams, a man projects films written by "Anna" about her relationships. The projectionist mocks her nostalgic attitude to her past, insinuating that it is insincere. His masculinity disparages female sentimentality; as a man, he believes he has greater access to Truth, and substitutes his judgment for hers. This dream reflects Anna's tendency to let men dictate and moralize, without questioning whether women's morality is different from men's.[12] In another set of dreams, she transforms into various male fighters she has known or read about: the anti-apartheid hero Mr. Mathlong, the rebel Charlie Tremba, and an Algerian soldier. In her dreams, the fictional Paul and the real-life Michael merge as one super-strong, heroic Man. While she becomes different women too (a Chinese peasant; a bitter old white woman), these experiences do not resonate like her male impersonations. These dreams prove the extent to which Anna is male-identified.

Because of this internalized patriarchal judgment, Anna even thinks that crazy Saul is stronger than herself: "that man is a thousand times more courageous than you are," she says to herself (592). She thinks that the desire to "submerge" into insanity is a female trait: "Anna, you are betraying everything you believe in; you are sunk in subjectivity, yourself, your own needs" (592). This sentence contains the proscriptions of both Communism and patriarchy. To be "subjective," to care about your own needs, is both bourgeois (the bogey man of communism) and female. In one dream, Anna feels sorry for a caged tiger. Believing it is Saul, she wants to free that psychic force. Jungians would see the tiger as a symbol of strength, yet Anna misses the message from her unconscious that this strength is her own to claim.

One of Anna's strongest depictions of male narcissism is Saul's "I I I I" monologue. He can only speak (and think) in the first person. His male egotism blots out the rational elements of his discourse. Instead of turning her anger on him, or on the patriarchal conditioning that makes him believe that men are superior, Anna turns it on herself, mocking her own "female" weakness: "And now the whisky had weakened me and saddened me, and I felt in myself the weak, soft sodden emotion, the woman betrayed. Oh boohoo, you don't love me, you don't love, men don't love women any more" (606). While Anna can be funny in her self-mockery, she sells herself short, failing to take her "subjective, weak and womanly" feelings seriously. She abjects the emotional, self-pitying part of her, which she dubs "female."

Related to her conviction that men are stronger, Anna suffers from a rescue complex that makes men necessary to women, who cannot save themselves. Although Saul's schizophrenia is worse in duration and degree, Anna feels that only he can save them, because he is a man. When she realizes the destructiveness of their relationship, she tells him to end it, saying, "I ought to, but I'm not strong enough. I realize you're much stronger than I am" (598).

In Lessing's depiction of patriarchy, she lets the male speak for the female. For instance, Saul tells Anna what she learned during her own breakdown. He instructs her to laugh more. The accusation of over-seriousness is a common device used to shut down women's thinking when it is perceived as threatening. Saul also instructs her to write. In a gesture that can be seen as both generous and domineering, he writes the first sentence of her novel for her. As we see from the last chapter of *The Golden Notebook*, which is also Anna's final chapter of *Free Women*, breaking through her writer's block *is* exactly what saves her sanity. However, the paradigm of man-as-savior only replicates relationships of unequal power. While the text shows that Saul is more broken than Anna, the author chooses him to be the agent of the woman's change.

Anna's problems with men, Communism, and writing chase her in a never-ending circle. Anna's writer's block precipitates her engagement with Communism. The source of her writer's block is the Communist prohibition against writing "the personal," the very subject at which Anna excels. Her Communist colleagues don't believe in monogamy, but her unsettled love relationships precipitate her breakdown. During her schizophrenic dreams, she is visited by poor people in third world countries who ask, "Why aren't you doing something about us, instead of wasting your time scribbling?"

(614). These visitations fuel Anna's deep-seated Communist guilt about the nature of her "women's" writing. Although she wants Communism to save her, it only perpetuates her self-defeating behaviors.

Anna's internal prohibitions against valuing women do not stem only from her Communist indoctrination; she is also afraid to be lesbian. She is afraid of taking the ramifications of her masochistic sexuality seriously enough to do something about it. Anna rejects as lesbian what her intelligence tells her about men and women. She writes, "I was an Anna who invited defeat from men, without even being conscious of it.... I was stuck fast in an emotion common to women of our time, that can turn them bitter, or Lesbian, or solitary" (466). And again: "Women's resentment is the disease of our time" (321). Gay and lesbian sexuality repelled Lessing. If lesbianism appeared the only alternative to Anna's problematic relationship to men, then she would blame herself for not understanding men. Devaluing or diminishing the importance of men was not an option for Anna.

Turning to the Irish world of Kate Brady, we note that one of the most prominent differences between Anna Wulf and Kate Brady is their fate. Lessing lets Anna live, even healing her to some degree by her writing and caring for her daughter. Conversely, O'Brien kills Kate, not finding any way to heal her. Killing the heroine is a common ploy of women writers to suggest that free-thinking women are too dangerous to survive patriarchy. Authors sometimes kill awakened women who "will not accept an adulthood that denies profound convictions and desires" (*The Voyage In* 46). Kate Chopin kills the heroine in *The Awakening,* who has dared to leave her marriage and have an affair. Elizabeth Bowen kills the heroine in *To the North,* who is fatally attracted to a cad. Virginia Woolf kills the heroine of *The Voyage Out,* who is about to marry a hopeless idealist. George Eliot kills the heroine of *The Mill on the Floss,* whose intellectual fervor and romantic idealism challenge regional norms. Olive Schreiner kills her heroine of *The Story of an African Farm* because she refuses to marry the father of her child. Edith Wharton kills the heroine of *The House of Mirth* because she contradicts the social code. In line with these examples, Edna O'Brien kills Kate because her idealization of heterosexual love makes her real life impossible.

In the *Country Girls Trilogy,* there is a doomed quality to Kate's experience from the first page, where she is fearful of her father's rage, and afraid her mother will die. As she matures, the masochistic nature of her involvement with Mr. Gentleman foreshadows the relationship with Eugene Gaillard. Kate's abjection of the maternal and the feminine, her self-abjection before chosen friends and lovers, and her inability to learn from her failures, all combine to make her breakdown and suicide believable. Without pointing a finger at the Catholic Church, O'Brien expresses Kate's indoctrination by this woman-fearing, male-dominated, guilt-provoking institution. Yet the Catholic Church never stands alone in analyses of Ireland's repressive ambiance. As we have seen, hegemonic discourses combine to make powerful restrictions on Irish women. Catholicism defines womanhood as domestic, pure, and obedient; the Irish nation adds a legal imperative that keeps them in the home (the Constitutional Amendment of 1937).

In contrast to Kate, Anna Wulf conceptualizes her breakdown as a breaking through. To cure Anna would strain the reader's credulity, but Lessing allows Anna visions and actions, like finishing her novel, that at least unblock her from paralyzing depression. Anna is unwilling to conceptualize her women's problems within a social framework of patriarchy. Yet Lessing gives her greater control over her fate than Kate, impelling her towards social connection at the end of the novel (new job, new political party, new volunteer work) instead of further isolation. Although the failure of Communists to produce a workers' state is what depresses Anna to the point of breakdown, she does continue to participate in social institutions. In comparison, Kate is isolated. Before her suicide she lives alone, works in a bookshop, and has dropped out of school. Communist ideology had trained Anna to devalue her own womanly experience, but it had given her positive opportunities as well, such as a vehicle to express her idealism, and a forum to share her deepest dreams with others. Kate's self-absorption may be partly a result of her Catholicism. I wouldn't want to posit Eugene as a knower of Truth, but his condemnation of Kate's religion as egocentric is interesting: "Only egomaniacs see Christ as God come especially to save them" (328). Even though Catholicism is not purely individualistic (indeed, it stresses the importance of communion in the worship of Christ), Eugene may have a point. Catholicism also stresses the maintenance of the cleanliness of one's soul, a project that is likely to isolate the individual.

Like many women writers, O'Brien and Lessing disavow their allegiance to feminist ideas. Yet each demonstrates profound awareness of the ways in which women's identity is constructed by patriarchy's expectations. *The Golden Notebook* spurred large numbers of men and women to reexamine their marriages and sexual relationships, but Lessing scorned publicity, because she did not want to be seen as a liberator of women. Such was not the goal of the Communist revolution. In contrast, O'Brien received negative press: she was an embarrassment to certain feminists for exposing the sadomasochism of many women engaged in abusive relationships. She was also an embarrassment to certain Irish conservatives, who resented the exposure of the hypocrisies of Irish institutions. Yet she would not assume a feminist viewpoint, instead asserting that men and women were both to blame for inequality. Her texts elicit instant recognition in Irish readers who have lived the experiences of her characters; they speak directly to a large proportion of the population. Because *Country Girls Trilogy* and *The Golden Notebook* create communities of men and women readers who discuss them and the patriarchies they unveil, I maintain that there is a powerful feminist content and feminist effect in both of the novels. They speak eloquently of the high costs of living in systems in which women identify with and internalize the misogynistic values of Catholicism and Communism.

CHAPTER FIVE

Turn of the 21st Century: Individualist and Communal Values in Fay Weldon's *Big Women* and Nuala O'Faolain's *My Dream of You*

Synopsis: The polarity of these two novels illustrates opposite directions that much literary feminism has taken in Ireland and Britain. While the characters in both books confront feminism after the Fall from the idealistic Eden of 1968, they do so in radically different ways. By giving emphatic voice to feminism's critics, Weldon mourns the death of idealism. Unlike O'Faolain, she doesn't raise a phoenix out of its ashes. O'Faolain's phoenix is the therapeutic journey inward to self, and back to Ireland. In embracing an ethnic identity she had too emphatically renounced, the protagonist confronts the repressed Irishness that is eternally returning to haunt her. In a perfect illustration of intersectionality, Cait can only heal her masochistic sexuality by positively identifying as Irish and being proud of it. The feminist impulses of these authors are different. Weldon uses the bludgeon of sarcasm to mask her mourning. O'Faolain demonstrates the third-wave belief that feminism also means a personal quest to confront the bogeyman within.

Historical Background

By the turn of the twenty-first century, three decades have passed since feminism's second wave. In both Britain and the United States, the movement fragments, prompting the press to claim the movement is dead. The backlash blames feminism for such general ills as women's tiredness and dissatisfaction, the increased incidence of rape,[1] and even for war itself.[2] Margaret Thatcher, Prime Minister from 1979 to 1990, heralded a new era of individualistic capitalism that did not advance feminism. In 1987, she asserted this ideology in the bizarre statement, "There is no such thing as society: there are individual men and women, and there are families" (Redfern 9). In the employment arena, Britain's 1975 Equal Pay Act had little effect on equal pay. Most women workers were employed in jobs that men shunned. In cases where a man and woman were doing the same job, an employer could skirt the legislation by re-classifying the woman's job.[3] As feminism took up a stronger position inside the academy than outside, activists worried that its political edge was blunted. The victory of establishing women's studies as a discipline had the cost, according to Imelda Whelehan, of "allowing the academic mainstream to forget feminism's political function within the academic institution" (134).

To discuss women writers in the third wave, and specifically in the turn-of-the-century period, I chose two women whose birth dates (Weldon in 1931, O'Faolain in 1940) signal their belonging, age-wise, to the second wave. However, in their turn-of-the-century novels, these two writers demonstrate timely trends in feminist thought in the two countries. Had I chosen younger writers who came of age in the eighties and nineties, I could have written about Zadie Smith (b. 1975), whose *On Beauty* was shortlisted for the Man Booker prize in 2005, and Irish writer Anne Enright (b. 1962), who won the Man Booker prize for *The Gathering* in 2007. However, Smith's work prioritizes male points of view, and finds questions of race more compelling than gender, like many post-feminists. In *The Gathering*, Anne Enright's subject is similar to Nuala O'Faolain's, insofar as she uncovers the guilt, repression, hostility, and abuse of an Irish family. However, the feminist emphasis is not nearly as strong.

For a British writer, I choose Fay Weldon because she typifies a trend in third-wave feminism; a former leading figure, she later recants her beliefs, blaming feminism for various social ills and for men's low self-esteem. In this reversal, she is similar to Germaine Greer and Betty Friedan, big-name second-wave feminists who have retracted some of their positions, confusing their adherents and feeding the delight of those media who portray feminism as a cause destroyed by its own infighting.

On the Irish side, I choose Nuala O'Faolain because her brand of confessional feminism typifies a late-century way of making the personal political. However, her determination to be painfully open and honest about her own pitfalls, deep needs, and vices differentiates her brand of honesty from a younger set of American third-wave feminists, whose bold confessions attempt to rationalize the subjectivity of the individual as a new, empowered stance. For instance, in *to be real* (1995), Rebecca Walker, self-proclaimed embodiment and founder of the Third Wave,[4] compiles an anthology of personal testimonies of the "new" feminism. Her requirement of contributors was simply that they be "personal, honest, and record a transformative journey taken." Eschewing an academic approach, Walker prefers personal testimonies "because they build empathy and compassion, are infinitely more accessible than more academic tracts, and because I believe that our lives are the best basis for feminist theory" (xxxvii). Walker struggles with the feminist label, because "it is tedious to always criticize world politics, popular culture, and the nuances of social interaction" (xxxiii). Yet at the end of her Introduction, she wonders whether her eschewal of public issues makes her a bad feminist: "What about the politics? What about the activism that people need to hear about?" (xxxix). She decides that had she written the book she "*should* have written," with "an incisive critique of the patriarchy," it would "not help her to learn more about herself, and thus about the nature of female empowerment" (xl). So, she sacrifices theorization because she believes it will not teach her about herself. Many American third-wave feminists share Walker's focus on the self. *Choice* and *empowerment* are their buzzwords; they find empowerment in their freedom to choose how to style themselves as feminists, whether they are "curious about pornography, attracted to a stable domestic partnership, desire to start a business and pursue traditional individual power, are interested in the world of S/M, and love people who flatly oppose their feminist beliefs" (xxx).

In contrast to such concerns, O'Faolain's brand of confessional feminism interrogates both her own psyche and the Irish culture that spawned her, in order to understand why she feels compelled to make choices that harm not only her feminist ideals, but also her basic wellbeing. Unlike leading third-wave American feminists, however, O'Faolain does not feel empowered by the sexual choices she has made. Like them, she recognizes that women from different walks of life experience and express their feminism differently. For instance, for the BBC and the RTE (*Radio Telefís Éireann*), she intentionally sought to interview women from marginalized groups such as the elderly and the poor, putting their voices on the air because she knew that she could not accurately represent them by speaking for them.

Regarding sexuality, Irish third-wave feminism has a character of its own, more similar to second-wave concerns about female objectification than third-wave concerns about free speech and sexual expression. Because female sexuality has been repressed for so long in Ireland, the so-called sex-positive trend of third-wave feminism has not been as prominent there as in Britain and the United States. Pornography and prostitution thrive in Ireland, as elsewhere, and leading feminists address this issue. At the 2010 Kilkenny Arts Festival, a forty-year feminist retrospective featured three speakers, Nell

McCafferty, Catriona Crowe, and Margaret MacCurtain, in a discussion of "Where we are, where we have been, and where we are going." The focus of their talks was first- and second-wave feminism; of the three speakers, only Crowe, archivist and former president of the Women's History Association of Ireland, addressed the sex-positive concerns of the third wave. She named pornography, sex trafficking, and vulgar commercialism as the three most serious problems facing feminists today. She dispensed with third-wave "choice" and "empowerment" arguments with characteristic Irish humor: "There's not a lot we can do about this [widespread use of pornography], except not to let ourselves be fooled by shallow assertions of so-called empowerment for women from this type of stuff. If turkeys could vote, some of them would actually vote for Christmas."[5] Leaving her audience with an optimistic message for the future, she said:

> A lot of the bad stuff [in today's movement] is around sex. Can we combine freedom of sexual expression for women with opposition to blatant, brutal, fabulously lucrative exploitation of our bodies? I think we can. I think it's time it got cool again to refuse sex to anyone unless you actually want to do it. I think it's time it got cool again to celebrate the female in her many manifestations, not just the horrible Barbie doll created by the porn industry.

The last few decades of Irish feminism find most energy in the academy, where contributions of Irish women writers and activists are being reclaimed. Crowe maintains that Irish women's history is thriving, despite attacks on women's history centers in some Irish universities.[6] She gives credit to the editors of Volumes IV and V of the *Field Day Anthology of Irish Writing: Irish Women Writing and Traditions*, which came about because of feminist outcry at the original *Anthology*'s exclusion of women. To compile this 3200-page addendum, eight women scholars commissioned over fifty editors to construct the entire history of Irish women writers from medieval times to the present. When the *Dictionary of Irish Biography* was published in 2010, its editors had learned a lesson from the Field Day fiasco, and included as many women as possible in its nine-volume expanse. Summing up the progression of Irish feminism between 1995 and 2005, Rebecca Pelan remarks on a shift in focus: "a significant part of feminist activity today involves a form of institutionalized vigilance to resist the erosion or depoliticization of those women's issues that have already entered the mainstream of social and political life, while topics of ethnicity and (anti)racism have overtaken feminism with a sense of urgency" (134). A sense of nostalgia for radical politicization of women's issues, which Ireland experienced during the second wave, permeates Pelan's and other historians' comments.

Lives of the Writers

Fay Weldon's Life as Told in Auto da Fay *(2002)*
and Mantrapped *(2004)*

In her 2002 autobiography, *Auto da Fay*, Weldon attributes some of the chaotic unpredictability of her life to the fact that she lived through a major earthquake in 1931 while still inside her mother's womb. This disaster set a pattern for her entire life, of long periods of boredom punctuated by crises. Another life pattern was one she inherited from her female relatives, that of marrying for economic convenience. "Women betray their daughters," she writes, by marrying philanderers who will not provide a lasting home. Weldon's own father, Frank Birkinshaw, disappeared when the earthquake destroyed their New Zealand home, only to reappear three months later. Weldon's mother was "clever, determined, and tough"; she worked in the kitchen of a sheep farm until Frank came back to claim his family.

Like Germaine Greer and Doris Lessing's fathers, Weldon's father suffered PTSD caused by his military service. Weldon believes that Frank passed on his emotional stoicism to her. Weldon's habit of deflecting the pain in her own life, through humor and denial, supports her theory (30). In discussing the most difficult events of her life, she tends to blame her mistakes on naïveté or sex drive, and to make a joke about herself. Her father Frank was charming, sociable, and pragmatic. He met his future wife, Margaret Jepson, because he had charmed her parents at a nightclub so thoroughly that they took him home. Edgar Jepson was an astrologist, writer of popular novels, and philanderer; his son, Selwyn, was a well-known mystery writer and screenwriter. The Jepson house was a gathering place for bohemians whose names read like a syllabus of Modern British Literature. H.G. Wells, Rebecca West, Ford Madox Ford, Jean Rhys, Violet

Fay Weldon (Photofest).

Hunt, George Bernard Shaw, Ezra Pound, Arnold Bennett, Joseph Conrad, Walter de la Mare, and Arthur Machen frequented Fay Weldon's mother's home. But rather than adulating them, Fay's grandmother criticized these writers, perhaps teaching Fay to question the authority of the English canon of literature and to write, instead, in her own uniquely irreverent style.

By the time Fay was three, Margaret was fed up with Frank's philandering. She returned home to England, intending to send for her daughters once she found work. In Margaret's absence, several women shared Frank's bed. Nobody told Fay why her mother had left, or whether she would return. Only when four-year-old Fay contracted polio, did her mother return. On her six-week steamer voyage back to New Zealand, Margaret penned her first romance, *Via Panama*. Yet her real passion was a more serious subject; for years, she worked on a book about the relationship between morality and aesthetics. Realizing the high intellectualism of her mother, Weldon began to see her mother and herself as opposite sides of a whole, where Fay represented the flesh and Margaret, the spirit. This polarizing view of her closest relationship expresses Weldon's tendency to create characters as abstractions in her fiction.

When Fay was six, her father left for the North Island, to become medical superintendent of a rural area that Weldon remembers with fondness. She and sister Jane spent summers there for six years. Back home in Christchurch, life was chaotic. Child support payments were often late, Margaret's wages never sufficient, and frequent moves were necessitated by the fluctuations in her pay. Just as Weldon saw the contrasts between her mother and herself, she felt a split between herself and her sister, who was quieter, prettier, and better liked by teachers. Given her mother's spiritualism and her sister's incipient mental illness, Fay became the caretaker of the small, female family. She was expected to cheer them up during times of crisis. The arrival of Margaret's mother, Nona, brightened the atmosphere with her piano playing and tales of the famous writers at Adelaide Road. But Nona had a darker side, too. Abandoned by Edward for his mistress, she subsequently abandoned her own daughter Faith, who had become schizophrenic after incestuous sexual abuse by her uncle. Impressed by these early examples, Weldon vowed never to abandon her own family; this may explain in part her long marriage to Ron Weldon.

Fay was very sociable at school, but frequent disruptions hurt her relationships. At thirteen, she was close to the school's star pupil, Molly Banks, but the teachers saw their affection as unnatural, and even Margaret accused her daughter of lesbianism. Weldon's despair at her mother's disapproval made her suicidal for several weeks. During this period, she lost all trust in her mother. The event was deeply shocking, and began a pattern in her life, in which periods of healthy contentment would alternate with "the grey desolation of limbo," where she was stuck in "the dead lava landscape" (134–5). Her psychoanalyst later diagnosed her condition as masochism and low self-esteem; note that Weldon is the third author of my study suffering from these conditions. Weldon's visions of death and greyness suggest that depression played a role as well — a quite natural response to the number of crises that she experienced in her life.

In 1946, an event occurred that would literally change Weldon's landscape for good. Upon receiving a nine-hundred-pound legacy from her aunt, Margaret decided instantly to leave New Zealand for London. Because of Fay's attachment to her father, stepmother, and friends, she looked upon this move as the end of her life. Newsreels showed London as an ugly, bombed-scarred, grey city (like the grey limbo of her depressive inner landscape) — the same apocalyptic London that Doris Lessing would move to, three years later. Always more practical than her mother, Weldon knew they didn't have enough money to move. On her farewell visit, Weldon wanted to beg Frank to keep her in New Zealand, but she couldn't find the courage to ask. Adding to her trauma, they landed in London on Fay's fifteenth birthday, which nobody remembered. That night, Weldon promised herself to "get the better of this town."

The next three years see Margaret, Jane and Fay living in a series of dingy rooms. Margaret may be poor, but she makes sure that the girls get a good education. Fay begs to go to the South Hampstead School for Girls, which prepares females for Oxbridge careers. But she loses her chance by changing majors too often. Another disappointment is that her peers ostracize her for being on scholarship. By using her given name, Franklin, Fay manages to get into the University of St. Andrews. But Weldon's proud entrance into the adult world of university and independent living was marred by news of her beloved father's death in New Zealand.

At university, Weldon is still unpopular. As a boost to her confidence, she sleeps with the first boy who offers, who happens to be her roommate's boyfriend. Today, Weldon is still haunted by this relationship, not because she stole her friend's boyfriend, but because he committed suicide. Young Fay must have been wondering, "Do I ruin everything I touch?" Uninterested in her studies, Weldon vows never to talk to a professor. This was no problem for her misogynistic philosophy professor, since he refused to speak to women students on principle. Yet it was from his class that Weldon learned a form of dialectical argument that typifies her voice. In speaking and writing, Weldon adopts an extreme position, in the expectation that her interlocutor will counter, and that the debaters will modify each other's view till they arrive at a synthesis. Instead, her extreme statements often infuriate people; her fiction is full of them, often propounded by an intrusive narrator.

Although she claimed a disinterest in academics, Weldon's studies in economics and psychology strongly influenced her philosophy of life. She often views feminism in the context of economics, saying that women's entry into the workforce was not necessarily good for the economy, as it drove wages down. From her psychology professor Cyril Burt's work on twins, she developed a fascination with the effects of biology and environment on character formation, very apparent in the psychoanalytic components of her fictional characterizations.

In 1952, Weldon graduates from St. Andrews, and moves to London. After a few low-paying service jobs, she lands a good job at the Foreign Office's Information Research Department. Her friends set her up with Colyn Davies, a folk singer and nightclub bouncer, who woos her with bad poetry and the story of his dysfunctional upbringing. When Weldon gets pregnant, Davies offers marriage, but she turns him down because she does not want to be the wife of a pipe-fitter. To avoid scandal, her mother advises her to quit her job. Briefly, Fay, her mother and sister live together in Saffron Walden, trying to run a bakery.

The next period of her life is one that Weldon would like to forget. She shares a London bed-sit with her mother, working as advice columnist, advertising copywriter, and pollster, all at lower wages than her male counterparts. Finally, Weldon decides she must marry someone, in order to prevent the State from taking away her child. Ronald Bateman is twenty-five years older, with a respectable job as headmaster in a technical college in Acton. His only reason for marrying is to attain the appearance of respectability. Bateman doesn't like sex, but he is a voyeur and sadomasochist, who encourages his wife to sleep with other men for payment. Although Bateman finds Fay a job in a strip club, she stops short of prostitution, because "she would rather give it away for free than feel indebted to those who paid her" (309). Finally, she runs away from Bateman and has an affair with a married advertising man, who finds her a job in the industry where she proves most successful. At a party, she meets antiques dealer Ron Weldon, and they marry.

Fay likes Ron because his bohemian ways remind her of her father. He is also like her mother, because he could read her thoughts, and he took the moral high ground. As a condition of marriage, Ron makes her undergo psychoanalysis. Although Ron and Fay enjoy a happy honeymoon period, his thirteen-year-old daughter rejects Fay as stepmother. Weldon's description of what Ron probably found attractive about her reveals her low self-esteem:

> She was educated but not too bright, so far as could be observed. She was well-read, easy-natured, six years younger than he was, a good earner, albeit in advertising, had a child of her own, and so would be responsive to his. A port-and-lemon good-time girl, relatively unsophisticated, so he

could teach her wine, music, politics. She spoke softly, moved softly, did not irritate overmuch, would cook and clean and look after his house, while not moving his things, and was no sort of rival [340].

What seemed promising to Fay Weldon in 1961, reads like a recipe for disaster to readers today, but after her feminist phase was over, Weldon longed for the simplicity of the age when "men proposed and men disposed," and silent marriages were the norm. She regrets the loss of mystery and power in our current "therapized" age, when men and women spill the contents of their hearts and minds to each other in an effort to make their marriages egalitarian and intimate.

Auto da Fay (2002) ends with the arrival of son Daniel, but Weldon's life-story continues in her autobiographical novel, *Mantrapped* (2004). To justify the combination of biography and fiction, Weldon compares contemporary readers to consumers of reality TV. Readers like to know the author's life story. The protagonists of the novel are a man and woman who accidentally swap souls as they brush by each other on a narrow stairway. With this premise, Weldon might be parodying Virginia Woolf's *Orlando*, or perhaps this fictional androgyny helps Weldon to understand Ron. The memoir portion of *Mantrapped* tries to see the problems of the Weldon marriage from both sides, since Weldon does not like to blame men for bad relationships. The term *mantrapped* is used to describe women's plight in love. They may be able to see the sins and weaknesses of their man, but are helpless to leave him (much the same as Lessing and O'Brien described entrapment in their relationships). Also, they are destroyed if he leaves them. Ron and Fay separated several times before ending their thirty-year marriage.

In 1991, Weldon was invited to a psychoanalytic conference to present a paper on archetypes in literature. This experience solidified her convictions about the corruption of therapists. She was shocked to witness a group of therapists deciding to split up a couple that had been together for decades. She believed that therapists treated human lives as though they were fictional; they played God, and turned people's lives into narratives, giving them the ending that their training suggested (191). From this point on, Weldon becomes strongly anti-therapy. In many novels, she satirizes therapists and therapeutic ideas. In the meantime, Ron obeys the advice of his own therapist, to split up with Fay and marry the therapist. This was just one of Ron's many affairs. On the very day of his divorce from Fay, Ron dies of heart failure. One of Weldon's novels couldn't have timed it better.

Fay's writing success was an area of contention in the marriage. Ron had not known or suspected that she would be so successful. He called her books "trash," and assumed that she neglected the children because of her attachment to writing. Even before she began writing novels and screenplays, the family lived on Fay's income, not Ron's. Fay's output was large, entailing thirty novels, six collections of short stories, five non-fiction works, numerous plays and screenplays, and magazine and newspaper articles. In addition to publication, many honors came her way. *Praxis* was shortlisted for the Booker Prize in 1979; she was Chair of the Booker Prize in 1983; she was awarded the Commander of the British Empire in 2001. Meantime, Ron was just an antiques dealer.

Upon Ron's death in 1994, Weldon married her agent, Nick Fox. They live in an 1840s townhouse in Shaftesbury, Dorset, where Weldon has given a number of interviews. At least four interviewers for *The Guardian* and *The Telegraph* independently expressed their confusion about Weldon's intentions. When she criticized feminism, the interviewers did not know whether to take her seriously. In 2009, Elizabeth Grice commented, "It is part of her persona now to appear ever so slightly daffy."[7] Grice believes that Weldon uses her plumpness and her sense of humor as a "convenient disguise for her clever-ness." However, Weldon's body type and her giggle have not managed to deflect hostility from feminists over Weldon's views on rape. In a 1998 inter-view, Weldon said that rape is not the worst thing that can happen to a woman. She would like to see rape "deglamorized" by returning it to the category of aggravated assault. Contrary to Catherine MacKinnon and Andrea Dworkin's views, Weldon believes that rape is more about sex than power. About a sexual assault upon her in a taxi, Weldon comments, "that man simply wanted sex."[8] Also problematic for feminist audiences is Weldon's idea that men are the "casualties" of the gender wars. She believes that women cause men unnec-essary suffering because their expectations are too high, and that most men are bent upon pleasing women: "It is a rare man who dares to ill-treat a woman." She feels sorry for men, because women treat them as sex objects.[9]

Recently, Weldon had a near-death experience, which made her take stock of her life. She decided that she felt guilty about her contribution to the women's movement: "The contemporary culture is partly my fault. If you shift the balance in gender, you feel a vague responsibility."[10] Weldon feels that feminism undermines men, and is therefore not worth it.

Nuala O'Faolain's Life as Told in Are You Somebody? *(1996) and* Almost There *(2003)*

The subtitle of O'Faolain's first memoir, *The Accidental Memoir of a Dublin Woman*, captures the recurring theme of chance in her life. Through-out the narrative, she builds a list of blessings, without which she feels she would have lived the typical life of a poor Irish woman from a family of nine children, an alcoholic mother, and an absent father. These blessings include her Catholic boarding school; her patronage by three people (an unnamed Jesuit priest who gave her school fees; an older doctor friend who looked after her during university; Sean Mac Réamoinn, a fellow broadcaster and Irish culture enthusiast); not marrying or having a child by her first boyfriend, Michael; the patronage of labor historian Raphael Samuel at Oxford; and the 1973 Merriman Summer School in west Clare. Despite many tragedies and disappointments in her life, includ-

Nuala O'Faolain, 1996 (photographer Paddy Whelan, courtesy *The Irish Times*).

ing depression and drinking, O'Faolain manages to start each new phase of her life with optimism, gratitude, and humor.

Born in 1940 Dublin, the second of nine children, O'Faolain was lucky to come early in the birth order, as her parents' neglect grew much worse after their third child. Writing as Terry O'Sullivan for Dublin's *Evening Press*, Tomas O'Faolain rose from the working class by using his charm and wit. Although Nuala saw her father's glamorous public life as a charade, she also learned how to put on a pose. Being a *bon vivant* was not only part of his job, but a welcome escape from the complaints of his lonely, depressed wife and too many children. In her memoir, O'Faolain tells that she forgave her parents once she realized that, given their limited choices, she would have become just like them. By humanizing them, she is able to let go of her anger.

Without a functioning mother, O'Faolain's childhood was chaotic. Despite their small lodgings, cousins crowded in the kids' bedroom, and neighborhood boys would sneak into their beds without the parents' notice. The children slept on the floor, under coats. Because Mrs. O'Faolain assigned her three eldest daughters specific roles, they did not develop self-confidence in other areas. Gráinne, the eldest, was the pretty one, Nuala the brainy one, and Deirdre the nice one. At least one benefit of being called brainy was that Nuala was a feminist from the time she knew what it meant.

Her first "blessing" was being sent to a boarding school at fourteen, after expulsion from public school for walking with boys. Her mother got her into St. Louis's Convent in Monaghan, on the Northern Ireland border, while her father sold his car to subsidize her education. Perhaps O'Faolain counts convent school a blessing because she fears if she hadn't been supervised, she would have been pregnant. In 1950s Ireland, that meant either early marriage or social ostracism: "Lives were ruined at that time, thousands and thousands of them, quite casually, by the rules the patriarchy made for young women" (52). Although she was a feminist, O'Faolain experienced typical Catholic guilt about her sexuality. She recounts her shock when an acquaintance unexpectedly shoved his way into her during a petting session. As penance, she briefly considered a vocation as a nun, but the more lasting effect was that she was "enthusiastic with boys from the waist up, but the rest of me was so self-conscious that I wouldn't even say that I wanted to go to the Ladies" (40). Even in middle age, a sense of shame for her female body continued to resurface.

At University College Dublin on scholarship, O'Faolain pursued English literature, finding a passion for American male poets. Like Weldon, she was far more interested in social than academic life. In the late fifties, Dublin sported a strong bohemian subculture. Heavy-drinking writers would party and sleep at poet Leland Bardwell's basement flat, where Nuala for a brief period slept in the same room as alcoholic poet Patrick Kavanah. It was a new dawn of cosmopolitanism after the provincialism of De Valera's reign. Everyone shared their literary projects, acting out plays and correcting each other's drafts. When O'Faolain entered professional life, she would miss this collective aspect of working.

Being caught up in her social life, O'Faolain missed her first-year exams. Losing her scholarship, she had to support herself by washing dishes at a London hospital, an experience that would lead to her first depression. Novelist Mary Lavin helped her to study for exams, while her Jesuit patron paid her school fees, enabling her to re-enroll at UCD. After graduation, her active social life paid off, when the well-known broadcaster Sean Mac Réamoinn asked her to write for Radio Éireann. O'Faolain's early writing was as conservative as that of her compatriots. Although Dubliners were beginning to watch foreign films and read foreign literature for the first time since the Free State, their point of reference was still Catholic. O'Faolain was no exception; her first published essay was on the visual references to the Via Dolorosa in Bergman's *Wild Strawberries*.

Under the aegis of her Old English professor, O'Faolain applied for a scholarship in Medieval English at the University of Hull. The greatest challenge in going to England was moving away from her first serious boyfriend, Michael. Because she had experienced orgasms with him, she believed that their love was true, and that Michael would immediately divorce his wife and marry her. In retrospect, O'Faolain understands the typical self-delusions of young Irish women of that time. Even though she knew how miserable her mother was made by her young marriage and too many children, O'Faolain believed that the same could not possibly happen to her. She followed the elation of her orgasms to the next logical step; marriage could be the only right outcome of passion.

After just one year at Hull, O'Faolain returned to Dublin to be with Michael. As this relationship deteriorated, she had several short affairs and one-night stands with professors, poets, and drinkers. The astounding success of *Are You Somebody?* stems largely from the candor with which O'Faolain admits to such behavior; she challenges an Irish cultural taboo on speaking about women's sexuality. Thousands of readers told her that they admired her courage in breaking that taboo. Once she goes to therapy in her fifties, O'Faolain understands that her high rate of sexual activity reflects her low self-esteem. She also blames Ireland's Catholic culture for depriving her of any moral sense in dealing with the opposite sex (85). Paradoxically, the experience of being told by the Church exactly what was sinful precluded her from developing her own moral compass for quite some time.

In the mid-sixties, O'Faolain received the coveted all–Ireland scholarship, and used it to enroll at Oxford University. Her thesis topic was the reception of Irish author George Moore's novel, *Esther Waters* (1894). This choice reflected O'Faolain's own quest for a meaningful sex life in a restrictive culture. In the novel, Esther is seduced and abandoned by a footman at the estate where she is a maid. Struggling for survival with an illegitimate son, Esther's poor chances remind us of Moll Flanders' a century earlier. However, as the Victorian incarnation of Moll, Esther is "purer"; her interest in men is elevated by her romantic ideals. Although O'Faolain grants her thesis a mere sentence in her memoir, its significance to her life deserves more mention. Forty years later, she would write a biography, *The Story of Chicago May* (2005), about a historical figure with a similar problem: how to survive decently in the face of society's opprobrium towards poor, disgraced women. In 1890, Chicago May stole her family's savings to escape poverty in west Ireland. At the age of nineteen, she fled to Chicago. Finding she could live on prostitution, May moved in and out of prosperity, dodging marriage proposals, and generally making unwise choices. Because of O'Faolain's understanding of May's poor Irish background and the limited choices of women in poverty, she identifies and sympathizes with May. In trying to understand this prostitute, O'Faolain plumbs the depths of her own condition, which she calls "sexual availability." Again and again, O'Faolain gives voice to downtrodden Irish females, attempting to erode readers' sexual, class and ethnic prejudice.

At Oxford, O'Faolain began another important relationship, falling in love with Rob at least as deeply as she had with Michael. Admiring his intelligence, she thought she had found a soul mate: he was "loud and happy and shabby and vivid — and impersonal" (94). In that last word lies the probable root of her dissatisfaction. Like Michael, Rob was uncommitted. Although they once agreed to marry, O'Faolain recognized in time that it was a desperate measure to get him to stop cheating, and called off the engagement. Both her father and grandfather advised her against the marriage, on the grounds that Rob was a "pagan" (Protestant). O'Faolain does not say whether their advice influenced her; she was simply astonished that her neglecting father had taken the trouble to visit her.

After graduation, O'Faolain spent a year teaching at UCD, where she was disappointed in both her student and collegial relationships. Some students did not appreciate her sarcasm, and her male colleagues had the upper hand because of entrenched academic sexism. Only after some years' experience did she realize that the only way females got ahead in academia was by male patronage. She had thought that academia was just an assortment of "nice men and nasty men," not registering that it was 99 percent men, and that she was finding favor, when she managed it, largely on sexual terms (98).

In 1970, O'Faolain started producing educational programs for the BBC, as part of a new Open University program for nontraditional students. The job allowed her to travel, work collaboratively, and do a job whose mission she believed in. In retrospect, she wishes she had learned the technical aspect of filming, and laments the fact that many women avoid technical information. She loved the sense of belonging to a group, but there was a limit to her identification with the male bastion of BBC. The Open Door program afforded underrepresented groups the opportunity to make programs, but she feels it was only done for public relations: "the access idea was largely a piece of empty rhetoric" (122). Her most interesting assignment was reporting on the Bogside Community Association in Derry, though O'Faolain humbly admits she had no business reporting on the politics of Northern Ireland, since neither she nor the BBC had enough background to adequately represent them.

At the ending of the relationship with Rob, O'Faolain begins to apply the teachings of the women's movement to her own life. She had been reliant on men for her own happiness; she wanted to change this dangerous propensity. Although she proceeds to her next affairs with greater awareness of them, she remains stuck in the same behavioral patterns. O'Faolain finds she is willing to compromise her feminism in order to bask in the glow of two charismatic lovers, Harry Craig and Clement Greenburg. Harry Craig, married Irish socialist turned Hollywood screenwriter, lures many women into his arms with his animal magnetism. Clement Greenberg is a New York Jewish art critic, who tries to imitate Henry Miller by being vulgarly explicit about his sexual needs and emotional unavailability. He signs his letters to O'Faolain, "in hopes of another orgasm."

Just at a point when these "old school" relationships begin to depress her, O'Faolain is saved by Sean Mac Réamoinn's invitation to matriculate in his new Merriman Summer School in Scariff, County Clare. It is 1973, and the folk movement is not limited to Ireland but flourishes throughout Europe. In retrospect, O'Faolain marvels at her girlish enthusiasm for the course on folk arts. She had idolized her instructors simply because they appreciated the *real* Irish culture. Nonetheless, the experience changed her life: "A new concept of home came into my life when I realized that Ireland, in all its aspects, present and past, was mine. That I belong to Ireland, just because I am Irish" (143). Quitting her job, she buys a cheap house in a Dublin slum and begins writing for *Radio Telefís Éireann* (RTÉ), where she meets Nell McCafferty. A charismatic feminist journalist from Derry, Nell was to be O'Faolain's domestic partner for fifteen years.

RTÉ turned out to be an uncomfortable environment. Its male employees were relentlessly antinationalist: "Direct public, personal abuse of anyone deemed to be either nationalist or insufficiently antinationalist was allowable" (149). They were misogynist: "Women were excluded by the rough, macho management style often in play just underneath the good manners of formal management" (148). They were Irish, "bigger-than-life personalities." After stodgy Englishmen at the BBC, her Irish coworkers' energy was exhilarating, but their work ethic was lacking: "Some of the people in RTÉ, compared to the BBC, seemed to want to be charmed or amused or pushed by superior force of will into doing their job ... doing it well for its own sake didn't satisfy them" (148). Despite its misogyny, RTÉ sponsored programs on women; O'Faolain took the helm on *Women Talking, The Women's Programme,* and *Plain Tales* (a show about older women which won the 1985 Jacob's Award). By another stroke of luck, an *Irish Times* editor heard O'Faolain reminiscing on the radio and invited her to be opinion columnist for the most respected newspaper in the country. Being listened to for her political opinions was unusual for an Irish woman at that time. O'Faolain found she had to cultivate a confident voice to do the job, reminding her of her father, whose cheery work voice was unlike his angry home voice (4).

The return to Ireland was not entirely redeeming, however. Living close to her ailing parents, she had to face painful memories, which she had evaded while living in London. Two weeks after her father's death in 1980, O'Faolain broke down and checked into St. Patrick's psychiatric hospital. Homeless, drinking, and in shock, she bottomed out. Nell McCafferty gave her a home. The sense of security O'Faolain derived from living with a woman instead of a man gave her "the deepest pleasure." Why go to a pub, when she felt a sense of belonging in her own home? Yet the relationship would become tempestuous. They disagreed on most things, especially nationalist politics. Because

Irish nationalism doesn't support feminism, O'Faolain couldn't support it. In a public debate in Derry, she said, "feminism is about human development and is therefore incompatible with killing.... Southern women had little or no sympathy with Northern nationalist women.... the men of Sinn Féin were just another layer of patriarchs among the many in Northern Ireland that oppressed women" (173). Despite their different political position regarding The Troubles, the McCafferty family extended hospitality to O'Faolain.

Although she had instigated the breakup, O'Faolain entered a deep depression after leaving McCafferty. Her gay friend Luke rescued her from this funk by moving in with her and taking her out to socialize. He is the basis for the character Jimmy, Cait's beloved friend in *My Dream of You*. Nuala's next affair, with a married truck driver called Joe, takes place in a motel room at the Northern Ireland border. They meet infrequently over the next four years. Although Joe is obviously the prototype for Caitleen's lover in *My Dream of You*, the real-life person is far less friendly and less available than Shay. Whereas Shay and Caitleen spend hours talking about their Irish childhoods, Joe typically sits wordless for many minutes in Nuala's presence. When he does speak, he expresses stock working-class prejudices and cynicism. While his "old-school" attitudes might disturb her feminist consciousness, she is attracted to those very attitudes because she believes they are a form of caretaking (Shay calls her his "little girl"). O'Faolain knows that more is going on than sensual pleasure. Joe reminds her of her grandfather, a frightening patriarch. Well into the relationship, Joe confesses that he is married. O'Faolain's feminism dictates that she should leave, out of self-respect and respect for the other woman. Yet she carries on compulsively, until he retires to Portugal with his wife.

On the strength of her memoir's sales, her publisher advises her to write a novel, and *My Dream of You* is born. Desiring to put some distance between herself and the Ireland of her imagination, O'Faolain takes a series of sublets in Manhattan, the last one dramatically positioned with a view of the twin Trade Towers. Returning after the 9/11 attacks, O'Faolain felt like she was viewing Paradise Lost. Her friends were scattered, and she no longer felt like she belonged. Writing novels was difficult, because of her inexperience, and her characteristic desire for authenticity. These feelings are replicated in her character's insecurities about writing a historical romance. However, poetic license allows Nuala to make her protagonist stronger than herself. By pulling her character out of a destructive relationship, Nuala gains the courage to look for a love of her own.

Through Match.com, O'Faolain meets a lover who presents her with the usual set of conflicts. John is affectionate, educated, and responsible; he shares custody of his eight-year-old daughter with his ex-wife. But he is also "old-school" (by which she means sexist), over-indulgent towards his daughter, and absorbed in his work at a law firm. O'Faolain's jealousy of his daughter surprises her, though she begins to understand that it is due to her own lack of parental love. Although she convinces herself that the path to health lies away from this painful relationship, the ending of the memoir sees O'Faolain talking herself back into it: "If I could love more steadily than I ever thought I could — I know I would be saved" (274). This statement reveals a question at the very heart of feminism: is love the savior of the soul, despite its struggles, or is it a trap that women stay in because they blame love problems on themselves?

O'Faolain's last two books contain the same themes that had always engrossed her: middle-aged, childless women seeking comfort, if not love, in a couple-oriented world; Irish versus American identities and their different paths to happiness; and women's quests for identity. The biography of Chicago May is immeasurably enriched by its author's identification with May. The posthumous novel, *Best Love, Rosie* (2009), satirizes the self-help industry, and paints an encouraging portrait of a happy 70-year-old. But O'Faolain's contentment is quickly destroyed when she learns that she has metastasized lung cancer. She dies in May 2008. The only consistent and outspoken feminist writer in this book, Nuala O'Faolain has much to offer this study, in part because she concedes the difficulty of acting in a feminist way in the midst of a search for love. Another valuable aspect of her work is its exposure of Irish social problems with neither excessive euphemism nor excessive judgment. When her sister read the first draft of *Are You Somebody*, she told O'Faolain that it was an act of revenge against all the people who had hurt her. After O'Faolain's revisions, the memoir is noteworthy for its honesty and fairness. So is O'Faolain's speaking persona. When she spoke at an Irish Studies conference in Missouri, I felt I was in the presence of genius: the genius of speaking the truth regardless of patriarchal expectations.

Synopses of the Novels

Big Women, *by Fay Weldon*

The novel opens in 1971 London, as Stephanie and Layla hang posters declaring, "A woman needs a man like a fish needs a bicycle." A few days later, these twenty-something feminists host a consciousness-raising session in Stephanie's apartment, at which time they launch Medusa, a feminist publishing house. Meanwhile, distinctly un-feminist activities are occurring in the next room. While the other women are dancing in the nude, Daffy is sleeping with Stephanie's handsome husband, Hamish. In the midst of this Dionysian evening, Zoe's husband Bull comes to retrieve Zoe from this unseemly gathering. The memory of this night will push Zoe's daughter Saffron away from feminism forever. When Stephie discovers her husband in bed with Daffy, she leaves the marriage. Determined to be independent, she takes nothing of the marriage with her. She walks out of the marriage, nude.

Part 2, "A Nest of Randy Vipers," sees Stephanie living rent-free in Layla's attic. Layla is independently wealthy. Since she finances Medusa, she thinks she can control its operation. Also renting from Layla are Richard and Johnny, gay paramours who provide comic relief from the constant tensions among the ladies of Medusa. Layla steals Hamish from Daffy, though this makes her a "weak sister." Enter Nancy, a New Zealander so naïve that she is attracted to Johnny, a gay man. Stephanie tries political lesbianism with a butch-dyke, whose violence eventually repels her. The lone asexual woman, Alice is a stereotypical academic who pursues ideas instead of people. Losing her focus, she ends up worshipping The Goddess at Glastonbury. In Alice's absence, Nancy takes care of Alice's parents. Clearly, Weldon's broad brush is allegorical, each Medusa woman an archetype: Layla the rich bitch, Stephanie the moral crusader, Alice the sexless intellectual, Daffy the working-class nymphomaniac, Zoe the good wife, and Nancy the do-gooder. Nancy is the only character that attains some degree of roundness by gradually learning to assert herself, yet even her feminism is eventually thwarted when she gets back with her ex-boyfriend.

The plot thickens with the tragedy of one member's death. Throughout her marriage, Zoe has secretly been writing a sociological monograph, *Lost Women: The Fate of the Graduate Housewife,* which she submits to Medusa for publication. Stephanie calls Zoe's house to announce the book's acceptance, but she leaves the message with Bull. In a drunken rage, Bull pretends that Medusa rejected it, and burns the manuscript. Later that day, Zoe overdoses on sleeping pills. At the memorial service, the sisters get sidetracked from mourning by debating whether it was patriarchy or feminism that killed Zoe. Suddenly, a female stranger stands up to announce that Zoe died of a broken heart, as the stranger had stolen Zoe's husband.

Part 3, "Saffron's Search," takes place in 1983. At fifteen, Zoe's child Saffron has become the caretaker of her alcoholic father and younger brother. Naturally, she does not want to believe that her mother committed suicide. Although she doesn't like them, she seeks out the Medusa feminists to learn the real cause of Zoe's death. Saffron follows Layla to the Greenham Common Peace Camp, where she is protesting the nuclear bomb. Attracting the media by her good looks, Layla's interviews with them alienate the purists, who want to evict her for talking to men. By this time, Layla's feminist politics have mellowed so that men are no longer the enemy. Like her author, she has begun to feel sorry for the effects of the women's movement on men's potency.

In Part 4, "Well, I'm Sorry," the year is 1997. The narrator apologizes for feminism's casualties. Women cannot find love and have stopped nurturing children, while men can't achieve erections or find confidence. Stephanie's son Roland sleeps with Saffron and would like a commitment, but Saffron is only sleeping with him to get information about who really funds Medusa. Saffron edits a women's magazine, where she ruthlessly fires all of the "dead wood" on her first day at work. Roland's twin brother Rafe marries kind, earnest, unattractive Marly, who is training to be a psychoanalyst. A product of feminism, their household reverses traditional gender roles, so Marly works while Rafe stays home with the baby. Hamish doesn't understand these and other repercussions of the movement; he escapes to live in the countryside. Despite his many infidelities, Daffy follows, and has his child. Layla breaks up with her long-time lover, a rich Egyptian who has been secretly financing Medusa with his wife's money. Stephanie rescues Alice from her increasingly delusional relationship to The Goddess, bringing her back to London to attend a Medusa board meeting.

At the final board meeting, Layla announces her intention to sell Medusa to a captain of industry, Sir Marcus Liebling. None of the original founders agrees with this choice, but Saffron and Layla outvote them (Saffron has secretly purchased enough shares to constitute a majority with Layla). The four founders, Layla, Stephanie, Nancy, and Alice, make a million each out of the sale. The narrator claims that they are now free—that is, free to do whatever they want with their money.

My Dream of You

This novel's title refers to both the narrator's love affair and the one that she tries to write a novel about, concerning lovers from 1848. It also refers to Cait's tendency to construct an ideal lover and project this imago[11] onto strangers. The novel proceeds by way of flashbacks and flash-forwards, connecting a few weeks in the present day life of its protagonist, Caitleen de Burca, with memories of her past. Woven into these accounts of Cait's Ireland sojourn, and her past, is the story she is writing about two lovers in Ballygal, taking place between 1848 and 1854.

As the novel opens, twenty-two-year-old Cait is blissfully cohabitating with her English boyfriend in London. Hugo, a law student, shows Cait *The Judgment*, an 1854 divorce case brought by English landowner Richard Talbot against his wife Marianne and her lover, the Irish groom William Mullan.

Cait is fascinated by this story for two reasons. First, she has always been compelled by true love stories. Second, she has always been fascinated by the Famine because she thinks her parents' joyless lives are somehow genetically passed down from Famine times as a race memory. Her own romance with Hugo ends on the day he finds her in bed with their roommate.

The novel now jumps forward twenty-five years to the present, when Cait writes for the magazine *TravelWrite*, lives in a small basement apartment in Bloomsbury, and shares confidences with a gay American coworker named Jimmy. He is her only friend. She frequently has one-night stands with men met during her travels. When Jimmy dies of a heart attack, Cait is devastated. She goes to a psychiatrist, who betrays her by allowing his trainee to eavesdrop from behind a curtain. Impulsively quitting her job, Cait goes to Ireland to research the Talbot affair, hoping to adapt it into a novel. Before leaving her apartment, she sleeps with her married, unattractive landlord, who says he will excuse the rent if she has sex with him. Cait's inability to say *no* to unwanted sexual advances is a recurring problem; by the end of her stay in Ireland, she will gain at least some understanding of her problem.

Cait has avoided returning to Ireland for thirty years. She holds a grudge against the country that let her mother die. When her mother was pregnant, she was diagnosed with uterine cancer, but the Catholic hospital would not give her a hysterectomy to save her life. Cait's father and brother supported the hospital's decision. Because of this and other traumas, Cait's trip becomes a search into her own past for the causes of her alienation. Long-blocked memories flood her mind while she drives her rented car through west Ireland. Aspects of the Talbot case bring up suppressed incidents of her own life for analysis. Cait knows that she has inherited her mother's belief that passion is worth any cost. This is why she identifies so strongly with Marianne Talbot. She also relates to Marianne's depressive nature. Like Marianne, Cait knows that she sabotages all of her intimate relationships.

On a ferry ride, Cait meets another lone traveler, Shay the gardener. They have little in common except their Irish background and their choice to live in England. Shay is an Irishman who works in England, but often visits Sligo in order to help his father. Both Cait and Shay believe that passion should be enough to sustain them, but Shay is married with children. On their third meeting, Shay proposes that they rent a love nest where they can meet for sex once a month. Cait takes a few days to think this over, bringing up much unresolved material from her past.

When she finds a document that proves Marianne's complete innocence in the affair, Cait's research reaches a crisis. Can she still write the book, when the story is untrue? Only with great reluctance does Cait relinquish her ideal of Marianne and William's true love. The final straw is finding documentation of a firsthand witness who caught Marianne in the act with yet another man, neither William nor Richard.

Imagining this scene recalls to Cait's mind her own coupling with her best friend's ex-husband, several years before. Once again twinning herself with Marianne, Cait deduces that it is not its erotic promise that made the Talbot story so meaningful to her, but rather her own craving for punishment. On some level, she is convinced of her unworthiness; she repeatedly debases herself to prove this. She sees her infidelities and sexual availability as part of the larger pattern that she analyzes as a peculiarly Irish form of self-hatred.

Cait's decisions to stop seeing Shay and stop writing the Talbot book are intertwined. Removing her romantic projections from Marianne helps her to reject a future with Shay. Waiting for his once-a-month visit would be too much like her mother's sad life. At the novel's close, Cait is flying to London to rescue her friend Alex from taking religious vows. Gazing at Ireland from her airplane window, Cait imagines William Mullan as he lies dying in the woods. He sees a deer whose smooth flank reminds him of Marianne, proving he carried the torch till his death. Both Cait and William make peace with the difficult choice of leaving their lovers.

Big Women (1997) and *My Dream of You* (2001): Collective, Communal, and Individual Values in British and Irish Feminisms

Despite their author's age at the time of publication (Weldon 66, O'Faolain 61), these novels show third-wave influences in the following ways. Neither author blames the oppression of women directly upon male characters. Each writer uses an intersectional approach,[12] insofar as ethnic influences (in O'Faolain) and economic forces (in Weldon) upon the female protagonists are considered in equal measure as their gender. Both offer implied (O'Faolain) and direct (Weldon) critiques of second-wave idealism. As in third-wave feminism, each author adopts a highly individualistic model in which the protagonists interrogate their personal relationships to feminism, rather than affirming the idealized collective practices of 1970s feminism. Although Weldon's novel opens upon a consciousness-raising meeting, its protagonists later find that the sisterhood does not cohere, and each woman must journey on an increasingly lonely path.

The question of the relative roles of collectivity and individualism in feminism is central to its definition. Does a feminist have to act collectively in order to earn her "feminist credentials"? Since definitions of feminism are fluid, the requirements of collective action vary from person to person. It is tempting to say that liberal and socialist feminists *always* act collectively because their objectives are to change the law and employment sector, in the first case, and the whole structure of socioeconomic life, in the second. Similarly, why not say that radical feminists act in the most collective way of all, because they create all-woman communities? Are cultural feminists supremely individualist because they work on their own projects in art or literature? By extension, is a feminist professor acting collectively because she reaches a wide audience of students, or is she highly individualistic, because she chooses her own curriculum and holds the ultimate authority in the classroom?

These questions revisit some of the terms considered in the previous chapter, where we saw Lessing and O'Brien rejecting the feminist call to interrogate their affective life through the feminist lens, because the Communist and Catholic-nationalist hegemonies of their communities taught them that such individualistic interrogation was bourgeois (Lessing) or sinful (O'Brien). However, there is a significant difference between the time periods. Being influenced by patriarchal hegemonies in the 1950s is not the same issue as deciding to take individual or collective action as a third-wave feminist; one striking contrast between the second-wave novels *The Golden Notebook* and *Country Girls Trilogy* and the third-wave novels *Big Women* and *My Dream of You* is the later characters' relative security in adopting the terminology of feminism, and agreeing with its general premise that they live in patriarchal societies which oppress women.

In her seminal *Irish Women Writers: An Uncharted Tradition* (1990), Ann Owens Weekes recognizes that to speak about Irish writers accurately, she must make significant distinctions between separate Gaelic and Anglo traditions in Irish writing. These distinctions are also helpful when we consider Irish-Catholic and British-Protestant writers. Weekes finds that the most important difference lies in these groups' adoption of communal versus individualist values, which they imbibe from their cultural heritage of Catholicism and Protestantism, respectively. Weekes contrasts the "agentic" or individualistic emphasis in Protestant ethics to the "communal" emphasis in Catholic ethics. The Protestant's relationship with God is private and individual. The association between Protestantism and progress (both economic and scientific) "exaggerates" individualism at the expense of communal values. Weekes cites Max Weber and David Bakan to prove that the Protestant ethos is quite different to that of the Catholic. According to Protestants, "Each person is on his own with respect to grace. The major business of life is a private affair between each person and God. This is associated with a considerable alienation of each individual from other persons, including the members of his family.... In place of sociability he substitutes formal social organization" (Bakan 15).

Applying Bakan's theory to novels by Anglo-Irish Jennifer Johnston and Gaelic-Irish Julia O'Faolain, Weekes finds that their protagonists act in accordance with Protestant "agentic" and Catholic "communal" drives. In Johnston's *Railway Station Man*, the heroine rejects a marriage proposal from a man who promises happiness, because her happiness can only come from her individual relationship with God (this is despite the fact that she is not religious). In Julia O'Faolain's *The Obedient Wife*, on the other hand, the protagonist leaves her lover to return to her volatile husband. She accuses her lover of being incapable of truly needing her because he is Protestant: "You believing Christians have an enormous ego.... I imagine it comes from the notion that your first duty is to save your own soul — that's breathtaking egoism, and you learn it as a duty, a maxim and foundation-stone to your moral system" (quoted in Weekes 216). It is humorous to remember that such egotism is exactly what Eugene Gaillard accuses Catholics of having, when he resents Kate's belief in the Catholic Mass. Perhaps both comments reflect the jealousy that can occur when one member of a couple appears to have more faith than the other, regardless of their denomination. According to Weekes, Julia O'Faolain sends her heroine back to her marriage because her Catholic culture "recognizes the richness of even deeply flawed relationships" (215). There is a pattern in Anglo- and Gaelic-Irish novels, in which the Anglo-Irish protagonists find fulfillment in independence, whereas the Gaelic-Irish, though entirely aware of marriage's "restrictions," still value communion over independence.

Since they carry such weight in Weekes' argument, the terms *communal* and *collective* deserve examination. Bakan uses *communal* to describe a particularly Catholic cultural value. This word is related to *collective*, but their difference is crucial, for purposes of this discussion. *Communal* derives from Greek and Latin words meaning "sharing in common," while *collective* derives from Latin *collectivus*, "a gathering together." Predating the sacramental meaning of the term, communion also meant "the suffering of others" "the commonality between Gentiles and Jews," and "the bodily nature all have in common." In secular contexts, *communal* refers to shared interests, ideals or experience. The accent on the word *share* differentiates *communal* from *collective*, which simply means involving all members of a group as distinct from its individuals. A collective does not necessarily signify that its members share common values. This apparent digression into the etymologies of the words matters to our discussion of Gaelic communal values and Anglo individual values, because the texts to which I will apply the distinction take place in secularized contexts. Yet because of the generation-to-generation power of hegemonies, the perspectives of Protestantism and Catholicism persist, even in a generation of nonbelievers. The Protestant work ethic is a good example of how secular and religious values coalesce into an ideology that is neither strictly religious nor strictly secular.

In regard to individualist versus communal values, *My Dream of You* and *Big Women* are structurally opposite. O'Faolain's protagonist starts off intensely lonely, but achieves community by the end, while Weldon's six protagonists start out by forming a collective, but end up alone (albeit rich). *My Dream of You* features a lone protagonist whose journey *seems* to entail the loss of one important relationship after another, though I will argue that she both consciously and unconsciously establishes many fertile bonds that heal her disintegration. In the present-time of the novel, Cait loses Jimmy, Nan, and Shay; while in the past, she has lost mother, father, brothers, Caroline, and Hugo. In Cait's work, she deals with Marianne's loss of Mullan, Richard, and her community. In contrast, *Big Women*'s six protagonists start out by making Medusa Publishing Collective, but end up selling the business to a capitalist mainstream publisher. Theoretically, Weldon provides the four founding members with the Protestant-inflected "success" of becoming millionaires, with the wherewithal to do whatever they please. Yet the happy ending feels false; it is based on the collapse of the collective, and the loss of its ideals. Medusa is wealth without *communion*, which points to the hollowness in the center of the novel.

My Dream of You and the Construction of the Communal

In the beginning of *My Dream of You*, Caitleen feels lonely and depressed; she is cut off from family and community, which her Irish heritage has taught her to esteem more highly than individuality and commercial success. Jimmy's death is the impetus for her journey of self-discovery, but the journey uncovers several other unmourned losses. As Cait begins her research on the Talbot affair, each aspect of her study recalls a painful memory from her own past. She feels guilty for leaving her family as her mother lay dying, particularly since her younger brother had to become caretaker for her father and brother Sean. She feels guilty for seducing her best friend's husband. She still feels guilty for betraying her first lover, Hugo, thirty years ago. She is ashamed of having bedded her boss one night, and having never addressed the painful subject afterwards. She feels perplexed about why she had sex with her landlord in return for rent. Betrayed by the psychiatrist she visits in order to address her overwhelming burden of grief and shame, Cait turns to historical research instead. The exercise of entering the mind of her subject, Marianne Talbot, helps her to confront her own demons. She intentionally makes the academic quest a personal one: "Could I move beyond some momentary imagining of the past towards finding a meaning for it? Not an explanation, but a meaning? And not a meaning in history but in my own life?" (72).

Along this journey, Cait meets several people who help fill in the blanks of her ignored past. During the course of the few weeks that she spends in Ireland, Cait unconsciously replaces the most important relationships that she has allowed to wither, making a new family, and setting up the psychic conditions necessary for healing. I will argue that Cait allows new figures to play essential archetypal roles, thereby bringing repressed portions of herself back to life. Bertie the innkeeper and Nan the librarian fill the roles of Good Father and Good Mother; Danny and Annie come back into their roles as Good Brother and Good Sister; Oliver and Lilian play the Children that Cait never had; Alex fills Jimmy's shoes as Best Male Friend; and Caro fills the role of good female friend that Cait's real sister Nora had relinquished. The only role that Cait consciously empties instead of filling is that of Lover; in letting Shay go, she also relinquishes the Marianne in her, a positive act since Marianne represents self-destructive love. At the end of the novel, Cait switches her identification from Marianne, the female Lover, to Mullan, the male Lover. She identifies with Mullan because he leaves Ballygal and his lover behind, as she leaves Ballygal and Shay. Identifying with the "agentic" male at this moment is positive for Cait, because in the past she has passively accepted any sex that came her way.

In theorizing that Cait's construction of this new archetypal family helps fulfill her Irish need for communal existence, it is useful to consider historian Clair Wills' description of Irish community. In her 2001 article, "Women, Domesticity and the Family," Wills reported that Catholic rural culture shows "inherited patterns such as identification with the community as much as the family, and a *recourse to collective memory and shared symbolic forms of orientation*, as much as to individual experience" (37, emphasis mine). When Caitleen finally returns to her native country after thirty years, she begins to identify with the community by means of this collective memory and shared symbols. Cait, Nan, and Bertie share the collective cultural memory of the Famine. Cait intentionally engages her new friends in her research and imaginative reconstruction of Ballygal at the time of the Famine. One of Cait's simple but profound discoveries is that her descendants "must have survived the Famine, because we Burkes are here." This realization gives her a sense of pride in her ancestors' strength. While Bertie and Nan denigrate the Talbots, making them represent all evil English landlords of the time, the opportunity to debate and temper each other's positions is helpful to Cait. Both Bertie and Nan are humorous in their contempt for English colonization, but Bertie's attitude is softer than Cait's father's. This enables her both to recall her dead father, and to replace him, in a psychic sense, with a better model.

Wills claims that a collective symbol can unite a community. The symbol of Mother Ireland had a powerful sway over generations of Irish. The archetypal martyr who represented purity and pain, Mother Ireland dominates Cait's conscious, and to a degree, her unconscious life, in both the private sense (her own Irish mother) and public sense (her Irish identity). In large part, the objective of her trip is to forgive her unloving mother so that she can move on with her life. Cait's struggle to avoid repetition of her mother's faults, particularly her romantic desperation, means coming to terms with her Irish identity as well as her inherited depression.

In her associations of Mother Ireland as a country for which she has ambivalent feelings, Cait engages in a shared orientation with other Irish people. Cait's response to English bigotry has never been assertive; rather, she has tended to internalize their belief of her inferiority. For instance, she sleeps with her unattractive landlord out of gratitude that he, an Englishman, rented to her, an Irish person. She accepts Sir David's "gropes" because she imagines he thinks that all Irish are servants and whores. She does not even defend Ireland to a woman who throws a potato at her face. Nor does she confront a psychiatrist whom she believes is treating her differently on the basis of her ethnicity. To some extent, Cait seems intent on performing a kind of stage–Irishry in her drinking, volatility, irresponsibility, and impulsive sexual choices. Living in her basement apartment for thirty years, she is irresponsible to the part of herself that wanted children, family, health, and self-understanding. For years, travel writing had kept her anxieties at bay. When Jimmy dies, the loss is painful, but also an opportunity to address her unlived life.

Many feminists try to avoid repeating their mother's patterns by avoiding marriage and motherhood. In Ireland, the question of family is further complicated by its particular political and economic history. Clair Wills demonstrates that Irish families were historically quite different from English or European families. Until the latter half of the twentieth century, Irish families tended to be so "open-ended" that the Enlightenment view of companionate marriage did not necessarily apply to the Irish situation. Until the early twentieth century, servants and their employers living together constituted a family quite different from the nuclear model. After the Famine, widespread emigration meant that wage-earners were absent from the Irish household, though they sent their money home. The west of Ireland retained some older customs until quite recently. A 1983 study of west Kerry concluded that the closest and most enduring ties that most villagers formed were with members of the same sex, or with parents or siblings instead of lovers or spouses.

Although villagers agreed that male sexuality was very repressed, they thought that marriage was problematic for many in Ireland, "exactly because it tends to intrude on other affections and primary relations" (quoted in Wills 48). In particular, the brother-sister bond can be quite strong.

Another component that makes Irish families unusual is that postcolonial Ireland valorized a form of domesticity that was without privacy or intimacy. The family home, so cherished that De Valera wrote it into the 1937 Constitution as the basic unit of Irish life, was a symbol of domestic order and discipline, charged with sustaining the wider public order. Middle class domesticity was the very foundation for the conservative nationalism of the Free State (Wills 46). The rural culture disapproved of love and romance, preferring calculated business matches because of economic requirements of "the continuity of settlement on the land" (47). Because the history of the family in Ireland is different from that of its European neighbors, Wills cautions against trying to "automatically map western concepts of modernity" (such as intimacy, sexuality and female emancipation by way of companionate marriage) onto other cultures such as Ireland's (49).

Taken together, Wills' and Weekes' research supports the idea that Irish Catholic-nationalist hegemonies value communal ties over the primacy of the individual. Irish people in exile often speak of a kind of homesickness, certainly not unique to their culture, but that nevertheless carries an Irish stamp.[13] O'Faolain, for instance, fully acknowledges her need for Ireland. At the end of the second memoir, although she has had many positive American experiences, she chooses to return to Ireland because of its communal sense:

> [Irish] people — another landscape, a frieze, people in public, people putting themselves at risk for the sake of entertaining others, people drinking so as to feel the happiness of the present moment more intensely. There's a kind of occasion at home that I have never had in America. It is in a pub, not a house, and it is communal, not individual. It builds toward a plateau of utter contentment and then goes, because it must, over the top [237].

As a writer, O'Faolain is aware of needing more than pub community; she needs a readership too. After living in America for some time, she quits her job with the *Irish Times* because she feels she has lived abroad too long to be relevant. Yet she mourns the loss of this kind of community, her readership: "The people who read my *Irish Times* column were my community — more than that, a family, almost, because my thoughts and feelings were known to them" (234).

In her roman à clef, *My Dream of You*, O'Faolain's protagonist attains a degree of healing by returning to Ireland to confront her past. One reader complains that O'Faolain's own healing is not equivalent to that of her character because she does not leave her own lover; therefore it is "difficult to take seriously O'Faolain's feminist claims" (Ebest 69). Yet O'Faolain does believe that writing Caitleen was therapeutic:

> What happened to [Caitleen] wasn't just a by-product of the making of a fiction. I was changing, myself, in symbiosis with my heroine. Happiness— or if not happiness, a robust vision of how to manage its absence and live well — had crept up on me. It subverted my character's fatalistic progress toward self-immolation.... She had become too widely life-loving to ruin her own life, even for honest passion perfectly expressed [*Almost There*, 149].

Although it takes longer for O'Faolain to leave Joe than for Cait to leave Shay, the writer does embody Cait's strengths in other ways, such as finding contentment in her life as a single woman.

In characterizing Caitleen's assembly as a cast of good characters who will substitute for old family members and become her new internal family, I draw on the psychoanalytical concepts of *introjection*, *good objects*, and *psychic reality*, as presented in Kleinian Object Relations theory. *Objects* are both real others and one's internalized image of them. The infant's early relations with caregivers constitute its psychic reality. Infants first perceive the breast as a *part object*, not as the whole being of the mother. But as the child passes through the Oedipal complex, he or she comes to see the mother as a *whole object*, to which s/he experiences ambivalence and guilt. *Projective identification* is the result of the denial of parts of the self, and their displacement onto an object, while *introjective identification* results from the ego incorporating qualities of the object. *Internal objects* are those introjected into the ego. *Good objects* are felt as sources of life, love and goodness, but are not ideal; their bad qualities are recognized and may be experienced as frustrating in contrast to the ideal object. The *ideal object* (breast or penis, to an infant; perfect lover to an adult) is experienced as a result of splitting and denial of persecution. All the infant's good experiences are attributed to this ideal object, with which it identifies and which it desires to possess.[14]

It should be clear from this description that idealization causes the psyche trouble, and that introjection of good, rather than ideal objects, is the goal of therapy and healing. *Psychic reality* is the experience of one's internal world, including the experience of impulses and the internal objects. According to Klein, all infants pass through, and all adults repeatedly pass in and out of, the *depressive position*, which entails "the mourning and pining for the good object felt as lost and destroyed, and guilt, a characteristic depressive experience which arises from the sense that he has lost the good object through his own destructiveness" (70). Cait's constant longing for the ideal mother that she never had frequently puts her in the depressive position. Her Ireland journey enables her to recollect good times with both mother and father. Largely through her introjective identifications with Bertie and Nan, she is able to experience the basic premise, stated by Nan, that "the world is wonderful" (419). In other words, Ireland lightens her psychic reality, making her burdens more tolerable.

The development of Irish relationships helps Cait to heal. The most important figure for this purpose is Nan Leech, the 70-year-old Ballygal librarian with cancer (like Cait's mother). Nan both criticizes Cait's history project (acting as bad object) and reinforces its value (good object). From the start, their relationship is startlingly open and honest, in accordance with the warm, direct interactions Cait has with all Irish, and different from the alienating relationships she has with most British people. For instance, on their second meeting, Nan asks, "Do you believe in the Creator?" to which Cait responds, "I believe there is a Creation. I see and hear things every day that make me think there must be a Creator. But ..." (74). The fact that Nan agrees with her "but" brings them closer already than Cait and her mother, who sacrificed her life for her Catholic beliefs. Although Nan attempts to be empirical about history, she also shares Cait's sentimental fantasies. Nan goes so far as to imagine that the 300 tenants living on the Talbot farm in 1847 were happy, because of their "unbroken heritage of language and music and stories and customs and traditions ... and the faith.... It was a whole civilization" (79).

Nan shares some of the physical reserve of Cait's mother, as well as her valorization of sexual passion. When Cait seeks advice about Shay's offer, Nan responds that if it were her choice, she would accept the offer to be his mistress. It both surprises and relieves Cait to learn that her romantic and sexual proclivities are not odd or sinful in Nan's opinion. On the other hand, Nan's answering *as though Cait were her daughter* gives Cait a sense of belonging, and replaces the introjected bad mother with the good. Nan answers, "I'd want more than that for a daughter. I mean, I'd like a companion for you, not a visitor.... Someone you could respond to with the best in you. Because you are a good girl" (419). There were only two times that Cait's mother had told her she was good: when she won an essay contest and when she won a scholarship to Trinity College. Thus, Cait is more than usually moved by this affirmation of her worth. Nan also confronts her own death in a more positive way than Cait's mother did. Nan Leech provides a model of good mother, because she is both similar and different enough from Cait's real mother to create an imago that elicits healing.

Cait and her father had a strained relationship; he was usually absent, and cruelly dismissive of her mother. In adulthood, Cait realizes that the restrictive Irish 1940s culture had created the monstrous aspects of him: "such willfully stunted lives, the lives of respectable Irishmen of my father's generation." She is afraid she might have inherited his coldness: "I was terrified that I was as unloving as he, and that the only reason I hadn't done as much harm was because there was no one dependent on me" (190). In contrast to her father's coldness, Bertie the innkeeper provides a model of the good father. Typical of Cait, her first impulse towards Bertie is sexual, even though he is sixty-three years old, to her fifty. When Bertie shows her a secret statue in an ivy-covered archway, they lean against each other intimately. Cait recalls the desire she had felt in "a similar configuration" when she and a fellow traveler had looked at a statue in rural Cambodia. But the moment passes without incident for Bertie and Cait. Bertie has several positive traits, some similar to Mr. Burke, others different, but with enough on each side to form the imago, or object relation that reminds her of the father.

Like her father, Bertie loves his Irish heritage. He is strongly attached to his dog, his daughter, his home and the village where he has lived all his life. Unlike her father, he supports her in her dream (of writing the history) and takes care of her physical and emotional needs. Because the inn will be filled with wedding guests on the weekend, Bertie lends her his cottage in the country. He feeds her, shares his grandchildren, relays messages from Shay, takes her to the Talbot estate, and brainstorms with her about her book. When she leaves for the cottage, he tells her, "Don't get into trouble, now!" This moves her to tears because these were the last words her mother ever said to her. But Mammy said them from the opposite side of a room, while Bertie said them while hugging her. Bertie is the Good Father, with traits of the Good Mother as well; being around him begins to lighten Cait's psychic reality.

Success at Ballygal gives Cait the courage to visit her real brother and sister-in-law, whom she has barely seen since her flight from Ireland thirty years ago. During her brief stay, Cait introjects the objects Good Brother and Good Sister, for Annie is far more of a friend than her own sister Nora, who left for America and never came back. Meeting Annie at the old family farm, Cait thinks: "We were like survivors, finding each other after a disaster" (202). Annie's warmth allows Cait to "be natural." Contrasted to her hugs with Nora, which were "bony, wary," she warmly hugged Annie back. Cait's next thought expresses a simple but profound truth, with implications for her healing: "I know what goodness is like. Annie is good" (202). Introjecting good objects that are similar in age, gender, and background entails a different, but still important identification, compared to introjecting parental objects.

Annie particularly fits the definition of a good object, not an ideal one, when she criticizes Cait of being thoughtless for giving Danny money (because Danny spent it on a drinking binge). Rather than either attack Annie or condemn herself, Cait understands the otherness of Annie, seeing her as a whole person rather than internalizing her condemnation. Both Danny and Annie ask Cait to come back into the fold. When Danny uses the phrase, "belonging to the Burkes," Cait goes limp from the impact of the word, *belonging*. Annie directly asks her to "start coming home" (460). "It would help Danny, to have a sister like you around. Full of life. And I'd love you to be an auntie to Lil" (460). Since Cait suffers greatly from her alienation from the family, these words are profoundly meaningful.

Finally, Cait's relationship to the children, Lilian and Oliver, completes the new psychic family. They expose her to the healing powers of children's innocence. Spending time with them assuages her sadness that she has no children of her own. Lil is a particularly affectionate eight-year-old who proudly introduces her aunt in the village, sits in her lap, and holds her in the bed during sleep. Lil's trusting and full-hearted affection reminds Cait of Shay. Bertie's grandson, Oliver, sparks another bittersweet memory when he calls her "Atlee," just like her little brother Sean had done. On the brighter side, watching Oliver take his first steps makes her think of the possibilities of the life still ahead. When Bertie begins praising Oliver, Cait feels an inner release, of "a tension [she] hadn't known [she] felt" (383). As Ollie began a long life of walking, she felt as if she "had crossed a threshold too. To be absorbed by watching a child learning to walk! Me! To have arrived somewhere where I knew people who taught children to walk!" (383). Enmeshed in the life of a single career woman, Cait had not realized that spending time with families could heal her.

Although imaginary (as imagos are), the fictional Marianne and William also contribute to Cait's psychic reality. In the beginning of her research, Cait over-identifies with her projection of Marianne because she believes that Marianne had that rare thing, true love: "All the more because it was a journey I had failed to make, I believed that the body was the way to the heart, and the heart was the way to the soul. When I told the story of William Mullan and Marianne Talbot, I would be preaching that belief" (65). As she begins to find evidence that this love affair did not actually occur, Cait tries to believe that the evidence is wrong, because she wants so badly for her version of events to be right. Not until she receives incontrovertible proof that Marianne didn't love Mullan does Cait manage to relinquish her identification. On the plane ride back to England, she constructs the end of the romance, making Mullan the central character, and switching her identification to him. She believes that he would have kept his love for Marianne intact through the years, just as she prays she can do for Shay. She explicitly compares the development in her relationship to Marianne to that with her own mother. At the moment that she forgives her mother, she also relinquishes the Marianne in her: "I have to watch the Marianne in me dying from now on" (499).

Fortunately for Cait, she still has a friend in England. In fact, she finds the strength to leave Shay and return to England in part because of her boss Alex's need for her. Jimmy has been the closest companion of her life; there is every possibility that Alex can replace him as the Good Male Friend. At Jimmy's funeral, Alex finally broke his long silence about their one-night affair. He revealed a secret kept for eighteen years, that he is a priest. Learning this, Cait is able to relinquish the feelings of guilt and rejection that she has been carrying. She has always deeply admired and trusted Alex; taking care of him in his state of depression over his mother's death will help Cait form another nonsexual friendship with a man (Alex is off-limits because of his religious status; Jimmy because of his sexual orientation). Alex might be even better for her than Jimmy. Although she confided in Jimmy, he did not really like her serious side. Implied by Alex's profound soul-searching is the potential for a deeper (spiritual) relationship with him than she'd had with Jimmy. Finally, Cait will return to live with her friend Caro, who has forgiven her for her betrayal with Ian, promising the renewal of a female friendship as well.

If Ireland, as I argue, renewed Cait's potential for positive relationships, then the return to England might tend to erode this newfound quality. However, since Cait has quit a job of eighteen years, it is possible that she will return to Ireland to work, after the end of the novel. Even if she does not return, she may be able to sustain herself on the community she has formed. The replacement of the Bad Objects—split-off parts of the father, mother, sister, brother, lover, children, and friend—with Good Objects, whether they are replacements or improved relationships with existing people, represents the formation of community based on a commonality of collective memory and cultural symbols. Regaining touch with her good Irishness begins to heal Cait, as O'Faolain's return to Ireland in mid-career started her own journey of healing.

Big Women *and the Failure of Sisterhood*

Whereas *My Dream of You* progressively opens the protagonist's world to greater possibilities of fulfillment, *Big Women* is structured in an opposite way. The ending dashes every hope born of the initial consciousness-raising scene. Yet Weldon's narrator is not so much destructive as conservative. She believes that feminism is only a wave of history that came and went, leaving us with the normative social structure of patriarchy. Layla's beliefs are sometimes indistinguishable from the narrator's; when she sells Medusa to a mainstream company, she announces that feminism's time is over: "The wave did its work, receded, passed on elsewhere, and has left us foundering in the shallows" (342). Among the casualties of second-wave feminism are "the death of love, lost children, and the diminishing of man" (267). Although this is a harsh verdict on feminism, there are ways in which this novel can be construed as feminist. Its protagonists are women; the female characters are stronger than the males; patriarchy is at one time recognized as the most influential social force; and feminist theory is recited by many of the characters. However, several anti-feminist aspects confuse the issue: the sisterhood is fragile; the strongest women are either selfish or deluded; no character is rewarded for her feminism; the costs of feminism are judged higher than its gains. In fact, feminism itself is targeted as the reason for several characters' demise. The second paragraph of the novel asks, "If in achieving so much they all but destroyed themselves, who should be surprised?" (1).

In "The Bloodless Revolution," Imelda Whelehan addresses this ambivalence of *Big Women*. Its protagonists are "lost women"; their plight constitutes an "enigma at the heart of the narrative" (37). In the course of the novel's thirty-year span, the women's movement loses its way, but its premise remains valid. Although Weldon's narrator "seems to relish the corruption of feminist values," the characters' dissatisfaction with their domestic arrangements proves that the conditions of oppression still exist (46). In other words, Weldon clearly paints the picture of oppression that these women face, yet tears down the ideals of feminism, putting nothing in their place.

Anglo-Protestant culture values individualism as the path to salvation. *Big Women* doesn't so much assert this value as prove it by dooming its opposite, the sisters' attempts at collective action. In this novel, individualism seems not so much an affirmative value, but "merely" the way of the world, and the nature of the human heart. Rather than a path to grace, individualism appears as a necessity for survival. The lack of any belief in progress, or optimism about collective human endeavor, suggests hollowness at the core of the novel, what Whelehan called both a *gap* and an *enigma*. The narrator's cynicism implies that profit is the bottom line of all collective endeavors, with desire for power a close second. In addition, she asserts that women are at least as competitive as men, making their hopes of bonding in common cause unlikely to be fulfilled.

If this kind of bottom-line cynicism were all that the novel is about, it would be a very boring read. But Weldon's humor allows us to laugh at feminist idealism, and in the process, to interrogate its forms. Studies have found that women's comedy operates by debunking male comic forms, especially the reintegration into society of the male hero after making his funny mistakes. Writing on comedy and feminism, Judy Little states, "Women's comedy mocks the deepest possible norms" (quoted in Barreca, *Untamed*, 29). Judith Wilt claims that the woman writer "hesitates, laughing at the edge, withholding fertility, humility, community"—all the traits and values associated with women in male comedy (quoted in Barreca, 29). By definition, feminist comedy resists resolution, since resolution of conflict within a patriarchal setting implies acceptance of patriarchal norms.[15] Judged in this light, Weldon's humor seems more feminist, for she definitely withholds *resolution, fertility, humility*, and *community*. The only *resolution* is that the four founding members of Medusa receive a million pounds out of its sale. The only initially *humble* member, Nancy, learns to assert herself in the face of Layla's tyranny. *Fertility* is denied to the feminist Layla, and granted to the non-feminist Daffy. The *community* is fragile from the very start of Medusa in 1971, and is finally dispersed by the sell-out in 1997, never having achieved its promise of uniting the founders in common cause. This is not to deny that Medusa was successful in achieving its goal of publishing writing by women authors about feminist causes. Yet Weldon never hands out success without taking away happiness. Zoe's book *Lost Women* is Medusa's best-selling title, yet Zoe died for this book. Layla founded the first feminist press in England, yet lost the opportunity to have children. Alice received the first honorary doctorate in the Philosophy of Gender from Oxbridge, but nearly lost her mind when trying to correct her over-rationalism with new-age mysticism. No sooner does Nancy gain self-esteem in her professional context than she leaves publishing for marriage. Stephanie gained her freedom from Hamish but lost her friendship with Layla. Medusa is an economic success, but as a social experiment of communalism, it is a failure.

Weldon's appreciation of the individualism that is fostered by capitalistic values harks back to her university major in economics. As Max Weber argued in *The Protestant Work Ethic and the Rise of Capitalism*, the Protestant mindset (that one makes one's own salvation) is a cultural precondition for free market capitalism. In a long passage that describes socioeconomic changes in the interval between the 1970s and 1980s, Weldon's narrator expresses nostalgia for the "innocent" socialism of pre–Thatcher days:

> [In the old days] the pupils [were] mixed boys and girls, black and white, rich and poor: the children of those who aspire and those who despair coming together in a great social experiment. There is as yet no national curriculum: there is no homework: there are occasional exams, which entail some hard work in the run up to them, should you want to pass, otherwise your life is your own. Your teachers are not chided and punished for your failures. A job can always be had, when this purgatory is over. The air you breathe, the water you drink, the bus you ride on, seem freely given: yours by social right. No one notices that the tide is turning, that market forces are seeping in, as is the notion that the only way to keep inflation down is to keep unemployment up. That for most to be comfortable quite a few must go to the wall, and society is prepared to do it [197].

Weldon sees British socioeconomic policies as the macrocosm of increasing individualism; she creates the troubles in Medusa as its microcosmic reflection.

From its very inception, Medusa members cannot agree on a mission, and do not support each other enough personally. On the evening of their creation, two of the sisters betray their ideal of standing in solidarity against patriarchy. Daffy goes to bed with Stephanie's husband, and Zoe leaves her sisters for Bull. She may just as well have been pulled back to Bull's cave by the hair as far as the sisters are concerned. They label her a "weak sister" and use her as a negative example. By implication, this exclusion contributes to her suicide. During the long scene of Medusa's initiation, Weldon takes every opportunity to break the rules of consciousness-raising (CR) as set out by second-wave feminists. CR's purpose was to give each woman an opportunity to express herself. Listening was as important as speaking. Because CR tried to avoid the trappings of male organizations, rules were not part of the plan. So, criticism was not forbidden, yet mutual support was the very bedrock of sisterhood.

Instead, Weldon depicts very little verbal support among the women at any time during the twenty-six years of Medusa's existence. On the contrary, some of the founders speak with gratuitous cruelty. When Daffy asks Stephie what "metaphorically" means, Stephie replies, "You're such a fool it's hopeless telling you" (20). In this short exchange, Weldon satirizes the tendency of educated, middle-class sisters to intimidate their uneducated counterparts, echoing a complaint that would predominate in the third wave. Stephie's refusal to define a term contradicts the very meaning of consciousness-raising. Later, Layla demonstrates the same condescension to their sister Nancy. When Nancy reproaches Layla about her frequent use of the f-word, Layla retorts, "Oh for fuck's sake, Nancy, you're the dogsbody, not the nanny" (83). Stephie and Layla put each other down as well, but their hostility is less egregious because they are equally matched. In fact, their disagreements form the dialectical tension for which the reader is grateful, because Stephie's radical feminism contrasts and contests Layla's increasing anti-feminism.

In Medusa meetings, Layla represents the voice of commerce, while Stephie represents the radical feminist ideal of empowering women. "We exist to raise female consciousness," says a radical sister, to which Layla replies, "In order to exist at all, we have to break even" (80). "Money should be the last of our considerations when it comes to choosing the list," says Stephie, and Layla replies, "So what's for dinner today? Oh, goodie, look! It's integrity" (81). "[We need not] be a prey to crude commercialism. That's the male way," says a sister. Layla retorts: "I disagree. Since the male way keeps men so comfortable, I don't see why women shouldn't do the same" (81).

In addition to their ideological differences about which titles Medusa should publish, Layla and Stephanie's friendship suffers from their competition. Both are beautiful women, and neither interferes with the sexual relationships of the other, but a struggle for personal power dominates their friendship. As the narrator relates, "They would have laid down their lives for each other, but not without a one-up remark as each expired" (123). In their effort to outwit the other, they are like characters in an Oscar Wilde play, but sometimes deadlier. And, like George and Martha in *Who's Afraid of Virginia Woolf,* they go for the jugular. Their struggle dramatizes the narrator's essential premise that women are too competitive to be able to put aside their differences for a common good. Yet Medusa does survive, and sometimes even thrives.

Weldon based Medusa on the real-life model of the Virago Press, a successful women's publishing company founded in 1973 by Carmen Callil. If Virago had not been so successful, Weldon might have destroyed Medusa earlier in its life, to prove her point that a female collective is nothing but "a randy nest of vipers." Instead of destroying Medusa, however, she strips it of its principles. Intended as a collective, Medusa initially obeyed the second-wave logic that women should eschew the hierarchical and bureaucratic models of male businesses, and its members share equally in power and profit. Yet Medusa soon converted into a shareholding company, "for reasons never fully explained" to its members (81). Those with more shares could obviously control the outcome of votes on policy and other issues. The suspense of the final chapter rides on Layla and Saffron's scramble to buy a majority of shares so that Layla can sell out. Both women earn the money to buy the stock by sleeping with married men, thus betraying two or more principles of enlightened feminism at once.

At the final Medusa board meeting, Layla is not content just to announce the sale of the concern to a mainstream publishing company with no feminist agenda. She also wants to sever emotional ties with her founding sisters. Pretending to justify the sale, she insults each founding member. Alice is "more interested in life forms on Sirius than in the philosophy of feminism." Nancy is boring. And Stephanie went "down the PC drain. No one wants to know about women as victims. These days it's girls on top.... Our readers can't live by gender alone; and women mustn't end up as unpleasant to men as they ever were to us" (341). This begs the question, why not? However, Layla was never one to explain her choices. As the wealthiest member, she had always called the shots. The women often suppressed their dissent because she had the funds to bail them out of personal disasters as well as keep Medusa afloat. Although the collective had initially intended to keep one another in line, Layla was never susceptible to any individual or group corrections: "There was a feeling around the table that she lacked the capacity for constructive self-criticism" (80). Layla is by no means presented as a role model for readers, feminist or otherwise, yet she is the most powerful of the founding Four Furies. Her daughter inherits her selfishness, and converts her own magazine into a vehicle for third-wave, sex-positive "feminism." Her readership would "rather have a boyfriend than a promotion." Although Weldon's very funny novel can be seen as a satire whose purpose is to entertain, most readers hear the serious, unspoken question at the heart of the narrative: if second-wave radical feminism does not work, then where do we go from here?

Comparing two popular novels at the turn of the century is one way to draw conclusions about third-wave feminism's different manifestations in Ireland and Britain. O'Faolain's confessional realism and Weldon's satire of second-wave idealism capture the *Zeitgeist* of their respective countries. Numerous priest sex scandals in the early 1990s destroyed Ireland's perception of herself as the world's spiritual leader. Good Mother Ireland had turned into the Bad Mother. These events left many Irish people feeling that Catholicism itself was wrong, that as a system it had failed to practice the virtues it so ardently preached; "the very concept of Catholic Ireland was, by the end of the century, gone" (Kenny 309). O'Faolain's brand of self-investigation fills the cultural void left by Catholicism's defection. Cait's efforts to understand and forgive her family, country, and self reflect the spirituality of her national heritage, without the dogma or fatal flaws of Catholicism. Her strong feminism operates as an undercurrent throughout her narrative, instructing her to overcome her socialization as a female with low self-esteem who looks for momentary release in her sexual encounters with inappropriate others. Her cultural heritage of communal orientation drives Cait to a healing reconstruction of her psychic reality, one that includes Irish community instead of excluding it.

On the other hand, Weldon's world-weary narrator eschews any spiritual response to her characters' ideological problems, and her secularism reflects her adopted nation, for England is a secular nation.[16] The great social movements of the twentieth century, including socialism, civil rights, and feminism, fulfilled for many the "religious need" that Freud argued was essentially human. But Weldon's characters do not obtain fulfillment by the adoption of feminist values and practices; she even goes so far as to say that feminism destroys them. Satire allows the narrator to stand at a distance from her characters, and from human nature itself. The satiric genre gives the author great power to judge. While the satirist takes on a God-like role, the Protestant ethos gives the individual a singular relationship to their own god and their own salvation — if salvation is of any interest.

Conclusion:
Comparative Analysis

A substantial body of Irish gynocritics has come into existence since the early eighties, to stand alongside the larger body of British women's literary history. Some anthology introductions helpfully generalize about Irish women's styles and subjects. In *Woman's Part: An Anthology of Short Fiction by and about Irish Women, 1890–1960* (1984), Janet Madden-Simpson unites Irish women writers of the first half of the century by their shared attention to realistic details of ordinary lives, a practice which garnered them a reputation for low writing, or popular fiction. Yet Madden-Simpson found that even when the characters inhabited traditional female roles, their authors' awareness of the difficulty of being women sparked recognition in their readers: "this common awareness is a bond which to some extent makes most Irish female writing feminist; that is, in the sense that the reader is almost without exception expected to identify with the heroines and to participate in their stories."[1]

In *Contemporary Irish and Welsh Women's Fiction* (2007), Linden Peach notes that Irish and Welsh women frequently employ notions of family, history and community to further the public discourse of nationhood. We have seen this phenomenon in the feminization of Ireland, and in Ireland's valorization of the family throughout the past three centuries. In fact, Irish, Northern Irish, and Welsh women's writing bears more traces of modernism than of postmodernism. In contrast to British writers' "ultimate skepticism about meaning, myth, and language," Irish writers retain the conviction that an ultimate truth or meaning does exist (14). Turning to my selected Irish writers, I find that Peach's characterization is highly accurate with regard to O'Faolain, less so with regard to O'Brien and Bowen, whose protagonists do not find a Grand Narrative of their own to put in place of the romance myth (O'Brien) or Anglo-Irish identity (Bowen) that fails them. However, I argue that their very nostalgia for a possible time or state of mind in which such entity existed or could exist, marks them with modernist angst more than postmodernist detachment.

In 2002, the publication of volumes 4 and 5 of the *Field Day Anthology,* titled *Irish Women's Writing and Traditions,* is the largest Irish gynocritical project undertaken by feminist scholars, tracing the contributions of women writers from medieval to present times. It certainly meets the gynocritical objective of providing a literary history of women, but has been criticized for its lack of attention to other important gynocritical aspects, such as literary interpretation. One of its first reviewers, Eileen Battersby, disliked what she called the sociological agenda "stalking" the volumes, saying, "We don't need roll calls or inventories at this stage of our cultural evolution. We want exploration and textual analysis."[2] It is true that the purely literary scholar might be disinterested in the bulk of historical and political writing within the volumes, and their lack of literary analysis, but both women's studies and Irish studies pride themselves on their interdisciplinarity. Perhaps this groundbreaking project is not the place to look for literary gynocriticism, but rather a base from which to build it. Anthologies of women's writing need to be compiled first, before broad criticism or the attempt to generalize about a specifically Irish literary tradition can take place.

Among these attempts to define the tradition of Irish women's writing, several are germane to my query. Christine St. Peter's *Changing Ireland: Strategies in Contemporary Women's Fiction* (2000) treats novels from the 1990s, and thus is focusing on a very small part of the twentieth century, but her discoveries about Irish women include the concept of *voice* in ways I find true and empowering. St. Peter describes women's fiction as a particularly empowering place from which to speak and challenge patriarchy. In the last decade (the nineties), women are "new kinds of subjects," and women's writing "allows women to discover or create places from which to speak" (3).

Echoing this concept of women's writing as a place of resistance, and extrapolating from Julia Kristeva's theory on women's writing and nationalism, Heather Ingman writes, "Literature, in an Irish context, may provide a space in which to resist the homogenization of the nation brought about by the discourse of Irish nationalism" (*Twentieth Century Fiction by Irish Women* 5). Kristeva believes that women are well positioned to fight totalitarianism because they are treated as exiles from the public life of the nation. Ingman notes, as I do, that Irish women's literature is a place for this resistance. In telling their stories, Irish women are revealing the truths of their social conditions.

In "These Traits Also Endure," Sally Barr Ebest compares Irish and Irish-American women novelists writing between the 1960s and 2003. Irish writing by both genders explores themes of "the domineering mother and submissive daughter; lives ruined by alcohol, drugs, violence, and abuse; lives saved by family, friends, or religion; and a penchant stylistically for formal experimentation, linguistic exuberance, and satiric modes."[3] To this list, Ebest adds other traits that Irish women writers share with Irish-American women writers:

> They feature female protagonists coming of age despite, and often in defiance of traditional expectations regarding a woman's role. They decry sexism, alcoholism, violence, and abuse. They promote independence yet reiterate the importance of motherhood. They emphasize the strength that comes from family, friends, and community. They show the rise and warn us of the fall of feminism. They point out the church's weaknesses in dealing with women, while they remind us of the need for faith [71].

Indeed, Ebest finds that spirituality is the defining trait of Irish women writers on both sides of the Atlantic. Though it may be unspoken, the "mix of conscience and guilt continues to guide most plots" (72). Citing Mary Kenny and Edna O'Brien on the topic, Ebest asserts that even in the face of rising secularism and waning Catholicism, the Irish continue to be a spiritual people.

In addition to their spiritual lives, realism thrives as a means of expression for Irish women. In *Two Irelands*, Rebecca Pelan claims that Irish women writers' use of realism is their predominant characteristic, and a strong vehicle for feminism. As postmodernism has become the predominant mode of fiction since the sixties, a certain academic prejudice against realism has appeared. Calling realism "an ideology that conceals the socially relative or constructed nature of language" and is "complicit with patriarchal systems of representation," some critics believe realism is a tool of conservatives to maintain status quo (116, 117). Some poststructuralist theorists pose experimentalism as the opposite to realism, in its potential to subvert patriarchy or capitalism; because it challenges the representational nature of language, experimentalism at least appears to question all ordering systems. However, when I test this hypothesis on key Irish texts, I do not arrive at the same conclusion as these poststructuralists. Consider, for instance, Joyce's *Ulysses* next to O'Brien's *Country Girls Trilogy*. Does Joyce unseat Irish hegemonies any more effectively by his rhetorical experimentation than O'Brien does by her realism? No, both texts unsettle Irish pieties at very deep levels; Leopold Bloom's humanitarianism transcends sectarian prejudice, and Kate Brady's tragedy exposes the costs of Catholic taboos around female sexuality. Pelan even goes one step further, believing that realism has *more* potential than experimentalism to incite challenges to existing orders because (a) it is more accessible to readers, and (b) readers who identify with oppressed female protagonists reflect on their own lives, and begin to stage their own challenges to oppression.

The earliest theorist of Irish women's writing, Ann Owen Weekes, contributes much to this dialog by describing the "uncharted tradition" of Irish women's writing in her 1990 monograph. Distinguishing between Protestant- and Catholic-inflected novels, Weekes echoes Ebest in noting that contemporary Irish writers lament the demise of Catholicism because of their sense that it was a source of "human warmth and communion in the face of a hostile world" (219). A study of Irish women writers from 1800 to 1990 reveals several trends. Quoting Adrienne Rich, Weekes finds that Irish women writers like to "dive into the wreck" of their common Irish history, feeling the need to reassess its meaning to them as women. Women's lives are notoriously absent from Irish historical narratives, yet Irish women writers receive an unconscious heritage from their mothers' labor, similar to the Irish culture's "double grammatical and double cultural mode" that arises from the imposition of English language and laws on Gaelic-speaking people (218). Another common theme in Irish women's writing is an undercurrent of awareness of both the value and cost of relationships (23). Most importantly for the present study, Irish women repeatedly return to the *bildungsroman*, re-writing this classic genre with a feminist twist. Unlike male counterparts, feminist protagonists do not reach maturity by engaging in fulfilling sexual relationships, but rather by banishing traditional romantic expectations (214). Thus, Bowen's protagonist Lois Farquar would rather marry or kiss a woman than a man; O'Brien's Kate and Baba both find tragedy at the heart of romance; and O'Faolain's protagonist, Cait, leaves her lover in order to protect her own health.

Building upon these characterizations by Ebest, Ingman, Pelan, St. Peter, and Weekes, in the present book, I add to their list of Irish writers' traits, intending to sharpen their portrait by contrast to their British counterparts. My selected British writers show an antipathy to feminist activism, yet an affinity to cultural feminism, in that they find women the most interesting subject of fiction (until the third wave, when writers such as Zadie Smith and Monica Ali focus on race and ethnicity). Woolf's fiction makes suffragettes into caricatures because they are so single-minded, yet her nonfiction, particularly *Three Guineas*, is radically cultural-feminist, as it advocates the separation of women from men in order to attain their own goals in education and politics. Lessing's antipathy to feminist activism is most strongly stated in her dictum, "Everything I dislike about politics is enshrined in the women's movement. It's just petty and stupid" (Klein 192). She portrays this attitude in Anna Wulf, who is ashamed for thinking that her plight could possibly represent all women's plight. Anna's womanly self-denigration reminds me of Rick's famous sentence of condescension to Ilsa at the end of *Casablanca*: "It doesn't take much to see that the problems of three little people don't add up to a hill of beans in this crazy world." Cultural feminism says that relationship problems *do* matter, and are part of a larger social order. Weldon resembles both Woolf and Lessing in her satiric attitude towards feminist activism. Her entire novel shows women's liberationists as objects of satire. Although in the 1990s, Weldon writes nostalgically of pre–Thatcher days, she is not a socialist. In fact, her capitalist critique appears in the form of sarcastic comments about the bottom line. If she is aware of one dominant form of hegemony in British society, it is capitalism. Yet she separates that particular form of oppression from patriarchy. In Weldon's worldview, people are consumed by their drive to succeed at the most basic levels on Maslow's Hierarchy of Needs. By this standard, feminism would be one of the higher Maslovian needs (self-actualization), that gets marginalized as long as basic needs predominate. This view, however, ignores the needs of working class women, who do require the feminist struggle for equal rights and equal pay in order to meet their most basic survival needs.

Despite Weldon's disavowals, it is British feminism's long alliance with socialism that may account for these writers' reticence to put gender first in their hierarchy of values. All three of my British subjects tried in various ways to transcend their own essentialist tendencies in regard to gender difference, finding ways to universalize suffering instead of blaming women's suffering on patriarchy. When Bloomsbury was compelled by the fervor of the Russian Revolution, Woolf felt guilty about being so comfortably middle class: "I'm one of those who are hampered by the psychological hindrance of owning capital." Her greatest artistic attempt to transcend gender boundaries lay in her valuation of androgyny as the artist's *sine qua non*. Only by cultivating his or her inner male and female halves, could the artist achieve any balanced approach to character. Lessing's universalization of suffering was also along class lines, as taught by the Communist Party. Although communist ideology couched its misogyny in universal, non-gendered terms, I show in Chapter 4 that its prohibitions against personal, emotional literary expression dovetailed with patriarchy's denigration of such attributes in women. Communism's motto might as well be Carol Hanisch's in reverse, saying "the personal is *not* political," and adding a guilt factor that many female Communists would internalize when they wanted to write about women's inner lives. Weldon, too, tends to universalize human suffering, rather than gender it. Her default explanation for suffering is "human nature," not patriarchy, making her unpopular with poststructuralists who refuse to recognize such an essentialist entity as human nature. Targeting human weakness as the cause of suffering aligns Weldon with a long tradition of British satire.

If British feminism has had a long alliance with socialism, Irish feminism has had a close association with nationalism. Gender is written into Irish identity through the feminization of the Irish state, which proscribes sexual behavior ("only for procreation") and sexual identity in women. Many women's novels written since 1950 have to do with women's sexual lives, precisely because Catholic-nationalist hegemony has directed so much attention to that sphere. The Irish protagonists in this study struggle to form identities that can push back against social pressure with a modicum of individuality. Bowen's character, Lois, doubly orphaned by family and nation, identifies with a mentor (Marda) who, though older, has not won that social battle, and whose form of answering-back is mere social wit. O'Brien's Kate is asphyxiated by the hegemonic pressures described in Chapter 4. She internalizes Eugene's scorn towards the Irish, so much that she identifies with the negative stereotype. Finally, the only identity she wishes to achieve is the negative one of the "deject," submitting to her desire for non-being through suicide. O'Faolain's character, Cait, is the only one of the three who is victorious in this regard, regaining much of what she had lost by fleeing Ireland in her twenties. Her return trip gives her back an Irish identity in its good manifestation; vanquishing the Bad Objects of her dysfunctional Irish family, Cait now finds a resiliency in Irishness that bodes well for her future development.

Conversely, we cannot say that the British protagonists are engaged in a search for their British identity. If Clarissa Dalloway, Anna Wulf, and Layla Lavery have anything in common, it is the individualism of their struggles for meaningful life in a meaningless world. They are very lonely people. Each character reifies the cultural angst stemming from major twentieth-century political events, all taking place on an international scale, in direct contrast to the Irish focus of the Irish novels. Clarissa identifies so eerily with Septimus, a male, post-traumatic-stress victim of World War I, because her life too has been traumatic, though in the distaff world of family relations. Anna Wulf's absorption of Stalin's atrocities, Communism's failure, and her comrades' betrayals leads to a schizophrenic breakdown in which she hallucinates, and changes places with, heroes and victims of third world countries. Though on a different scale (being written in the satiric mode), Layla Lavery loses the political consciousness that made her a 1970s feminist leader, and turns into a capitalist narcissist. In Weldon's broad-brush caricature of social change, Thatcherism changed the consciousness of good English people until their former selves were unrecognizable.

Besides their difference in world awareness, the Irish and British novels differ in their literary genres and tones. As mentioned, most contemporary Irish women write in a realist mode. Confessional realism is a subgenre in which novelists discuss matters relating to their personal lives, only thinly disguised as fiction. They use intimate details and psychoanalytic terms to express painful experiences. O'Faolain's novel exemplifies this mode. Because of O'Faolain's two highly successful memoirs, the reader knows that Cait's quest and her sexual experience are close to the author's own. The Irish writers are not the only ones to be working in this mode; notably, Weldon's novels of the last decade, such as *Chalcot Crescent* (2009) and *Mantrapped* (2004), have tracked her own life closely. However, Weldon's principal genre is satire, and she makes her own life an object of satire. This satiric tone makes hers a different confessional style than O'Faolain's.

The tone of the three British texts, on the other hand, shows their narrators at a certain remove from self, using irony more than earnestness to express their feelings. Woolf's *To the Lighthouse* is sometimes cited as a model of high modernism, synonymous with an aestheticism that features rarefied moments of heightened consciousness. *Mrs. Dalloway* shares some of this quality, as it jumps from one character's perceptions to another's. The tone of *The Golden Notebook* is characterized by Anna's self-deprecation. Her interior monologue represents an endless struggle to justify her writing, loves, and communist activities. In Anna's stream of consciousness, Lessing replicates the solipsistic nature of the mind in crisis. In contrast, both O'Brien and O'Faolain's highly relatable characters invite the average reader to identity with them; to a greater extent, the authors seem to be talking to an imagined audience rather than themselves. Although Fay Weldon sometimes addresses the reader directly, the tone is not intimate, but aggressive, as when she complains that novel-readers have been spoiled by reality TV.

In both traditions, irony is a key element of feminist literature. The double-voiced discourse of women writers offers an implied critique of the dominant order, often through ironic, satiric, or parodic modes. Yet Irish irony is different from British. Their people's long experience of being the underdog has added a fatalistic edge to Irish humor, which is often self-deprecating, utilizing ethnic humor against themselves. This self-ironic stance may derive from the Catholic practice of confession, in which the supplicant abases herself before a Father Confessor. She depends upon an outside authority to judge her behavior. O'Brien works cleverly with situational irony. For instance, Kate's romanticism contrasts with the reality of her so-called lovers' terrible behavior. Baba swears copiously in defiance of her Catholic upbringing, yet the reader senses that behind this tough exterior, lives a hurt little girl. Baba satirizes the live-in nurse who cares for her husband after his stroke: "I don't think old Cooney herself ever bled, couldn't part with it. Old Cooney begrudges me every bit of malarkey I've ever had, like a Reverend Mother, always eyeing you and telling you about widows and divorced women and women with cancer, wanting you to join in lugubrious confraternity" (527). Baba sees that the Church pretends to care about young girls' futures, but is only interested in controlling their sexuality. Her cynical voice addresses an audience that she assumes is as weary of religious hypocrisy as she is.

O'Faolain's wit is often turned against the naïveté of her younger self. In *Are You Somebody*, she reports: "I had a messianic belief in the capacity of the academic study of English literature to change a person utterly" (99). Bowen's Anglo-Protestant humor carries a tone of world-weary sophistication. One of my favorite lines of *The Last September* is Lady Naylor's putdown of Hugo Montmorency, the ineffectual man who can't decide where to live or whom to love. Naylor says that maybe Hugo will die, as "that would be just his way of avoiding things." The absurdity of many of the characters' lines in *The Last September* exhibits the dandy quality discussed in Chapter 3, and associated with Oscar Wilde's silly aphorisms. This distancing from the inner voice, this assuming of a pose, is a characteristic that I associate with Anglo-Irish and British voices.

The sense of humor and irony found in the three British novels illustrate this distance between self and subject. *Mrs. Dalloway* is not a funny book, but situational irony abounds. For instance, in one of the most amusing segments, both Clarissa and Miss Kilman think about how much they hate each other, and try to rationalize or deny that hatred. "But Miss Kilman did not hate Mrs. Dalloway ... she felt, Fool! Simpleton! You who have known neither sorrow nor pleasure; who have trifled your life away! And there rose in her an overmastering desire to overcome her; to unmask her" (189). Situational irony consists in the fact that both women try to justify their hatred based on class values, but neither realizes the humanity in the other, despite their commitment to humanity in the abstract. Dramatic irony consists in the fact that the reader knows more than Kilman, having seen that Clarissa lives in anxiety and grief, while Kilman thinks that she is only a superficial person.

Weldon's irony is obvious, even splashy. One-liners saturate the text of *Big Women*. "Catty? Felines are nothing compared with women" (6). "Unable to change themselves [the feminists], they turned their attention to society, and set about changing that, for good or bad" (1). Stephie: "Feminists don't lie to one another. Sometimes I wonder if you're a feminist at all." Layla: "That is not such a terrible accusation as you might fucking think" (126). Weldon's is a challenging, satirical humor, which asks us to laugh at the human desire for self-improvement. No one is spared Weldon's attack, though kind and naïve people like Nancy take less flak. Weldon's pose of toughness keeps her writing self at a distance from her suffering self. In *Auto da Fay*, she switches from first to third person when telling of her first marriage because "Fay Bateman is more than the current 'I' can bear." Weldon tries to keep herself at a safe distance from the sources of her pain.

Both Weldon and Bowen use irony to keep overwhelming feelings at bay. Discovering the colonial prejudices of her ancestors, Bowen begins to feel a certain embarrassment at her legacy. She satirizes Anglo-Irish complacency, while keeping her fears and guilt at a distance. Weldon demonstrates the antipodean immigrant's insecurity about never being able to acquire British sophistication. Unlike Woolf or even Lessing, Weldon does not appear to identify as British when she blasts her adopted country's various institutions and social trends. Her aggressive wit may be an overcompensating attempt by a "colonial" to acquire British cynicism. On the other hand, it might also be a protective reaction for one whose life has been riddled by betrayals and abandonment.

The choices and voices of all six writers are amalgams of their experiences and the psychodynamics of their biological families, in addition to the cultural hegemonies that they imbibed from living in particular times and places. As the preceding discussion demonstrates, comparative literary criticism needs to contend with several sensitive factors before it can offer general conclusions about national, ethnic, religious and gender influences upon literary production. The concept of intersectionality asks us to examine multiple influences as a composite, rather than isolating them, or neglecting some at the expense of others. Disclaimers aside, I have come to the following conclusions about Irish and British twentieth-century women's writing, using six iconic writers as examples. The British writers had an antipathy to feminist activism, yet an affinity to cultural feminism, meaning that women's lives were the most interesting subject of fiction. Yet there was also a reticence to put gender first in their anatomy of the "diseases of our time," to use Lessing's phrase. British feminism's long alliance with socialism made women see class struggle intertwined with gender wars, creating a sense of guilt when they isolated their gender as the root of women's suffering. This guilt may account for the adoption of ironic poses, and their choice to write in genres that place a certain distance between writer and suffering self, such as satire, high modernism, or science fiction. Their irony is world-weary, and at all times conscious of the world outside Britain as the bigger canvas upon which the human condition is painted.

The Irish Catholic writers are divided on feminism. Both O'Brien and O'Faolain demonstrate that Catholic-nationalist patriarchy influenced generations of families, who passed down their dysfunction. O'Brien believes there is a strong biological and psychological difference between men and women that damns them to repeat these tragic patterns. O'Faolain appreciates the psychological difference between men and women, but believes in the power of the individual to overcome her inherited patterns through self-analysis. She is forthright about the Church's role in producing women's self-destructive tendencies. As Irish women become more aware of the ways in which Catholic-nationalist hegemony constructs feminine identity, their feminism will grow. Bowen's feminism was repressed by her childhood traumas and the Ascendancy's fragile status; she cultivated a crisp, satiric voice that would enable her to align herself with other survivors in Britain.

For many women, Irish feminism's early alliance with nationalism created a similar guilt complex as did England's alliance with socialism; in other words, they believed that pursuit of feminism detracted from these other dominant ideologies. Throughout the second half of the century, Irish women writers prefer realism and the confessional mode. Realism works well for them, in part because they have only begun to find their true voices. Ireland's permission to speak of women's sexuality is much more recent than Britain's. The nature of Irish irony is fatalistic, self-deprecating, and ethnically aware, in view of the country's long history of colonization and its citizens' experience of ethnic prejudice. Irish writers share a collective memory of their cultural and historical past. They recognize shared national symbols, giving a communal aspect to their experience, and the opportunity to forge a positive sense of their own national identity.

In the Introduction, I mentioned Elaine Showalter's historical model. British women's writing passed through three phases in the three centuries that the novel has existed as a form: (1) imitation of men's writing, (2) resistance and separation from men and (3) search for self-transformation. Postcolonial theorists use a similar model for decolonization: in newly independent nations, writers first imitate, later react against, the imported culture of their former colonizers. In the third stage, they acknowledge the influence of the colonizer culture, creating a hybrid cultural product that incorporates elements of both. England's colonization of Ireland was so long in duration that such cultural cross-pollination is particularly strong. All three of the Irish novels studied in the present book invoke England and Englishness as a central place, power and challenge to the characters' identities. Less apparent but equally important is Ireland's influence on British women's writing. Remembering Bataille's theory that the dominant cultural defines itself by its opposite, and Kristeva's model of abjection of the abhorred Other, we can say that British writers' identities are strongly reliant on their most proximate geographical Other, Ireland. Through literature, voices of Irish and British women writers can come into dialog.

Literature carries the voices of both repressed and oppressed aspects of humanity. It is a space for conflict to be expressed and mediated, even if that mediation involves such drastic resolutions as insanity, death, or the destruction of property. The intensity of these resolutions demonstrates the magnitude of the conflict. The feminist impulse in all six novels is to give voice to this intense conflict, demonstrating the roles that gender, race, and class oppressions play in women's and men's unhappiness. Staging these oppressions is the political act of the artist. One voice can heal another: this is the political and spiritual function of literature.

Chapter Notes

Preface

1. Quoted in Alcoff, "Cultural Feminism versus Post-Structuralism: The Identity Crisis in Feminist Theory," *Signs* 13:3 (Spring 1988), 409.

Introduction

1. Pankhurst, *My Own Story* (New York: New York Source Book, 1970), 66.

2. In 1987, postcolonial critic Gayatri Spivak justified studies about particular groups (in her case, Indian women) by saying that they serve a political interest. She called such projects a "strategic essentialism," one that is valid as long as it serves "a scrupulously visible political interest," such as identifying a group as a cohesive unit in order to present a political identity and position from which to fight. She has subsequently expressed dismay at how the phrase has been distorted in identity politics, but continues to stand by her original meaning. In *The Spivak Reader: Selected Works of Gayatri Chavravorty Spivak* (London: Routledge, 1995), 214.

3. Gilligan, *In a Different Voice* (Cambridge: Harvard University Press, 1993), xvi.

4. Poststructuralist French feminist theory describes this separate woman's language as *écriture féminine*, the inscription of the female body and female difference in language and text. The idea of dominant discourse is also expressed by the term *phallologocentrism*, the idea that discourse is organized through implicit recourse to the phallus as its prime signifier. In other words, culture is prejudiced towards language and logic made by men. This example shows that cultural feminism is not so antithetical to poststructuralism that the two cannot coexist.

5. Spaull and Pearce, "Gynocriticism," in *Feminist Readings, Feminists Reading*, ed. Sara Mills and Lynne Pearce (London: Prentice Hall, 1996), 100.

6. In *Women Writing and Writing about Women*, ed. Mary Jacobus (London: Croom Helm, 1979).

7. Bourke et al., *The Field Day Anthology of Irish Writing, Vol. v: Irish Women's Writing and Traditions* (New York: New York University Press, 2002), xxxvi.

8. Showalter, *A Literature of Their Own* (Princeton: Princeton University Press, 1977), 11.

9. Showalter, "Towards a Feminist Poetics," in *Modern Feminisms*, ed. Maggie Humm (New York: Columbia University Press, 1992), 383.

10. Sex-positive feminism is a third-wave variant; it claims that women's right to have sex and display their bodies in pornographic ways is a feminist achievement. Ireland's long-standing reticence around sexual expression has had the positive effect of reducing the incidence of this kind of propaganda in Ireland.

Chapter One

1. Ward, *Unmanageable Revolutionaries: Women and Irish Nationalism* (London: Pluto Press, 1983), 18. Here, and throughout this section, Ward is paraphrasing Anna Parnell's 1907 memoir, *The Land League: Tale of a Great Sham*, National Library of Ireland, MS. 12144. Police confiscated the manuscript in 1909. It was retrieved in the 1950s and placed in the National Library archives by Professor T. W. Moody.

2. Iseult Gonne's upbringing raises the question whether most famous people lack the qualities that would make them good parents for sensitive children. For instance, Margaret Mead's daughter, Mary Catherine Bateson, confessed that even though her mother was called Mother of the World for her tireless work in anthropology, she was not present or nurturing enough to be a good mother to her own nuclear family. The question of why Gonne did not tailor Iseult as well as Sean for the role of Ireland's savior should interest psychoanalysts concerned with the psychology of gender and mothering.

3. Constance's daughter, Maeve Markievicz, was born at Lissadell, the Gore-Booth estate, and was brought up by Constance's mother. Some critics fault de Markievicz for abandoning her child, and Maeve reports feeling somewhat neglected. But Constance felt that her bohemian lifestyle was not as healthy for a child as the country life at Lissadell. Anne Haverty is one biographer who has addressed the issue of Markievicz's neglect. It is interesting that both Maud Gonne and Constance de Markievicz were less nurturing of their daughters than one might expect from feminists, but few people would agree on what constitutes a good feminist.

4. "The personal is political" is a motto coined by Carol Hanisch, a radical New York second-wave feminist who led the Miss America protest in 1968. The motto means that the bedroom or the kitchen — in short, the marriage domain – is as political as the public sphere. Personal relationships between the sexes are political because they deal with power imbalances stemming from patriarchy.

Chapter Two

1. Ward, "Conflicting Interests: The British and Irish Suffrage Movements," *Feminist Review* 50 (Summer 1995), 127.

Chapter Three

1. What Naomi Black here describes as a "social feminist" is what most academicians would call a radical feminist, one who believes that biological differences define men and women, and that the genders should work separately because of these differences. Black's term is confusing for another reason: it should not be confused with a "socialist" feminist, nor was Woolf socialist enough to warrant that label.

2. In her book *Gender Trouble* (London: Routledge, 1990), Judith Butler argues that gender is "the stylized repetition of acts through time," in other words, a performance (192). Because this performance is necessary for survival, the consequences of failure are dire. The idea of gender as a performance predicated on "compulsory heterosexuality" stems from Adrienne Rich's essay, "Compulsory Heterosexuality and Lesbian Existence" (1980). This work claims that heterosexuality is a default sexual orientation that people assume, regardless of their actual sexual preference. Heterosexuality is a learned behavior, required by patriarchy. Rich argues that heterosexuality limits women's full sexual and emotional potential because it denies them a way of being sexual that is unrelated to male pleasure.

The melancholy of gender performance derives from Freud's essay on mourning and melancholia. The relinquishment of the mother as the primary love object in childhood results in an internalization of that object. The ambivalence the ego once felt for that object now reverses, so that the anger the ego once felt towards the mother is now directed by the internalized object onto the self. The melancholic refuses the loss of the object, but the identification the ego once felt with the object now becomes anger against the self. The ego changes place with the internalized object, giving it moral agency and power, making it the ego ideal. This ego ideal consolidates gender identity through rechanneling and sublimating desire.

The ego ideal implements and polices society's homosexuality taboo, but the repression results in sadness. "Because identifications substitute for object relations, and identifications are the consequence of loss, gender identification is a kind of melancholia in which the sex of the prohibited object is internalized as a prohibition" (86). In my reading, gender performance is melancholic (for Lois and other characters in *The Last September*) because it is based on prohibition, repressions and anxious self-criticism.

3. In Joyce's autobiographical novel *Portrait of the Artist as a Young Man* (Harmondsworth: Penguin, 1993), Stephen Dedalus vows to leave Ireland to "forge in the smithy of my soul the uncreated conscience of my race." He cannot become a true artist in his homeland because its institutions are too controlling: "When the soul of man is born in this country there are nets flung

at it to hold it back from flight. You talk to me of nationality, language, religion. I shall try to fly by those nets."

4. In *Virginia Woolf: The Impact of Childhood Sexual Abuse on her Life and Works*, (New York: Ballantine, 1991), Louise DeSalvo places most of the cause for Woolf's breakdowns and suicide upon sexual abuse by her two half-brothers. Fear of German invasion and reading Freud were the proximate causes of Woolf's suicide. In 1896, Freud published his seduction theory, saying that the cause of female hysteria was childhood sexual abuse and its antidote was the talking cure. Virginia took heart, and hoped to cure herself by writing *To the Lighthouse*. Later, Freud retracted the seduction theory, shifting the cause of hysteria to a child's unconscious desire for the parent. With this revision, Woolf lost the grounds of support for her own attempts to exorcise her past traumas. Jane Marcus and Elaine Showalter have also analyzed Woolf's madness and questioned why she did not seek psychoanalytic treatment. Marcus points out that psychoanalysis was believed to be destructive for fragile patients, and that sequestration was the gold standard of the time, so that Leonard should not be second-guessed in his choice of treatment for Virginia. See Nicole Ward Jouve, ("Virginia Woolf and Psychoanalysis," *The Cambridge Companion to Virginia Woolf*, ed. Sue Roe and Susan Sellers (Cambridge: Cambridge University Press, 2000), 246-52.

5. Fredric Jameson, *The Political Unconscious: Narrative as a Socially Symbolic Act* (Ithaca: Cornell UP, 1981).

6. Kristeva, *Powers of Horror: An Essay on Abjection* (New York: Columbia University Press, 1982).

Chapter Four

1. In "Compulsory Heterosexuality and Lesbian Existence," Adrienne Rich observes that patriarchy compels women to identify with men, since men are the ones who hold power in the system. Women are expected to have sexual relations with men, and to rely on them for economic security, employment, and social acceptance. In order to take back responsibility for their own self-definition, women should separate themselves from men and engage in some form of lesbian relationship to determine whether heterosexuality is really right for them. Because their earliest relationship is with a woman, Rich believes that all women identify somewhere along a *lesbian continuum*, whether they have had sex with other women or not. "Compulsory Heterosexuality and Lesbian Existence," *Blood, Bread, and Poetry: Selected Prose* (New York: Norton, 1986).

2. In *A Literature of Their Own* (Princeton: Princeton University Press, 1977), Elaine Showalter describes three stages of women writers' emancipation: the Feminine period, 1840-1880, when women writers imitated men; Feminist period, 1880-1920, when women writers protested male dominance; and Female period (1920–present), when women writers seek self-transformation.

3. "The personal is political" was a popular motto coined by Carol Hanisch in 1970 to express the idea that patriarchal power relations have as prominent a role in the home as in public life (see Chapter One, note 4). This phrase was particularly useful to heal women's sense that their personal lives were not of interest to the women's movement. The Women's Liberation Movement's greatest contribution was to focus feminist consciousness inwards, upon women's domestic and sexual relationships.

4. Besides biological and constructionist feminism, there are many other types. The following list is partial, but defines some types that pertain to this discussion. *Liberal feminists* believe that men and women are equal, and strive to attain equal rights under the law and through changes in economic policy. *Socialist feminists* believe that economic oppression causes gender discrimination, and strive to change the state apparatus to a socialist model. *Cultural feminists* believe that men and women are different, and that women have inherently feminine characteristics that make them better at certain tasks than men, such as nurturing. I have used the term *literary feminism* in this book to mean both awareness of this psychological difference and the production of art that stages the problems of patriarchy. *Separatist feminists* also believe in biological difference, and strive to create women-only lifestyles. Some other types of feminism are lesbian, radical, ecological, and black.

5. Wilfred Owen's 1917 poem, "*Dulce et Decorum Est*," is the most famous of the World War I poems. The brutal imagery of gas victims refutes the "old lie" that says it is sweet and fitting to die for one's country. Instead, this poem brings home the opposite message, that war is brutal and inappropriate for humanity.

6. World Fairs were a kind of the turn-of-the-century TV, advertising the allure of foreign lands. For example, Paul Gauguin decided to move to Tahiti when he saw bare-chested women at the Tahitian booth of the 1899 World Fair Exhibition in Paris. The move changed the way he

painted; and this change contributed to Post-Impressionism in unprecedented ways. I have written extensively about his choice to live in Tahiti in *Islands and the Modernists: The Allure of Isolation in Arts, Literature, and Science* (Jefferson, NC: McFarland. 2006).

7. As Sandra Gilbert and Susan Gubar explain in *Madwoman in the Attic: The Woman Writer and the Nineteenth-Century Imagination* (New Haven: Yale University Press, 2000), the *bildungsroman* is adapted to a male quest because it enables the hero to find his own voice in the community he inhabits, whereas a female *bildungsroman* entails the opposite, the silencing of her individual voice so that she can find a safe place in patriarchal society.

8. Quotations in this and the following paragraph are from Shusha Guppy's interview with O'Brien, in summer of 1984, published in *The Paris Review* 92.

9. From the definition of *hegemony* in *The Bedford Glossary of Critical and Literary Terms*, 3d ed., eds. Ross Murfin and Supryia M. Ray (Boston: Bedford/St. Martin's, 2009), 221.

10. To achieve individuation, Freud holds that the infant must resolve the Oedipal complex in which it wishes to bond exclusively with the mother, and destroy the father. The child's belief that the father will castrate him in retribution leads to his attempts to identify with the father and create an independent identity from the mother. In Lacan's theory, the pre–Oedipal existence is called the Imaginary Order, in which nonverbal communication occurs between infant and mother. The quality of that exchange determines how well adjusted the child will be. At about the age of eighteen months, when it can recognize its Self in the mirror, the child begins to enter the Symbolic Order. The Law of the Father rules the Symbolic Order, and derives from the patriarchal systems of language and authority that constitute identity after the original bond with the mother is cut.

11. The closeness of this bond and the near-fatal devastation upon its breaking resembles Paul and Gertrude Morel's bond in D. H. Lawrence's *Sons and Lovers*. In childhood, Paul defended his mother against his father's alcoholic rages. In adolescence, he discarded girlfriends because of his mother's jealousy, and chose opposite types of women to meet his spiritual (Miriam) and physical (Clara) needs, enacting the Virgin/Whore complex that devalues and makes Woman wholly Other. When Gertrude dies, Paul can barely summon the will to live. Without his identificatory bond with Mother, Paul feels meaningless, like Kate.

12. Carol Gilligan's groundbreaking work, *In a Different Voice* (Cambridge: Harvard University Press, 1982), establishes that women and men do have different moral codes, characterizing women's as an "ethics of responsibility" and men's as an "ethics of rights." Her work refutes Freud's assertions that men are more moral than women. Anna's keen sense of the difference of male and female needs predates second-wave feminism's theorization of these differences. Gilligan's work affords understanding and relief to many women who have internalized patriarchy's critique of the lesser nobility of "the female character."

Chapter Five

1. On the subject of rape being women's fault, see Katie Roiphe, *The Morning After: Sex, Fear and Feminism* (Boston: Back Bay Books, 1994) and Camille Paglia, *Sexual Personae: Art and Decadence from Nefertiti to Emily Dickinson* (New York: Vintage, 1991).

2. In *Post-Backlash Feminism* (Jefferson, NC: McFarland, 2007), Kellie Bean describes the Bush administration and the conservative media's efforts to scapegoat the Woman's Movement for the state of war and terrorism in the world. Feminists who did not endorse Bush's foreign policy after 9/11 were credited with "creating enemies angry enough to attack New York City" (146). Images of Middle Eastern women in burkhas and news of the Taliban's restrictions on women fueled the Right's ideological attack on the American Women's Movement because, in contrast, American women had so many freedoms (144). An American woman's participation in the torture of prisoners in Abu Ghraib was framed as proof that women do not belong in the military because they disrupt military order. Detractors argued that feminism had made Lynndie England perplexed about her gender identity, so that she took on the male role of torturing war prisoners, overcompensating because of her gender confusion (130).

3. Whelehan, *Modern Feminist Thought* (Edinburg: University of Edinburgh Press, 1995), 49.

4. In a *Ms.* magazine article in 1992, Rebecca Walker declares, "I am not a postfeminist feminist. I am the Third Wave" (Bean, 66).

5. Catriona Crowe, "Forty Years of Feminism," http://www.kilkennyarts.ie/bog/article/catrione-crowe-forty-years-of-feminism-notes/. 18 June 2011.

6. Ibid.

7. Fay Weldon interview with Elizabeth Grice, 12 March 2009, *The Telegraph*, http://telegraph.co.uk/culture/4980926/Fay-Weldon-Dying-I-Don't-Want-To-Do-That-Again.html.

8. *BBC Online Network*, 30 June 1998, http://news.bbc.co.uk/2/hi/uk_news/122813.stm.

9. Grice interview.

10. Interview with Stuart Jeffries, 5 September 2006, *The Guardian*, http://guardian.co.uk/world/2006/sep/06/gender.religion.

11. The term *imago* derives from Jungian psychology; it is the image that an individual constructs out of the best and worst aspects of their parents. In turn, they seek a romantic relationship with a person who has all of these traits, in a desperate attempt to rework the traumas of their childhood.

12. *Intersectionality* is a term coined by Kimberlé Crenshaw to express the matrix of identities intersecting in each woman. Born from the disillusionment of black and lesbian feminists with the capacity of the (mostly white, middle-class) American Women's Movement to represent them, this sociological concept stresses that components of identity (such as race, class, ability, orientation, and gender) are interwoven in a person, and none of them should be ignored when analyzing oppression.

13. For instance, the movie and television actor Gabriel Byrne wrote in his memoir, *Pictures in my Head* (Dublin: Wolfhound Press, 2001), and autobiographical film, *Stories from Home* (dir. Pat Collins, 2008), of his strong sense of exile while working and living in America. Like O'Faolain, he was running away from troubles he considered Irish, such as the trauma of abuse by priests in his childhood, family neglect, and alcoholism. At the same time, he recognized that Los Angeles and New York could never provide the sense of community to which he was accustomed.

14. Hannah Segal, ed., *Introduction to the Work of Melanie Klein* (London: Karnac Books, 1988), 125-28.

15. Toni O'Brien Johnson and David Cairns address this issue of the masculinist production of the literary canon in their Introduction to *Gender in Irish Writing* (Milton Keynes: Open University, 1991): "Since the culture that produced the texts examined in these essays [a selection of Irish literature] is patriarchal, and since accordingly it is the male and his constructed masculinity that dominates (for knowledge of what it is that make a man "masculine" is assumed to be universal and therefore unquestioned and unquestionable), it is inevitable that the main resistance to showing up the negative of the construction of "masculinity" should come from the male. It sometimes also comes from male-identified women, who have learnt all too well to accept a role that masculinism authorizes, and who resist the uncovering of the personal and psychological price they pay for such role-restriction. So long as one of the genders dominates the other, the dominant is unlikely willingly to forego the privileged position" (2-3). Fay Weldon is one of these male-identified women who resist the uncovering of the price they pay – despite her eight years of Freudian therapy and her consciousness of oppression.

16. In a 2007 survey, only 15 percent of United Kingdom respondents said they attended church. A 2005 poll reported that only 38 percent of United Kingdom citizens believed in God, contrasted with 73 percent of Irish.

Conclusion

1. Quoted in Pelan, *Two Irelands* (Syracuse: Syracuse University Press, 2005), 128.

2. *Ibid.*, xx.

3. Fanning, *The Irish Voice in America* (Lexington: University Press of Kentucky, 1990), quoted in Ebest, "These Traits Also Endure: Contemporary Irish and Irish-American Women Writers," *New Hibernia Review* 7:2 (Summer 2003), 55-72, p. 71.

Works Cited

Primary Sources

Bowen, Elizabeth. *Bowen's Court*. New York: Knopf, 1964.
_____. *The Last September*. New York: Knopf, 1952.
_____. *The Mulberry Tree: Writings of Elizabeth Bowen*. Intro. Hermione Lee. London: Virago, 1986.
_____. *People, Place, Things: Essays by Elizabeth Bowen*. Ed. Allan Hepburn. Edinburgh: Edinburgh University Press, 2008.
_____. *Pictures and Conversations: Chapters of an Autobiography with Other Collected Writings*. New York: Knopf, 1974
Lessing, Doris. *The Golden Notebook*. London: Grafton, 1973.
_____. *In Pursuit of the English: A Documentary*. London: MacGibbon & Kee, 1960.
_____. *A Small Personal Voice*. New York: Alfred Knopf, 1974.
_____. *Walking in the Shade: Volume Two of My Autobiography, 1949–1962*. New York: Harper Collins, 1997.
O'Brien, Edna. *The Country Girls Trilogy*. New York: Plume, 1986.
_____. *Mother Ireland: A Memoir*. New York: Plume, 1976.
O'Faolain, Nuala. *Almost There: The Onward Journey of a Dublin Woman*. New York: Riverhead Books, 2003.
_____. *Are You Somebody? The Accidental Memoir of a Dublin Woman*. New York: Henry Holt, 1996.
_____. *My Dream of You*. New York: Riverhead Books, 2001.
Weldon, Fay. *Auto da Fay: A Memoir*. New York: Grove Press, 2004.
_____. *Big Women*. London: Flamingo, 1997.
_____. *Mantrapped*. London: Fourth Estate, 2004.
Woolf, Virginia. *Mrs. Dalloway*. New York: Harcourt Brace Jovanovich, 1925.
_____. *The Mrs. Dalloway Reader*. New York: Houghton Mifflin, 2003.
_____. *Night and Day*. New York: Harcourt Brace Jovanovich, 1920.
_____. *A Room of One's Own*. San Diego: Harcourt Brace Jovanovich, 1929.
_____. *Three Guineas*. San Diego: Harcourt Brace Jovanovich, 1938.
_____. *The Years*. New York: Harcourt Brace Jovanovich, 1937.

Secondary Sources

Abel, Elizabeth, Marianne Hirsch, and Elizabeth Langland, eds. *The Voyage In: Fictions of Female Development*. Hanover, NH: University Press of New England, 1983.
Alcoff, Linda. "Cultural Feminism versus Poststructuralism: The Identity Crisis in Feminist Theory." *Signs* 13:3 (Spring 1988), 405–436.
Bakan, David. *The Duality of Human Existence: Isolation and Communion in Western Man*. Boston: Beacon Press, 1966.
Barreca, Regina, ed. *Fay Weldon's Wicked Fictions*. Hanover, NH: University Press of New England, 1994.
_____, ed. *Untamed and Unabashed: Essays on Women and Humor in British Literature*. Detroit: Wayne State University Press, 1994.

Bartley, Paula. *Emmeline Pankhurst*. London: Routledge, 2002.

Bassnett, Susan. *Feminist Experiences: The Women's Movement in Four Cultures*. London: Allen & Unwin, 1986.

Baumgardner, Jennifer, and Amy Richards. *Manifesta: Young Women, Feminism, and the Future*. New York: Farrar, Straus, and Giroux, 2000.

Bean, Kellie. *Post-Backlash Feminism: Women and the Media Since Reagan-Bush*. Jefferson, NC: McFarland, 2007.

Black, Naomi. *Virginia Woolf as Feminist*. Ithaca: Cornell University Press, 2004.

Blackwood, Caroline. *On the Perimeter*. London: Heinemann, 1984.

Bourke, Angela, Siobhán Kilfeather, Maria Luddy, Margaret MacCurtain, Gerardine Meaney, Máirín Ní Dhonnchadha, Mary O'Dowd, and Clair Wills. *The Field Day Anthology of Irish Writing, vol. v: Irish Women's Writing and Traditions*. New York: New York University Press, 2002.

Bowlby, Rachel. *Feminist Destinations and Further Essays on Virginia Woolf*. Edinburgh: Edinburgh University Press, 1997.

Briggs, Julia. *Virginia Woolf: An Inner Life*. New York: Harcourt Brace, 2005.

Bruley, Sue. *Women in Britain Since 1900*. London: Macmillan, 1999.

Butler, Judith. *Gender Trouble*. London: Routledge, 1990.

Byrne, Gabriel. *Pictures in my Head*. Dublin: Wolfhound Press, 2001.

_____. *Stories from Home*. Dir. Pat Collins, 2008.

Byron, Kristine. "'In the Name of the Mother': Reading and Revision in Edna O'Brien's *Country Girls Trilogy and Epilogue*." *Wild Colonial Girl: Essays on Edna O'Brien*. Eds. Lisa Colletta and Maureen O'Connor. Madison: University of Wisconsin Press, 2006. 14–30.

Castle, Barbara. *Sylvia and Christabel Pankhurst*. Harmondsworth: Penguin, 1987.

Coates, John. *Social Discontinuity in the Novels of Elizabeth Bowen*. Lewiston, NY: Edwin Mellen Press, 1998.

Connolly, Linda. *The Irish Women's Movement from Evolution to Devolution*. London: Palgrave, 2002.

Corcoran, Neil. *Elizabeth Bowen: The Enforced Return*. Oxford: Clarendon, 2004.

Coughlan, Patricia. "Killing the Bats: O'Brien, Abjection, and the Question of Agency." *Edna O'Brien: New Critical Perspectives*. Eds. Kathryn Laing, Sinead Mooney and Maureen O'Connor. Dublin: Carysfort Press, 2006. 151–170.

Crowe, Catriona. "Forty Years of Feminism," http://www.kilkennyarts.ie/bog/article/catrione-crowe-forty-years-of-feminism-notes/. 18 June 2011.

Cullingford, Elizabeth. "Something Else: Gendering Onliness in Elizabeth Bowen's Early Fiction." *Modern Fiction Studies* 53.2 (2007), 276–305.

Curtis, Vanessa. *Virginia Woolf's Women*. Madison: Univearsity of Wisconsin Press, 2002.

Davitt, Michael. *The Fall of Feudalism in Ireland*. London and New York: Harper & Row, 1904.

De Meester, Karen. "Trauma, Post-Traumatic Stress Disorder, and Obstacles to Postwar Recovery in *Mrs. Dalloway*." *Virginia Woolf and Trauma: Embodied Texts*. Eds. Suzette Henke and David Eberly. New York: Pace University Press, 2007.

DeSalvo, Louise. *Virginia Woolf: the Impact of Childhood Sexual Abuse on her Life and Works*. New York: Ballantine, 1991.

Dougherty, Jane E. "Nuala O'Faolain and the Unwritten Irish Girlhood." *New Hibernia Review* 11:2 (2007), 50–65.

Dowling, Finuala. *Fay Weldon's Fiction*. Madison, NJ: Fairleigh Dickinson University Press, 1998.

Draine, Betsy. *Substance Under Pressure: Artistic Coherence and Evolving Form in the Novels of Doris Lessing*. Madison: University of Wisconsin Press, 1983.

Ebest, Sally Barr. "These Traits Also Endure: Contemporary Irish and Irish-American Women Writers." *New Hibernia Review* 7:2 (2003), 55–72.

Eckley, Grace. *Edna O'Brien*. Lewisburg, PA: Bucknell University Press, 1974.

Ellmann, Maud. *Elizabeth Bowen: the Shadow Across the Page*. Edinburgh: Edinburgh University Press, 2006.

Fanning, Charles. *The Irish Voice in America: 250 Years of Irish-American Fiction*. Lexington: University Press of Kentucky, 1990.

Faulks, Lana. *Fay Weldon*. New York: Twayne, 1998.

Fernald, Anne E. *Virginia Woolf: Feminism and the Reader*. New York: Palgrave, 2006.

Freidan, Betty. *The Feminine Mystique*. New York: W.W. Norton, 1963.

French, Amanda. "A Strangely Useless Thing: Iseult Gonne and Yeats," *Yeats Eliot Review* 19:2 (2002), 13–24.

Froula, Christine. "*Mrs. Dalloway*'s Postwar Elegy: Women, War and the Art of Mourning." *Virginia Woolf and the Bloomsbury Avant-Garde: War, Civilization, Modernity*. New York: Columbia University Press, 2005. 87–128.

Gilbert, Sandra, and Susan Gubar. *Madwoman in the Attic: The Woman Writer and the Nineteenth-Century Imagination*. New Haven: Yale University Press, 2000.

Gilbert, Sandra M. Foreword. *Reconciling Catholicism and Feminism?* Eds. Sally Barr Ebest and Ron Ebest. University of Notre Dame Press, 2003. xi–xx.

Gilligan, Carol. *In a Different Voice: Psychological Theory and Women's Development*. Cambridge: Harvard University Press, 1982.

Glendinning, Victoria. *Elizabeth Bowen*. New York: Knopf, 1978.

Greene, Gayle. *Doris Lessing: The Poetics of Change*. Ann Arbor: University of Michigan Press, 1994.

Greenwood, Amanda. *Edna O'Brien*. Tavistock, Devon: Northcote House, 2003.

Greer, Germaine. *The Female Eunuch*. New York: McGraw-Hill, 1970, 71.

Haverty, Anne M. *Constance Markievicz: Irish Revolutionary*. New York: New York University Press, 1988.

Henke, Suzette. "The Challenge of Teaching Doris Lessing's *The Golden Notebook* in the Twenty-First Century." *Doris Lessing: Interrogating the Times*. Eds. Debrah Raschke, Phyllis Sternberg Perrakis, and Sandra Singer. Columbus: Ohio State University Press, 2010. 183–201.

Humm, Maggie, ed. *Modern Feminisms*. New York: Columbia University Press, 1992.

Ingman, Heather. "Edna O'Brien: Stretching the Nation's Boundaries." *Irish Studies Review* 10:3 (2002), 253–265.

_____. *Twentieth Century Fiction by Irish Women*. London: Ashgate, 2007.

Jacobus, Mary, ed. *Women Writing and Writing about Women*. London: Croom Helm, 1979.

Jameson, Fredric. *The Political Unconscious: Narrative as a Socially Symbolic Act*. Ithaca: Cornell University Press, 1981.

Johnson, Toni O'Brien, and David Cairns. *Gender in Irish Writing*. Milton Keynes: Open University Press, 1991.

Jouve, Nicole Ward. "Virginia Woolf and Psychoanalysis." *The Cambridge Companion to Virginia Woolf*. Eds. Sue Roe and Susan Sellers. Cambridge: Cambridge University Press, 2000. 246–52.

Joyce, James. *The Dead*. Ed. Daniel Schwarz. New York: Bedford/St. Martin's, 1994.

_____. *Portrait of the Artist as a Young Man*. Harmondsworth: Penguin, 1993.

Kalven, Janet. "Feminism and Catholicism." *Reconciling Catholicism and Feminism?* Eds. Sally Barr Ebest and Ron Ebest. Notre Dame: University of Notre Dame Press, 2003. 32–46.

Kenny, Mary. *Goodbye to Catholic Ireland*. Dublin: New Island, 2000.

_____. "Irish Women Reconciling Catholicism and Feminism." *Reconciling Catholicism and Feminism? Personal Reflections on Tradition and Change*. Eds. Sally Barr Ebest and Ron Ebest. Notre Dame: University of Notre Dame Press, 2003. 150–167.

Killeen, Richard. *A Short History of Ireland*. Surrey: Quadrillion, 1994.

Klein, Carol. *Doris Lessing: A Biography*. London: Gerald Duckworth & Co., 2000.

Kristeva, Julia. *Powers of Horror: An Essay on Abjection*. New York: Columbia University Press, 1982.

Krouse, Agate Nesaule. "Feminism and Art in Fay Weldon's Novels." *Critique* 20:2 (1978), 5–20.

Laing, Kathryn, Sinead Mooney, Maureen O'Connor, eds. *New Critical Perspectives on Edna O'Brien*. Dublin: Carysfort Press, 2006.

Lee, Hermione. *Elizabeth Bowen: An Estimation*. Vision Press, 1982.

Levenson, Samuel. *Maud Gonne*. New York: Reader's Digest Press, 1976.

Liddington, Jill. *The Road to Greenham Common: Feminism and Anti-Militarism in Britain since 1820*. Syracuse: Syracuse University Press, 1991.

Maguire, Moira J. "The Changing Face of Catholic Ireland: Conservatism and Liberalism in the Ann Lovett and Kerry Babies Scandals." *Feminist Studies* 27:2 (Summer 2001), 335–358.

Marcus, Laura. "Woolf's Feminism and Feminism's Woolf." *The Cambridge Companion to Virginia Woolf*, 2d ed. Ed. Susan Sellers. Cambridge: Cambridge University Press, 2010. 142–179.

Mayhall, Laura E. Nym. *The Militant Suffrage Movement: Citizenship and Resistance in Britain, 1860–1930*. Oxford: Oxford University Press, 2003.

McCafferty, Nell. *A Woman to Blame: The Kerry Babies Case*. Dublin: Attic Press, 1985.

Mills, Sara, and Lynne Pearce. *Feminist Readings, Feminists Reading*, 2d ed. London: Prentice Hall, 1996.

Mitchell, David. *Queen Christabel: A Biography of Christabel Pankhurst*. London: MacDonald and Jane's, 1977.

Moloney, Caitriona, and Helen Thompson. *Irish Women Writers Speak Out: Voices from the Field.* Syracuse: Syracuse University Press, 2003.

Murfin, Ross, and Supryia M. Ray, eds. *The Bedford Glossary of Critical and Literary Terms,* 3d ed. Boston: Bedford/St. Martin's, 2009.

O'Brien, Edna. Interview with Shusha Guppy. *The Art of Fiction No. 82. The Paris Review* 92 (Summer 1984).

Owens, Rosemary Cullen. *Smashing Times: A History of the Irish Women's Suffrage Movement 1889– 1922.* Dublin: Attic Press, 1984.

Paglia, Camille. *Sexual Personae: Art and Decadence from Nefertiti to Emily Dickinson.* New York: Vintage, 1991.

Pankhurst, Emmeline. *My Own Story.* New York: Source Book Press, 1970 (unabridged republication of the 1914 London edition).

Pearce, Sandra Manoogian. "An Interview with Edna O'Brien." *Canadian Journal of Irish Studies: Special Edition on Edna O'Brien,* 22:2 (1996), 5–8.

Pearlman, Mickey. *Listen to Their Voices: Twenty Interviews with Women Who Write.* New York: Norton, 1993.

Pelan, Rebecca. "Edna O'Brien's 'Love Objects.'" *Wild Colonial Girl.* Eds. Lisa Colletta and Maureen O'Connor. Madison: University of Wisconsin Press, 2006. 58–77.

_____. *Two Irelands: Literary Feminism North and South.* Syracuse: Syracuse University Press, 2005.

Pierse, Mary S., ed. *Irish Feminisms, 1810–1930.* New York: Routledge, 2010.

Pugh, Martin. *The Pankhursts.* London: Penguin, 2001.

Redfern, Catherine, and Kristin Aune. *Reclaiming the F Word: The New Feminist Movement.* London: Zed Books, *2010.*

Rich, Adrienne. *Blood, Bread, and Poetry: Selected Prose.* New York: Norton, 1986.

Roiphe, Katie. *The Morning After: Sex, Fear and Feminism.* Boston: Back Bay Books, 1994.

Rubenstein, Roberta. *The Novelistic Vision of Doris Lessing: Breaking the Forms of Consciousness.* Urbana: University of Illinois Press, 1979.

Ryan, Mary. "A Feminism of Their Own? Irish Women's History and Contemporary Irish Women's Writing." *Estudios Irlandeses,* 5 (2010), 92–101.

St. Peter, Christine. *Changing Ireland: Strategies in Contemporary Women's Fiction.* Houndsmills: Palgrave MacMillan, 2000.

Segal, Hanna, ed. *Introduction to the Work of Melanie Klein.* London: Karnac Books, 1988.

Showalter, Elaine. *A Literature of Their Own.* Princeton: Princeton University Press, 1998.

Spacks, Patricia Meyer. "Free Women." *Doris Lessing.* Ed. Harold Bloom. New York: Chelsea House, 1986. 95–102.

Spall, Sue, and Lynne Pearce, "Gynocriticism." *Feminist Readings, Feminists Reading.* Eds. Sara Mills and Lynne Pearce. London: Prentice Hall, 1996. 91–124.

Stopper, Anne. *Mondays at Gaj's: The Story of the Irish Women's Liberation Movement.* Dublin: The Liffey Press, 2006.

Van Voris, Jacqueline. *Constance de Markievicz: In the Cause of Ireland.* Amherst: University of Massachusetts Press, 1967.

Van Wingerden, Sophia A. *The Women's Suffrage Movement in Britain, 1866–1928.* London: Macmillan, 1999.

Walker, Rebecca. *To Be Real: Telling the Truth and Changing the Face of Feminism.* New York: Anchor, 1995.

Wallace, Christine. *Germaine Greer: Untamed Shrew.* New York: Faber & Faber, 1998.

Walshe, Eibhear, ed. *Sex, Nation and Dissent in Irish Writing.* Cork: Cork University Press, 1997.

Walter, Natasha. *Living Dolls: The Return of Sexism.* London: Virago, 2010.

Ward, Margaret. "Conflicting Interests: The British and Irish Suffrage Movements." *Feminist Review,* 50 (Summer 1995), 127–47.

_____. "Gendering the Union: Imperial Feminism and the Ladies' Land League." *Women's History Review*m, 10:1 (March 2001), 71–92.

_____. *Maud Gonne: Ireland's Joan of Arc.* London: Pandora Press, 1990.

_____. *Unmanageable Revolutionaries: Women and Irish Nationalism.* London: Pluto Press, 1983.

Weekes, Ann Owens. *Irish Women Writers: An Uncharted Tradition.* Lexington: University of Kentucky Press, 1990.

Welch, Christina. "Spirituality and Social Change at Greenham Common Peace Camp." *Journal for Faith, Spirituality and Social Change,* 1:1 (2006), 50–67.

Weldon, Fay. Interview with Mickey Pearlman. *Listen to Their voices: Twenty Interviews with Women Writers.* Ed. Mickey Pearlman. New York: Norton, 1993.

_____. Interview with Elizabeth Grice. 12 March 2009. *The Telegraph.* http://telegraph.co.uk/culture/4980926/Fay-Weldon-Dying-I-Don't-Want-To-Do-That-Again.html.

_____. Interview with Stuart Jeffries. 5 September 2006. *The Guardian.* http://guardian.co.uk/world/2006/sep/06/gender.religion.

Werlock, Abby, ed. *British Women Writing Fiction.* Tuscaloosa: University of Alabama Press, 2000.

Whelehan, Imelda. "The Bloodless Revolution: Feminism, Publishing and the Mass Media in Weldon's *Big Women.*" *Women: A Cultural Review,* 19:1 (2008), 37–48.

_____. *Modern Feminist Thought: From the Second Wave to 'Post-Feminism.'* Edinburgh: University of Edinburgh Press, 1995.

Willls, Clair. "Women, Domesticity and the Family: Recent Feminist Work in Irish Cultural Studies." *Cultural Studies,* 15:1 (2001), 33–57.

Wilson, Elizabeth. "Yesterday's Heroines: On Rereading Lessing and de Beauvoir." *Notebooks/Memoirs/Archives: Reading and Rereading Doris Lessing.* Ed. Jenny Taylor. Boston: Routlege and Kegan Paul, 1982. 57–74.

Woods, Alan. "Marxism and Art: An Introduction to Trotsky's Writing on Art." http//:www.smarxist.com/ArtAndLiterature-old/Marxism-and-art.html.

Woods, Michelle. "Red, Un-Read, and Edna: Ernest Gebler and Edna O'Brien. *Edna O'Brien: New Critical Perspectives.* Dublin, Carysfort Press, 2006. 54–67.

Zwerdling, Alec. *Virginia Woolf and the Real World.* Berkeley: University of California Press, 1986.

Index

Numbers in *bold italics* indicate pages with photographs.